D0203075

THE CALENDAR OF THE
ROMAN REPUBLIC

THE
CALENDAR
OF THE
ROMAN
REPUBLIC

BY AGNES KIRSOPP MICHELS

PRINCETON, NEW JERSEY

PRINCETON UNIVERSITY PRESS

MCMLXVII

Publication of this book has been aided
by the Whitney Darrow Publication Reserve Fund
of Princeton University Press

Printed in the United States of America
by Princeton University Press
Princeton, New Jersey

L. R. T.

DOMINAE

DOCTISSIMAE

DILECTISSIMAE

PREFACE

The title of this book may be misleading because the calendar has usually been treated as a source of evidence for various branches of Roman studies rather than as a subject in its own right. I should, therefore, make clear that the title means just what it says. The book deals exclusively with the calendar of the Roman republic, commonly called the pre-Julian calendar. It discusses Roman religion, Roman history and chronology, and Roman institutions only when they can shed light on the nature and history of the calendar. Moreover, it deals only with what I take to be the official calendar of the Roman state, that is, the material inscribed in the *Fasti* in large letters. The material inscribed in small letters, which varies from inscription to inscription, I have used as evidence when necessary, but have not discussed for its own sake. In the illustrations, Plate 4 does include some of the notations made in small letters in *Fasti Antiates Maiores*, but not all, since it was designed to bring out the pattern and decorative effect of a republican calendar, not to be used as a source for the dates of *Ludi* or the dedication days of temples. These items will not be found even in Plate 3, which is a guide to the material in large letters and is intended to emphasize the relations between the nundinal letters, the character letters, and the named days, which seem to me vital for an understanding of the calendar.

The character of this book is the result of my own adventures with the subject. I first became interested in the calendar in relation to the history of Roman religion and concentrated on the *feriae*. As a result I published an article in 1949 in which I tried to date the introduction of the pre-Julian calendar to 450 B.C. I then spent some frustrating years trying to discover the meaning of the character NP. Readers who struggle through Chapter 4 will perceive that I have been no more successful in this than my predecessors, but, in the course of my attempt, I came across some observations made by J. Paoli concerning the history of the character letters in the *Fasti* which opened my eyes to new and, to me, fascinating problems. The attempt to solve these problems led me far away from the field of religion, into areas where I had never seriously ventured before. I en-

countered such difficulty in finding the widely scattered evidence
for the character and use of the calendar that I thought I might
be of service to other students of Roman institutions if I gath-
ered the evidence together and made it more easily available.
My interpretation of the history of the calendar I have written
for my own satisfaction, and I present it here as a hypothetical
reconstruction, although I fear that at times I may have been so
carried away by my own arguments that I have stated it more
positively than I should. No one knows better than I that, in
the present state of the evidence, any statements about the history of the calendar prior to the First Century B.C. can only be
hypothetical. I have, however, tried to construct hypotheses
which make as economical use as possible of the available evidence.

I have deliberately limited the scope of this book to the period of the republic, not because I am not interested in the earlier stages of the Roman calendar but because I have become
cautious. As my readers will discover, I am prepared to work
with very little evidence, but when the evidence becomes so
slight that it can be used to support an almost infinite variety
of theories, I now prefer to restrain my imagination.

I am uncomfortably aware of many loose ends in my discussion. The one that bothers me most is the problem of the
relation between *ius publicum* and the characters of the days.
I have not been able to find any evidence as to whether or not
the *quarta accusatio* of a *iudicium populi*, other than *de vi*, had
to be held on a *dies comitialis*. If I appear to have dodged this
issue in Chapter 3, it is not because I am unaware of it but
because I do not know what to do about it.

The study of the Roman calendar began in antiquity, continued through the Middle Ages, and then, from the sixteenth
century on, swelled to awesome proportions in the hands of
epigraphers and writers on chronology. It would be the work
of half a lifetime to read and digest all this material. Therefore
I have not tried to do so, nor have I given here a full bibliography, but have cited in the footnotes what I have found most
useful or interesting. Those who are interested in sampling the
work of the past will find much of it in the eighth volume of

Graevius' *Thesaurus*, although some of the most entertaining specimens are omitted.

I have, however, read enough in the field to know that many of these treatments of the calendar are sound, some of them brilliant, and some purely fantastic. I also know that practically every theory about the calendar which could conceivably have been devised has been proposed by somebody, and that many have been re-invented several times. I know that very little of what I have to say has not been anticipated, especially in the work of O. E. Hartmann, whose book, *Ordo Iudiciorum*, deserved a better fate than to be obscured by the *auctoritas* of Mommsen.

My justification for adding one more item to the bibliography of the calendar is that during this century new evidence has come to light of which full use has not been made. The number of inscriptions in which the calendar is recorded has almost doubled since 1893 when Mommsen published those that were then known in *CIL* 1². Among them we now have the unique example of a pre-Julian calendar, *Fasti Antiates Maiores*, which was published in 1921. Work on the calendar has recently been made much easier by Professor Attilio Degrassi's magnificent publication of the whole corpus of *Fasti*, with exhaustive commentaries and indices, in *Inscriptiones Italiae* XIII.2 (1963). With new material to work on and a new tool for research, the time seems ripe for a reconsideration of the character and history of the republican calendar.

In the course of my work on this book I have received generous help from many sources. In 1960-61, the John Simon Guggenheim Memorial Foundation granted me a Fellowship which enabled me to break ground. The Staff of the Bryn Mawr College Library has cheerfully met all my demands. I have enjoyed the hospitality of the libraries of the University of Pennsylvania, Princeton University, the Institute for Advanced Study, the British Museum, and of the American Academy in Rome, where Mrs. Inez Longobardi helped me far beyond the call of duty. I appreciate deeply the interest of the Princeton University Press in publishing this book, and have especially enjoyed working with Mrs. E. Baldwin Smith and Miss Harriet Anderson, who have made the process of production an enjoyable experience. Mrs. Robert Conner, who typed the manuscript, earned my gratitude by her unfailing patience and efficiency.

I have turned to my colleagues at Bryn Mawr for help many times. Professor Myra Uhlfelder has read much of the manuscript, has made valuable suggestions, and has helped me track down many an obscure reference. Professor Russell T. Scott did me the great favor of drawing the reconstruction of a calendar for Plate 4. I cannot estimate the depth of my debt to Professor T. Robert S. Broughton, who, during all his years at Bryn Mawr, with characteristic kindness and patience allowed me to avail myself of his profound knowledge of Roman history. Professor Mabel Lang has helped me in my efforts to understand the complexities of Greek calendar studies, as have my friends elsewhere, Professors Michael Jameson, Sterling Dow, and Benjamin D. Meritt. Since our undergraduate days Dr. Lucy Shoe Meritt has been an unfailing source of encouragement in all my work, but especially in this.

I should express particular thanks to Bryn Mawr students, past and present, who have helped me in many ways: to Professor Zoja Pavlovskis, for her help on bibliography, to Professor Anne Laidlaw, who, as Fellow of the American Academy in Rome, made herself my chauffeur and *cicerone*, to Miss Mary Lou Leavitt, who spent two hot summers as my research assistant, to Miss Sheila Dickison, Mrs. Lionel Lippmann, and Mr. John Hunt, who checked references; to Mr. Richard De Puma, who drew the chart for Plate 3.

I owe a unique debt of gratitude to Professor Degrassi for his scholarly generosity in allowing me to use the proofs of his commentary on the *Fasti* two years before it was published, and for his encouraging interest in my efforts. He was also kind enough to supply me with the photograph for Plate 2.

My husband, Walter C. Michels, Marion Reilly Professor of Physics at Bryn Mawr College, has debated the problems of the Roman calendar with me for some twenty years. I could never have written Chapter 1 without the help of his gift for explaining the mysteries of astronomy in simple terms. If I have gone astray between the sun and the moon, the fault is mine alone.

Professor Louise Adams Holland first introduced me when I

was a student to what she has called the fatal fascination of the pre-historic, and I have ever since been deeply grateful for the rigorous discipline of her teaching, and for the constant stimulation of her lively apprehension of all things Roman.

During an association of forty years Professor Lily Ross Taylor has taught, helped, encouraged, and enlightened me, and turned the penetrating edge of her criticism on my work. With endless generosity she has put at my disposal her profound understanding of the Roman republic. In the midst of her own work, she has taken the time to read and criticize most of my manuscript. Where I may have blundered in the interpretation of evidence, the responsibility is entirely mine. As a very inadequate token of my admiration and affection for her, I have dedicated this book to L.R.T.

Bryn Mawr College
April 10, 1967

CONTENTS

ILLUSTRATIONS

ABBREVIATIONS

AJA	*American Journal of Archaeology*
AJP	*American Journal of Philology*
AnnAcadScientFenn	*Annales Academiae Scientiarum Fennicae*
Botsford, *RA*	Botsford, G. W., *The Roman Assemblies* (New York 1909)
Broughton, *MRR*	Broughton, T. R. S., *The Magistrates of the Roman Republic*, 2 vols. (New York 1951-1952)
BCH	*Bulletin de Correspondance Hellénique*
BSA	*Annual* of the British School of Archaeology at Athens
CP	*Classical Philology*
CRAI	*Comptes Rendus de l'Academie des Inscriptions et Belles-Lettres*
D-S	Daremberg, Ch. et Saglio, Edm., *Dictionnaire des antiquités grecques et romaines* (Paris 1881-1889)
Degrassi	Degrassi, A., *Inscriptiones Italiae*, XIII, *Fasti et Elogia*. Fasc. II, *Fasti Anni Numani et Iuliani* (Rome 1963)
Degrassi, *I.I.*	*Inscriptiones Italiae*, XIII, Fasc. I and III. Referred to as 13.1 and 13.3
Degrassi, *ILLRP*	Degrassi, A., *Inscriptiones Latinae Liberae Rei Publicae*, Fasc. 1 (Florence 1957), Fasc. 2 (Florence 1963) = *Biblioteca di Studi Superiori*, vols. 23 and 40
FIRA	*Fontes Iuris Romanae Anteiustiniani*, ed. S. Riccobono, J. Baviera, C. Ferrini, J. Furlani, V. Arangio-Ruiz, vols. I-III (Florence 1941-1943)
Ginzel	Ginzel, F. K., *Handbuch der mathematischen und technischen Chronologie*, vols. 1-3 (Leipzig 1906-1914)
HThR	*Harvard Theological Review*
JRS	*Journal of Roman Studies*
Lange, *RA*	Lange, L., *Römische Alterthümer*, vols.

1-2 (3rd ed., Berlin 1876-1879), vol. 3 (2nd ed., Berlin 1876)

Leuze   Leuze, O., "Bericht über die Literatur zur römischen Chronologie (Kalendar und Jahrzählung) in den Jahren 1901-1928," *Jahresbericht über die Fortschritte der Klassischen Altertumswissenschaft* 227 (1930) 97-139

MAAR   *Memoirs of the American Academy in Rome*

Mommsen, *Staatsrecht*[3]   Mommsen, C. M. T., *Römisches Staatsrecht*, 3 vols. (3rd ed., Leipzig 1887; reprinted Basel 1952)

Mommsen, *RC*[2]   Mommsen, C. M. T., *Die römische Chronologie bis auf Caesar* (2nd ed., Berlin 1859)

MusHelv   *Museum Helveticum*

NS   *Notizie degli Scavi di Antichità*

PMAAR   *Papers and Monographs of the American Academy in Rome*

RE   Pauly-Wissowa, *Real-Encyclopädie der classischen Altertumswissenschaft*

REA   *Revue des Études Anciennes*

REL   *Revue des Études Latines*

RhMus   *Rheinisches Museum für Philologie*

RPh   *Revue de Philologie*

Rotondi, *LPPR*   Rotondi, G., *Leges Publicae Populi Romani,* estratto dalla *Enciclopedia Giuridica Italiana* (Milan 1912; reprinted Hildesheim 1962)

Soltau, *RömChron*   Soltau, W., *Römische Chronologie* (Freiburg 1889)

TAPA   *Transactions of the American Philological Association*

Warde Fowler, *RF*   Fowler, W. Warde, *The Roman Festivals of the Period of the Republic* (London and New York 1899)

Wissowa, *RK*[2]   Wissowa, G., *Religion und Kultus der Römer* (2nd ed., Munich 1912)

[xvi]

PART I

THE CALENDAR OF THE
FIRST CENTURY B.C.

CHAPTER 1

THE PRE-JULIAN CALENDAR

THE NATURE OF CALENDARS

A calendar is an invention of the human mind, designed for the convenience of human beings. It is based on the observation of the natural phenomena by which men calculate the progress of time in order to regulate their own activities. The accuracy with which the calendar represents the actual phenomena depends on the needs of the people who devised it. A primitive people, living in isolation in a small area, can manage their lives with a simple and imprecise calendar.[1] The more complex a society grows, and the wider its area of activities becomes, the more need it has to coordinate its activities, and its need for a more accurate method of reckoning time becomes greater. Increased accuracy depends on increased knowledge of astronomy and of mathematics, and the calendar can be improved as knowledge grows. But a calendar is the tool of the society which uses it, and, as long as it is adequate for the needs of that society, it may well lag far behind the knowledge of its scientists. The Greek astronomers, from the fifth century B.C. on, were constantly refining their calculation of the actual length of the solar year, but it was not until 45 B.C., when Julius Caesar introduced the calendar known by his name, that any state availed itself of this knowledge for a civil calendar.

Since, however, a calendar is designed for everyday use by people, it is often much more than a device for reckoning the passage of time. It not only lists days, but it indicates, for those who can interpret it, what happens, or may happen, or must happen, on particular days. A calendar is written in a code which is perfectly clear to the group which uses it, but will have to be learned by others. A foreigner visiting America and seeing a certain day marked as Thanksgiving might very well not realize that that day will be a legal holiday on which no busi-

[1] For a discussion of primitive calendars, see M. P. Nilsson, *Primitive Time-Reckoning* (Lund 1920).

[3]

ness is transacted, and he might well be puzzled to discover that Labor Day is one of the laziest days in the year. A church calendar is of use only to those who know the obligations connected with the festivals which it lists. If, however, one takes the trouble to learn the code of any particular calendar, one can learn a great deal about the customs and interests of the group or the society that it represents. One can also see reflected in it a good deal of history. For example, in an American calendar, the names of the months are Anglicized forms of the Latin names, the days of the week are named for Saxon gods, and the dates are noted in Arabic numerals. Holidays are religious festivals or anniversaries of historical events, or the expression of an idea, such as Memorial Day and Labor Day. All these elements are clues to the complex origins of American culture, and to its history.

The Roman calendar, as we see it in the inscriptions in which it is preserved, contains a great deal of information which can, to a large extent, be decoded by applying to it information found in the works of ancient authors. In this book I propose to describe and analyze the calendar of the last years of the Republic, which the Romans were using before Caesar changed it, and to discuss the various ways in which it served the needs of the Roman citizen and the Roman state. I shall then try to trace its history during the previous periods of the Republic and to show how it developed in response to the changing needs of Rome.

Before plunging into the details of this discussion, I should point out some characteristics of the Roman state and its citizens which must have predetermined many of the features of the calendar and which may seem strange to the modern mind. The fundamental point which must be made is that in Rome there was no dichotomy between church and state. The gods of Rome are part of Rome, on them the welfare of the state and its citizens rest. The control of the state cult is in the hands of the Senate, which delegates its administration to the priests, who are very apt to be Senators and magistrates themselves. Every activity of the state, and most of those of its citizens, in some way or other involves the gods. Without the sanction of the gods given through the auspices, no law can be passed, no

[4]

magistrate elected, no war undertaken. The *pax deorum*, the absence of divine anger, is sought by all the great religious ceremonies of the state on behalf of the *populus Romanus Quiritium*, the body of Roman citizens. All the activities of the state, those which to us seem secular as well as those which are clearly religious, must be carried out at times which meet with the approval of the gods, as it is interpreted by the priests, because the orderly conduct of public affairs is to the Roman both necessary for the maintenance of the *pax deorum*, and also evidence that it has been maintained. Disorder in the state is evidence that the gods are angry.

Because the Roman never separated religion from civic affairs, we shall find that a study of the state calendar leads into many areas of Roman life which at first sight seem to have little to do with religion, such as civil law, electoral and legislative assemblies, even market days. The rites of the state cult combine with all these affairs to make up what is truly a civil calendar, because it represents the life of a citizen, a *civis Romanus*, in all its phases. Throughout this book, when I speak of a civil calendar, I am distinguishing it from an astronomical calendar, and am not implying that it is secular rather than religious. To illustrate the Roman use of the word *civilis* in a religious context I would quote Cicero's explanation of why a Greek priestess brought to Rome to preside over a recently Romanized Greek cult must be made a Roman citizen: *Sacra pro civibus civem facere voluerunt, ut deos immortales scientia peregrina et externa, mente domestica et civili precaretur* (*Pro Balbo* 55). Prayers offered to the gods on behalf of the citizens must be offered by a citizen endowed with the mind, the understanding and point of view, of a citizen.

THE LITERARY SOURCES

The Romans seem to have been interested in their calendar and several of them wrote books about it which have been lost.[2] The only one which has survived is a literary rather than a technical treatment of the subject. Ovid's poem, the *Fasti*,[3] was in-

---

[2] These lost works are often quoted by other ancient writers, and we shall make use of these citations in the following discussions.

[3] The fullest modern editions are *The Fasti of Ovid* in 5 vols. by Sir

tended to be a day-by-day account of the whole Roman religious year, based on the calendar with one book for each month, but unfortunately for us he stopped writing with Book 6. His major interest was in the religious festivals, their origins and meaning, which provided full scope for his gift of narrative. Luckily, however, he began Book 1 with a description of the contents of the calendar and a brief sketch of its history. He is, of course, working from the Julian, not the republican, calendar, and in matters of history and interpretation he allows his fancy free rein, introducing Greek myths and Roman legends, so that his evidence must be scrutinized with care, but he had been an eyewitness of much that he records, and was moreover an intelligent and well-read man who had at his disposal historical sources not available to us. One of these was the complete work of the great antiquarian of the late Republic, M. Terentius Varro. Aside from scattered quotations in the works of other authors, all that we have from Varro which bears directly on our topic is the section in his *De Lingua Latina* in which he discusses the technical terms used in the calendar, such as the names of festivals and the adjectives that define the characters of individual days. Another of Ovid's sources may have been[4] the work of the Augustan scholar, M. Verrius Flaccus, of which only the *De Verborum Significatu* is known to us, and that only through the fragments of the epitome made by Pompeius Festus in the second century, and the epitome of Festus' work made in the eighth century by Paulus Diaconus. It is, however, more than probable that Verrius Flaccus also wrote the notes on various days of the year in a calendar inscribed on marble, the fragments of which were discovered at Palestrina, the ancient town of Praeneste.[5]

In a later period, Censorinus, in his book *De Die Natali* published in A.D. 238, had a brief but useful section on the character

James Frazer (London 1929) and *P. Ovidius Naso. Die Fasten*, by Franz Bömer (Heidelberg 1957). Those who wish to explore earlier work on the Roman calendar will find interesting, if very difficult, reading in the introduction to R. Merkel's *P. Ovidii Nasonis Fastorum Libri Sex* (Berlin 1841).

[4] Cf. Bömer, *op.cit.* (n. 3) 1.23.

[5] Suetonius (*De Grammaticis* 17) gives a description of a calendar set up by Verrius Flaccus at Praeneste which fits precisely the character of the inscription.

and history of the Roman year. The best single source for the lost literature on the subject is the work of Macrobius, who in the late fourth century included in his *Saturnalia* a detailed discussion of the calendar in which he often quotes or paraphrases earlier authors whom he cites by name. His material, however, must be handled critically, for he does not as a rule give the context of his quotations, and he frequently fails to note that a statement in one section of his book is apparently contradicted by one which he made elsewhere. Another author whose statements need careful scrutiny is Johannes Lydus, who in the sixth century wrote a book in Greek on the months, *De Mensibus*. While much of what he says agrees with information given by much earlier authors who were describing what they knew at first hand, when he is our only source one cannot always accept his evidence at face value. His interpretations, typical of the thought of his own period, would often baffle a Roman of the republic.

In addition to these authors who deal specifically with the calendar, there is a vast amount of evidence to be found in incidental comments throughout the body of Latin literature. Historians, Greek as well as Latin, and writers on agriculture and law are particularly useful. For an understanding of the way in which the rules and regulations embodied in the Republican calendar affected daily life the most valuable information is provided by the works of Cicero, especially the letters and the orations.

THE INSCRIPTIONS

The information provided by the literary sources, which is sometimes very puzzling, is illuminated and brought into focus by the inscriptions that show us the calendar as it was actually presented to Roman eyes (Pl. 2). More than forty of these have now been found and published.[6] They are called *Fasti*

---

[6] These have recently been published with an elaborate commentary and a volume of plates and indices by A. Degrassi, *Inscriptiones Italiae*, XIII. *Fasti et Elogia*, Fasc. II. *Fasti Anni Numani et Iuliani* (Rome 1963), hereafter cited as Degrassi. This volume includes not only the *Fasti* but other inscriptions containing special types of calendars, and two calendars, preserved in manuscripts, which come from the fourth and fifth centuries A.D. *Fasti Antiates Maiores* has also been published by Degrassi

and modern scholars have given each its own name, for convenient reference (for a list, pp. 187-90). None of them has been completely preserved, and in some cases we have only a tiny fragment, but, by combining all the pieces, we can obtain at least some information about every day in the year. Unfortunately only one represents the calendar of the republic with which this book is concerned. This is *Fasti Antiates Maiores* (Pl. 1) which, unlike most of the other *Fasti,* is not cut on stone, but is painted in red and black letters on white plaster. All the other inscriptions which can be dated belong to the times of Augustus and Tiberius.[7] However, by a careful comparison of the contents of all the *Fasti,* supplemented by the literary evidence, we can reconstruct the pre-Julian calendar of the republic with some degree of confidence (see Pl. 4).

Behind the literary sources and the inscriptions we must keep in mind another source which would have been available to Romans, if they chose to use it. The administration of the Roman calendar was always, as far as we know, the task of the pontifices, the college of priests who had general control over the religious rites of the state. Although, as we shall see, they sometimes neglected or misunderstood their duties in relation to the calendar, a knowledge of the theory on which it was constructed and the rules which it imposed must have been part of the equipment of a pontifex, and must have been contained in their archives. Since the men who were pontifices were also as a rule men who held public office, magistrates and senators, an understanding of the intricacies of the calendar would, during the republic, have given them something of an advantage in political life, and they would have found it worth their while to pay attention to the subject. Undoubtedly, some of the information preserved in our literary sources was originally de-

---

with a very brief commentary in his *Inscriptiones Latinae Liberae Rei Publicae* (Florence 1957), hereafter cited as Degrassi, *ILLRP,* No. 9. Before Degrassi's work appeared, the basic collection was Mommsen's edition, *Corpus Inscriptionum Latinarum* $1^2.1$ (1893), hereafter cited as *CIL* $1^2.1$, of which the first edition had appeared in 1863. The inscriptions which were discovered after 1893 and published in a variety of places have now been incorporated with the earlier collection by Degrassi.

[7] See Degrassi, pp. xxiif. Some contain additional notes added during the reign of Claudius.

rived from expert rulings given by a pontifex who had been cornered by an inquisitive scholar.

THE BASIS OF A CALENDAR

To understand some of the peculiar features of the pre-Julian calendar, it is necessary to understand first some of the problems that faced the Romans who designed it. This means that before we can consider the Roman calendar we will have to consider the nature of calendars in general.[8]

A calendar is a device for measuring time, by which men can plan for the future and keep a record of the past. The desire to record events develops at a comparatively advanced stage of culture when a community with the leisure to look backward as well as forward becomes self-conscious, and needs to find its roots in the past as well as to provide for tomorrow. The need to plan develops much earlier. Even a quite primitive society needs to know how long it can count on warm weather for the growing of food, or how long the winter for which it must provide will last. As soon as man becomes aware of the need to reckon the passage of time, he observes that nature has provided the means in the regular recurrence of certain phenomena. The most obvious and the most frequent is the alternation of day and night, the rising and setting of the sun. The appearance, phases, and disappearance of the moon mark longer periods of time. The third basic means is again provided by the sun, which at different times of the year rises and sets at different points on the horizon in proximity to the positions of different stars, and climbs at noon to a higher or lower point in the sky. The regular alternation of the seasons also provides means for calculating the progress of time, commonly used among primitive peoples, but it is of only relative value, because, although the seasons proceed in a regular sequence from year to year, they may vary considerably in length owing to variations in the weather. Thus other means must be used to

[8] My major source for the astronomical data used in the following pages has been F. K. Ginzel, *Handbuch der mathematischen und technischen Chronologie* (Leipzig 1906-1914), hereafter cited as Ginzel. For a practical demonstration of the problems raised by the moon, I recommend studying the tables published in the *Nautical Almanac*, and conveniently reprinted in the annual *World Almanac*.

devise a calendar by which to judge and allow for the irregularity of the seasons. Seasons also vary locally. In the vicinity of Rome, for example, in the sheltered area around Lake Nemi, which lies protected in the crater of an extinct volcano, spring comes long before it touches the slopes of the mountains only a few miles away. The best means of keeping track of the seasons is provided by the stars. The constellations change their positions in the sky according to a timetable which is repeated regularly every year, so that, for example, when a certain constellation is visible in the east just before sunrise or just after sunset, a farmer knows that in his part of the world winter is almost over, or autumn is beginning. This is why ancient writers on agriculture very commonly use the motions of the stars to date the different phases of the year's work. The stars, however, do not provide the smaller subdivisions of time, such as the month and the day, which become practical necessities for a society as soon as it develops beyond the primitive stage. The civil calendar of a community engaged in many activities will therefore usually be based on the movements of the sun and moon, although these calendars may be checked for accuracy by the observation of the stars.

Without any knowledge of astronomy, or mathematics beyond quite simple arithmetic, one can contrive a calendar which, it is true, would not meet modern standards, but would meet the needs of a society less obsessed with time than ours. All that is needed is the patience to watch carefully the movements of the sun, moon, and stars, day after day and night after night, and the ability to count, to add, and to subtract. Men with an interest in such work become specialists in it, and assume the responsibility of timekeeping for the community.

Any one of the three natural means of time reckoning, the rising and setting of the sun, the progress of the moon, and the sun's annual course in relation to the stars, could be used independently as the basis of a calendar, but men have found it useful to work out a system which combines them, so as to be able to reckon in shorter and longer intervals of time simultaneously. It is this attempt to harmonize the three which makes the construction of calendars difficult, because the time spans which they measure are incommensurate. A solar day is the

[10]

period between one noon and the next, but the time between one new moon and the next averages 29 days 12 hours 44 minutes 2.9 seconds.[9] The solar year is the time which elapses from one vernal equinox to the next, and its average length is 365 days 5 hours 48 minutes 46.43 seconds.[10] Thus one cannot have months which all contain the same number of days, or a solar year composed of an integral number of lunar months. Moreover, these are only average lengths. The actual lengths vary by fractions which could not be observed precisely until astronomers developed refined methods, but over an extended period could upset the empirical calculations of a primitive calendar-maker without his knowing what had happened.

In antiquity, the inability to calculate exactly the fractions in the lengths of months and years inevitably meant that any calendar which men devised would need frequent correction based on observation. If the crescent moon did not appear on the day when it was expected, the beginning of the new month would be postponed, and the old month would have gained a day. If the equinox or solstice was not correctly observed, the year would gain or lose perhaps several days. The postponement in effect adds a day or more to the calendar month and to the calendar year. This accidental addition of a day leads men to recognize that they can correct their calendars by the intentional addition of a day or days. This process is known technically as intercalation, and is of fundamental importance in constructing any calendar. The different methods of intercalation used in antiquity will frequently be referred to in the course of this discussion.

THE CONSTRUCTION OF A CALENDAR

A simple and obvious form of calendar can be based on the moon. The months may have either 29 or 30 days,[11] while

[9] This is the synodic month, from one conjunction to the next, which determines the lunar months on which calendars can be based. The shorter sidereal month does not enter into calendar problems.

[10] This is the tropic year.

[11] A synodic month varies in length from 29.26 to 29.80 days, so that the sun may rise either 29 or 30 times during it. The variation in length is not regular. Cf. Pritchett and Neugebauer, *The Calendars of Athens* (Cambridge 1947) 5: "The months of a lunar calendar form rather

the year of 12 months is reckoned as containing 354 days (12 x 29.5). But the average time between new moons is actually 44 minutes 2.9 seconds longer than 29.5 days, so that an average lunar year is actually 354 days 8 hours 48 minutes and 36 seconds. This means that frequently in a lunar year the sun rises 355 times. Therefore, if the months are to keep in correct relation to the new moons, the extra hours must occasionally be taken into account by the intercalation of an extra day. If three years out of every eight have 355 days, the relation to the moon can be kept very nearly correct. This method could be worked out empirically on the basis of observation, without any knowledge of the astronomy involved, by men whose task it was to watch the moon in order to determine the beginning of the months. The disadvantage of this lunar year, however, is that it is a fraction more than eleven days shorter than the solar year, so that the months which are supposed to come in the spring, and the religious festivals assigned to them, will gradually slip back into the winter, the autumn, and the summer, until they come around to the spring again and then repeat the process. To avoid this one can, at stated intervals, intercalate a whole month into the year. A calendar of this type is called lunisolar.

Another practical difficulty in a lunar calendar which is based on observation of the moon is created by the relation between the real new moon and the first appearance of the crescent moon. The moon is "new" when it is in conjunction with the sun, that is when the earth, the moon, and the sun are more nearly in a straight line than at any other time in the

---

irregular sequences of intervals of 29 and 30 days whose arrangement cannot be predicted without a highly refined astronomical theory. . . . In a lunar calendar, sequences amounting to four consecutive 30-day months and to three 29-day months are possible, though rare. Pairs of 30-day months or 29-day months, however, are very common." Moreover, if the man in charge of the calendar really does wait to announce the new month until he has seen the crescent moon, a few days of rain might mean that the month would start late and run for only 28 or 27, even 26 days. An experienced moon-watcher would probably not wait so long, but trusting his own judgment, would proclaim what he considered the probable day. At this stage, no one would challenge the expert, or worry about minor inaccuracies.

month.[12] The conjunction may take place at any hour of the day or night. At the time of the moon's first rising and setting after the conjunction, it is so close to the sun that it is invisible in the brightness of the sun's light. Since the moon rises approximately an hour later relative to the time of sunset each day after the conjunction, in a day or so it will set long enough after the sun to be visible. On exactly which day this will happen in any one latitude depends on the time of day or night at which the conjunction took place and on the time of year. It may be the day after the conjunction, it may be the second day.[13] This means that until one has seen how wide the crescent moon is at its first appearance the number of days in the month cannot be predicted, nor how many days it will be until full moon, which may be important if the full moon is observed with religious ceremonies. The latter prediction is also complicated by the fact that the periods between the phases of the moon vary in length from month to month. From the conjunction to the first quarter, and from the first quarter to the full moon, the period may be from 6.5 days to a little more than 8 days. If one is depending on observation, it is fairly easy to be sure when the moon reaches the first quarter,[14] for the straight edge of the half-circle of the disk is clearcut, but it is not so easy to be sure whether the disk is really full or needs another day. This is especially true in the autumn, the season of the "Hunter's Moon" and the "Harvest Moon," when it appears to be full for two or three nights.

Another base for a simple calendar is the solar year, but here again a difficulty arises because this year consists of 365 days and about a quarter of a day more. If a solar calendar

[12] If, at the conjunction, sun, moon, and earth are very nearly in a straight line the sun is eclipsed.

[13] For more precise figures see Ginzel, 1.93. In observations taken in Athens the time between conjunction and visibility varied from 29.5 to 63 hours and was greatest in the autumn. R. A. Parker has a helpful explanation for the astronomical reasons for this variation in his *Calendars of Ancient Egypt* (*Studies in Ancient Oriental Civilization* 26, Chicago 1950) 4-6.

[14] It is also fairly easy to predict from the size of the crescent at its first visibility how many days it will take to reach the first quarter. I have experimented with this observation for several years, and have learned that it can be carried out with a quite gratifying degree of accuracy.

takes no account of the extra quarter of a day, it will lose one day every four years in relation to the actual solar year, and the calendar dates will shift through the seasons, coming back to where they started in approximately 1500 years. Once the existence and the length of the fraction of a day has been discovered, this difficulty can be corrected, as it is in our calendar, by intercalating a single day at regular intervals, but the discovery requires very precise methods of measurement, and throughout antiquity only approximate values for the fraction were known. Until Julius Caesar introduced his calendar, the fraction was usually ignored, except by astronomers, and for civil calendars the solar year was taken to have 365 days.[15]

The type of calendar which a community needs for practical purposes is one which is based on the solar year and day, but also provides subdivisions of the year, by compromising between the lunar and the solar years. In such a lunisolar calendar one has a year of 354 days and months of either 29 or 30 days. The months can be kept in correct relation to the new moon by the intercalation or omission of single days. The year can be kept in approximately correct relation to the seasons by intercalating a whole month at irregular intervals. The problem is to discover these intervals, and ancient astronomers applied themselves to it assiduously, refining their calculations century after century, but their findings seem to have had little effect on the civil calendars. A comparatively simple calculation, however, in early times, could have provided a guide to a crude system of intercalation. What one needs is to discover a number of years and a number of months in which the total number of days is the same. By empirical observation of the equinoxes or solstices, and of the moon, one can find out that 8 solar years contain 99 lunar months. If then, over a period of 8 years, one adds 3 months to the 96 months contained in 8 lunar years, one should be able to keep the calendar regulated by both sun and moon. Actually this system will never work exactly because of the incommensurability of the day, the month, and the year. It could be made to work fairly well by occasional cor-

[15] Censorinus (De Die Natali 19), after giving eight different opinions as to the precise length of the solar year, adds despairingly: Plerique praeterea incomprehensibile quiddam et inenuntiabile esse existimaverunt, sed pro vero quod proximum putabant amplexi sunt, dies scilicet CCCLXV.

[14]

rections, but it would always require the intercalation of months and of individual days.[16]

To avoid the difficulties inherent in a lunisolar calendar, the only solution is to use the solar year as a base and to divorce the subdivisions of the year completely from any dependence on the moon. Even this does not work out perfectly, because 365 cannot be divided into parts of equal lengths. The Egyptians in addition to their lunar calendar used a civil calendar of 12 months of 30 days each, and left the remaining five days unassigned, between the end of one year and the beginning of the next. Since they did not know, or ignored, the extra quarter day, their calendar year shifted in relation to the sun at the rate of one day every four years, but apparently the regularity of the calendar compensated for the inconvenience.[17] The Athenians kept to the lunisolar calendar, which was intimately connected with their religious life, but they also subdivided the year by prytanies, that is the term of days during which a prytanis, or subdivision of the Council, was on duty. Until the end of the fourth century B.C. there were ten prytanies, so that they never coincided with the lunar months. Athenian documents were dated both by the day of the month in the lunisolar calendar and by the day of the prytany, so that in effect Athens had two calendars.[18]

[16] The Greek astronomer Geminus states (8.33) that in an eight-year cycle months should be intercalated in the third, fifth, and eighth years. In the past this has been taken as evidence that the Greeks observed this cycle regularly, and it has been used as the basis of calendar studies. Recent work on the Athenian calendar, however, suggests that intercalation did not follow as regular a pattern as had been supposed, and Geminus adds that it makes little difference which years of the eight are intercalary.

[17] See R. A. Parker, op.cit. (n. 13) 51-56.

[18] This is a highly simplified statement of a highly complex situation. No *Fasti* of the Athenian calendar have been discovered and it must be reconstructed on the indirect evidence of dates given in documents recorded in inscriptions which present a mass of other, epigraphical, problems. The study of the calendar has raised controversies in which an outsider would hardly venture to intervene. See most recently B. D. Meritt, *The Athenian Year* (*Sather Classical Lectures* 32, Berkeley 1961); W. K. Pritchett, *Ancient Athenian Calendars on Stone* (*University of California Publications in Classical Archaeology*, 4. no. 4, Berkeley 1963); M. Lang, "The Abacus and the Calendar," *Hesperia* 33 (1964) 146-167; and the review of Meritt's book by P. A. Clement, *AJA* 69 (1965) 192-196, which includes an extensive bibliography.

THE YEAR IN THE CALENDAR OF
THE ROMAN REPUBLIC

We have considered briefly some of the major problems that arise in the construction of calendars. With these in mind we can now look at the Roman calendar of the late Republic and see if we can understand some of its peculiarities.[19] This calendar, commonly referred to as the pre-Julian, was based on a year of 355 days, and had four months of 31 days (March, May, July, October), seven of 29 days, and one (February) of 28. This was adjusted to the solar year by an unusual form of intercalation. The month of February was reduced to either 23 or 24 days, and was followed by an intercalary month of 27 days.[20] The religious observances that normally fell on the 24th and 27th of February were held on the 23rd and 26th of the intercalary month. Thus the calendar year was increased by 22 days, or, if the intercalary month began after February 24, by 23 days.

The length of this year is clearly related to the lunar year,[21] but the lengths of the months and the method of intercalation show equally clearly that we have here a calendar which has broken away from any relation to the actual phases of the

[19] It should be remembered that this is a purely civil calendar, designed to guide the religious, political, legal, and business activities of Roman citizens. When Cato in the second century B.C. writes about farming in his *De Agricultura*, he uses the civil calendar only for the dates of business affairs, such as contracts. For other purposes he reckons mainly by the stars. Polybius (9.14f.) discusses at length the need for a general to be familiar with astronomical matters such as the solstices and equinoxes, and the signs of the Zodiac, so as to be able to calculate the time available for his movements, but he nowhere mentions the use of a calendar. As we shall see, the Roman calendar of his day would have been useless for this purpose, as it had no regular relation to the seasons.

[20] Most modern authorities state that the intercalary month always began on the day after February 23, and alternated in length between 27 and 28 days. The evidence for the scheme which I have given here is presented in detail in Appendix I.

[21] The Romans have frequently been criticized for having been so ignorant of astronomy as to permit a lunar year of 355 days, instead of 354, but as a matter of fact a lunar year often does have 355 days (see p. 12). The 354-day year is a convention used for civil calendars, based on the acceptance of an average length for the month of 29.5 days, which is a little shorter than the real average. (Cf. Geminus, 8.3-5, where the point is made clear.)

[16]

moon. Months of 31 days, instead of 30, and an intercalary period of considerably less than a lunar month, could never have been expected or intended to stay in step with the moon. Thus we have something that is no longer a real lunisolar year, but has not yet made the transition to a genuine solar year. The intercalation of 22 days or sometimes 23, which over 8 years adds up to a total of 88 to 90 days, suggests that the inventors of this calendar knew that 8 solar years contain 3 more lunar months of 29 or 30 days than do 8 lunar years, and that one must intercalate a number of days equivalent to these three months. It also suggests that they wanted to intercalate every other year, not irregularly, as one must if one follows the moon. This they could have achieved by dividing the needed inter-calary days by four and adding 22 every other year,[22] ignoring the moon. They must have known from experience that it is difficult to determine the length of the solar year precisely, and thought that, by providing that the intercalary month could begin after either February 23 or February 24, they could allow for a slight margin of error.

In this calendar, of course, there is a serious mistake. Four solar years contain 1461 days, while four years of 355 days contain 1420. When, therefore, in a period of four years 44 or 45 days were intercalated, making a total of 1464 or 1465 days, the calendar year crept slowly forward in relation to the solar year. This could, however, easily be remedied by occa-sionally omitting an intercalation completely. To us this would seem very inconvenient, but to the Romans it would certainly have seemed an improvement over the juggling of odd days necessary in a calendar based on observation of the moon.

A peculiar feature of this method of intercalation is the date at which it took place. The obvious point for intercalation is between months. The twenty-two intercalary days could per-fectly well have been inserted between the end of February and the beginning of March. Why then did they lop four or five days off February and add them to the intercalary days to make up a month? The only plausible explanation which has as yet

[22] The basic addition was 22, but the option of beginning the inter-calary month after either the 23rd or 24th of February meant that the total addition over 8 years could vary between 88 and 90.

[17]

been propounded is that the two religious celebrations, the Regifugium and the Equirria, which normally come at the end of February, are in some way closely connected with those of March and could not be separated from them by a long interval,[23] a theory which gains support from the fact that the first festival in March is also called Equirria. It is sometimes stated by modern scholars that an intercalary month of 22 or 23 days was inserted into February after the 23rd, and that the last five days counted as part of February. This theory is disproved by the fact that these last days are regularly dated in the intercalary month.

MONTHS AND DAYS

In the short year of the Republican calendar March, May, July, and October had 31 days and February 28, but the other seven months had only 29. Their names are adjectival forms with which the noun *mensis* is always either expressed or understood. They are *Januarius, Februarius, Martius, Aprilis, Maius, Junius, Quinctilis, Sextilis, September, October, November, December.* The first six have names which are related to the characters of the months, while the last six are simply numbered.[24] The latter group indicate that originally the Roman year began in March, not January, since the numbers are reckoned from March. The names *Quinctilis* and *Sextilis* were changed in the Julian calendar to *Julius* and *Augustus*, in honor of Julius Caesar and the emperor Augustus. The correct name of the intercalary month was *mensis intercalaris*. The name Mercedonius, mentioned only by Plutarch (*Numa* 18.3, *Caesar* 59.2) must have been a popular nickname.

[23] Macrobius may have this in mind when he says (1.13.15): *reliquos Februarii mensis dies, qui erant quinque, post intercalationem subiungebant, credo vetere religionis suae more, ut Februarium omni modo Martius consequeretur.* The five days could hardly be identified as belonging to February except by the festivals which occurred during them.

[24] January and March are derived from the names of the gods Janus and Mars, whose rites are performed in these months. February is connected with the verb *februare*, "to purify," because of the purificatory nature of some of its rites. The derivation of April and May is uncertain, as it was in antiquity, while Junius probably comes from Juno, although perhaps from the Etruscan form of her name. For the ancient evidence on these names see Degrassi, pp. 317-323. For modern interpretations see Bömer, *op.cit.* (n. 3) 1.40-42.

[18]

As in the Julian calendar, each month was divided into three sections of unequal length by three days which have special names of their own. The first day of each month is called *Kalendae*, or Kalends. *Nonae*, the Nones, is the name of the fifth day of the short months, of the seventh day of the 31-day months. *Idus*, or Ides, often in the *Fasti* spelled *Eidus*, is the 13th of the short months, the 15th of the long ones. These names are all plural forms, and are identified by the same adjectives as the months.[25] The first of March, for example, is called *Kalendae Martiae* but is usually written in the abbreviated form *Kal. Mart.* Similarly the Nones and Ides become *Non. Mart.* and *Id. Mart.*

Certain ceremonies were carried out on these dividing days,[26] which, as we shall see later, are significant for the history of the calendar. They have been described briefly by Varro[27] and more fully by Macrobius.[28] Varro refers, judging from his use

[25] It is an interesting fact that in Latin and Greek the names of regularly recurring days are often plural, as are many of the annual religious observances which give names to calendar days. Why this should be true of some days and not of others is a puzzle. *Nonae* is the feminine plural of *nonus*, indicating that the Nones are always the 9th day before the Ides. *Kalendae*, always spelled in the archaic manner with a K, is in some way connected with a verb *calo* which occurs in the rites for the day (see n. 27). *Idus* may be of Etruscan derivation. For the ancient evidence on these names see Degrassi, pp. 327-330. Cf. A. H. Salonius, "Zur Römischen Datierung," *AnnAcadScientFenn*, 15. no. 10 (1922).

[26] I shall use the term "dividing days" to refer to the Kalends, Nones, and Ides collectively, when I wish to distinguish them from the larger group of named days.

[27] *De L. L.* 6.27: *Primi dies mensium nominati kalendae, quod his diebus calantur eius mensis nonae a pontificibus, quintanae an septimanae sint futurae, in Capitolio in Curia Calabra sic: "Die te quinti kalo Juno Covella, ⟨aut⟩ septimi die te kalo, Juno Covella."* (The first words in the formula are emendations for the MS readings *dictae quinque* and *septum dictae*.) 6.28: *eodem die* (the Nones) *in Urbe⟨m qui⟩ in agris ad regem conveniebat populus. Harum rerum vestigia apparent in sacris nonalibus in Arce, quod tunc ferias primas menstruas, quae futurae sint eo mense, rex edicit populus.* Cf. Servius Auct., *Aen.* 8.654: *ideo autem "Calabra," quod cum incertae essent kalendae aut Idus, a Romulo constitutum est ut ibi patres vel populus calarentur, id est vocarentur, et scirent, qua die kalendae essent vel etiam idus. a rege sacrificulo idem fiebat ut quoniam adhuc fasti non erant ludorum et sacrificiorum praenoscerent dies.*

[28] 1.15.9-13: *priscis ergo temporibus, antequam fasti a Cn. Flavio scriba invitis patribus in omnium notitiam proderentur, pontifici minori haec provincia delegabatur ut novae lunae primum observaret aspectum visamque regi sacrificulo nuntiaret. itaque sacrificio a rege et minore*

[19]

of the present tense, to what was done at the time when he was writing, presumably just before Caesar's reform of the calendar. According to his account, on the Kalends of each month the pontifices announced publicly, in the Curia Calabra on the Capitoline hill, the day on which the Nones would fall, either the fifth or the seventh of the month. On the Nones the *rex,* presumably the *rex sacrorum,*[29] proclaimed to the people on the *arx* of the Capitoline hill the first[30] festival (*feriae*) which would take place that month. Varro observes that one can see in these *sacra Nonalia* the vestiges of the old custom whereby the people came into the city from the countryside on the Nones to meet with the *rex.* Macrobius tells us that before the calendar was known to everyone, a *pontifex minor* was given the job of watching for the crescent moon, and reporting its appearance to the *rex.* He and the *rex* performed a sacrifice to Juno, while the *regina,* the wife of the *rex,* sacrificed to her in the Regia (1.15.19). Then he summoned the people to the Curia Calabra and announced how many days would elapse from the Kalends (the day on which he was speaking) to the Nones. This was done because on the Nones the country people would come into the city to hear from the *rex* the *causae*

---

pontifice celebrato idem pontifex calata, id est vocata, in Capitolium plebe iuxta curiam Calabram, quae casae Romuli proxima est, quot numero dies a kalendis ad nonas superessent pronuntiabat, et quintanas quidem dicto quinquies verbo καλῶ, septimanas repetito septies praedicabat. verbum autem καλῶ Graecum est, id est voco, et hunc diem, qui ex his diebus qui calarentur primus esset, placuit kalendas vocari. hinc et ipsi curiae ad quam vocabantur Calabrae nomen datum est, et classi, quod omnis in eam populus vocaretur. ideo autem minor pontifex numerum dierum qui ad nonas superesset calando prodebat, quod post novam lunam oportebat nonarum die populares qui in agris essent confluere in urbem, accepturos causas feriarum a rege sacrorum sciturosque quid esset eo mense faciendum. unde quidam hinc nonas aestimant dictas quasi novae initium observationis, vel quod ab eo die semper ad idus novem dies putentur, sicut apud Tuscos nonae plures habebantur, quod hi nono quoque die regem suum salutabant et de propriis negotiis consulebant. See also Lydus, De Mens. 3.10 (44f. Wuensch).

[29] The *rex sacrorum* (or *sacrificulus*), a member of the college of pontifices, was the highest ranking, although not the most powerful, priest in Rome, and in the republican period carried out those religious duties which formerly had been discharged by the Kings.

[30] Presumably in the past, before the calendar was written down (see p. 130), the *rex* had announced all the festivals and their details, as Macrobius indicates. By Varro's day the rite had lost its practical function and only a token announcement was made.

feriarum and to learn what had to be done that month. Macrobius (1.15.16) also reports that on the Ides a sheep (*ovis idulis*) was sacrificed to Jupiter by his own priest, the *Flamen Dialis*, on the *arx*, the northern peak of the Capitoline Hill.[31]

The interesting thing about these ceremonies is that they must have originated in a period when the Romans were using true lunar months based on the observation of the crescent moon. The Kalends then would have been the day after the evening on which the crescent had been first sighted,[32] the Nones would have been the day when the moon was at the first quarter.[33] The number of days between the Kalends and Nones would depend on how soon after the actual conjunction the crescent moon became visible. The Ides would be the day of the full moon. In the calendar of the late Republic the lunar months have disappeared and the days have been fixed into a rigid pattern.[34] The ceremonies which originally were the means by which the people kept track of their calendar could have been omitted in the first century B.C. but survived, as Varro says, as *vestigia*, and perhaps as reminders to the people, just as today holy days are announced, although they are clearly marked in the church calendar.

Besides the dividing days, 45 other days have names which are recorded in the calendar, presumably because they are the occasions of important religious rites. Many of the names are neuter plural adjectives formed from the names of the gods involved, such as the Saturnalia or Vestalia. Others are in some way descriptive of the rites, such as the Regifugium, the Feralia, or the Lucaria. The names of the most popular of these days are often used by Roman writers instead of dates, as we refer to Christmas instead of December 25th.

The Kalends, Nones, and Ides provide the basis for dating

[31] For the location see Varro, *De L. L.* 5.47, and Festus, 372 L.

[32] The Kalends must have been the day after the crescent moon was seen, because the observation must take place after sunset, and Romans did not hold public meetings after sunset (Mommsen, *Staatsrecht*[3] 3.1.378).

[33] The Nones are identified with the first quarter by Dionysius (16.3.2), and Lydus (*De Mens.* 3.10.45 Wuensch). But as long as they really marked the day of the first quarter, they could not yet have been called Nones, for reasons discussed on pp. 131f.

[34] This would have happened, in my opinion, at the time when the pre-Julian calendar was introduced. The date of this event will be discussed in Ch. 7.

each day of the month, which is identified as being so many days before the next dividing day in a backwards count. The day before the Kalends, Nones, or Ides is usually referred to as *pridie Kalendas, Nonas* or *Idus*, but if it is numbered it is the second day before the Kalends etc., because the Romans reckoned inclusively, that is, they include the day from which a series begins as the first of the series. Other days are identified by an idiomatic expression, *ante diem* followed by the number and the dividing day in the accusative, for example *ante diem III Kalendas Ianuarias* (December 28). The grammar of this is difficult to explain[35] but the meaning is clear enough. It is usually abbreviated to *a.d. III Kal. Ian.*, or *III Kal. Ian.*

For the modern reader of Latin the most irritating peculiarity of this system of dating is that the days after the Ides of any month carry the name of the following month. Thus *ante diem III Kal. Ian.* is actually December 28. In equating ancient dates with those in our own calendar one easily makes the mistake of putting an event a month too late. Another trap for the unwary lies in the fact that the Roman calendars given in most reference books are Julian, not pre-Julian. When Caesar added ten days to the Roman year he put them near the ends of the seven 29-day months, one or two in each. As a result, instead of the day after the Ides in all months being *a.d. XVII Kal.*, in these seven months it is either *a.d. XVIII Kal.* or *a.d. XIX Kal.*, and all the following days change correspondingly. *A.d. III Kal. Ian.* becomes December 30, instead of December 28. In translating dates from the period before 45 B.C. into modern dating, one must watch this detail carefully. For example, when Augustus was born in 63 B.C. on September 23, the date was *a.d. VIII Kal. Oct.*, but after the Julian calendar came in, in 45 B.C., September 23 was *a.d. IX Kal. Oct.*, a fact which led to some confusion about the celebration of the anniversary.[36]

THE CONTENTS OF THE *FASTI*

Most of the information presented so far about the Republican year can be found in the ancient authors, but for

[35] See Salonius, *op.cit.* (n. 25) 19-34.
[36] See the note on this day in App. 2.

further details as to the contents of the calendar itself and the form in which it was published, we must turn to the *Fasti*. Only one of these, *Fasti Antiates Maiores* (abbreviated as *Ant. Mai.*) gives us a republican calendar, but it proves that Caesar's reform did not change the basic pattern, and that only one new category of information was added after 45 B.C. Most of the details given in the *Fasti* are also mentioned by the authors, but without the visual representation of the calendar in the inscriptions we would not understand how they were put together, or how some elements in the calendar could be used.

The *Fasti* vary in size from the majestic *Praenestini* (abbreviated as *Praen.*) which is very nearly 2 meters high and about 5.5 broad, to ones that are relatively tiny. It seems probable that they were all built into the walls of buildings, either inside or outside, and served decorative as well as useful purposes. Most of them are cut on stone, but the oldest, *Ant. Mai.*, was painted on white plaster in red and black letters, which made it very effective (Pl. 4).[37] The letters were of two sizes. The essential elements that form the framework of the calendar are given in large letters, and vary from one inscription to another only in details which are usually obvious errors. Additional notes, which vary considerably, are given in small letters.

In the *Fasti* the months are arranged from left to right in vertical columns in which the days of each month are listed from top to bottom. Each column contains several elements. On the left-hand margin there run from top to bottom the large letters A to H in alphabetical order. These letters, known as the nundinal letters (see pp. 27f.), continue uninterruptedly from month to month throughout the year, from A on January 1 to C on the last day of December.[38] Across the top of each monthly column, after the nundinal letter of the first day, stands the large letter K (for *Kalendae*) followed by an abbreviated form of the name of the month. Similarly the names

[37] The reproduction in Degrassi's publication shows the lettering on a light blue background, presumably to differentiate the fragments more clearly from the white paper. A better impression of the colors can be obtained from the plate in the original publication, *NS* (1921) pl. 1. In the fragments themselves, in the storeroom of the Museo Nazionale in Rome, the colors are fast fading.

[38] In the Julian calendar, with 10 more days in the year, the last day is E.

[23]

Nonae and *Idus* (frequently spelled *Eidus*), whether in full or abbreviated form, are written in large letters across the width of the column. In most *Fasti*, the Nones and Ides are lined up across the inscription, which gives a pleasing effect to the total composition but means that the five days between Kalends and Nones in the long months and the three corresponding days in the short months are allowed the same space, which produces some irregularity in the size of the letters in this section.

The 45 other named days throughout the year are identified in large letters across the column by a word which is recognizable as an abbreviation of the name of some religious ceremony referred to by the ancient authors, for example, LVPER for Lupercalia. Each day of the year is also marked by a large letter, or pair of large letters, either F, N, C, NP, or EN. On unnamed days these letters come immediately after the nundinal letter. On named days they follow the name, on the right-hand margin of the column. Three unnamed days are marked by several large letters, twice Q.R.C.F., and once Q.ST. (or S) D.F. The meanings of most of these letters are, as we shall see, explained by the ancient authors.

Many days, including named days, carry notations written in small letters. These are of several different types. The commonest consists of the name of a divinity in the dative, or sometimes in the genitive,[39] occasionally followed by a reference to a place, for example, *Minervae in Aventino*. In the Julian calendars the god's name is often preceded by the word *Feriae* (holy day or holiday),[40] but this does not occur in *Ant. Mai.* Sometimes when these notes refer to named days, they are crowded in below the name, so that they appear to refer to the next day. When this happens in *Ant. Mai.*, which is painted, the correct relationship is indicated by a curved line which connects the note to the named day. The days of the great games in honor of the gods are noted as *Ludi* (sometimes spelled *Loedi*),[41] and the markets or fairs which followed

[39] On this usage see Degrassi, p. 370. The reference to the use of the ablative on p. 383 is obviously a slip, and should read dative.
[40] For a discussion of the meaning of *Feriae*, see pp. 69-73.
[41] A fragment of *Ant. Mai.* assigned by Mancini and Degrassi to September 8-10 contains three C's, each followed by a large M. Degrassi

some of the games are indicated by the word *mercatus*, abbreviated to *merc.* or *merk.* Two anniversaries are noted in the fragments of *Ant. Mai.* which have been preserved, the foundation day of Rome, April 21, and the *dies Alliensis*, July 18, on which in 390 B.C. the Romans were defeated by the Gauls at the river Allia. In the Julian calendars a great many anniversaries of events in the lives of members of the imperial family are noted, and many of them are referred to as *Feriae*. *Praen.*, the biggest of them all, also contains learned explanations of the technical words used in the calendar, or of the rites referred to. This type of commentary is not included in *Ant. Mai.*, which is only of medium size, but we know from literary sources that Fulvius Nobilior (*cos.* 189 B.C.) composed *Fasti* with a commentary,[42] so they may have occurred in more elaborate calendars which have not survived.

The total number of days in a month is often written at the bottom of the month's column. If the dates of the individual days are given, the numerals are placed immediately after the nundinal letters, but curiously enough, in about two-thirds of the calendars which are known, these dates are not given. One would think that they would form an essential element in any calendar, but apparently from the Roman point of view this was not so.

The features which I have described so far are found in both pre-Julian and Julian calendars. *Ant. Mai.* has another which occasioned some surprise when the inscription was first published in 1921. It has, after December, a thirteenth column.[43] The only possible explanation for this column is that it contained the intercalary month. It has two interesting

---

interprets this M(agni) as referring to the Ludi Magni or Romani. I am not convinced of this solution, as Ludi are not elsewhere identified in this way, and the fragment may belong elsewhere. The notation does not occur in any other *Fasti*.

[42] For details on Fulvius, see pp. 124f.

[43] There can be no doubt of this, although only two fragments of it exist. One fragment contains a C nundinal letter, followed by an E and the bottom of ID(=EID). The only month in the pre-Julian year of which the Ides come on a C day is December, and the Ides of December are also preserved. The second fragment contains the name of a day which comes on December 23, and to the right of this letters which must belong to the 13th column.

peculiarities. The Ides and the day following are marked as the C and D days in the nundinal series. Since this is a short month, the Ides must have fallen on the 13th. The first part of the month is lost, but if one works back from the Ides, one finds that the Kalends must have been a G day. This is surprising, because the month was intercalated after February 23 or 24 which are marked D and E, so that one would expect the intercalary Kalends to be E or F. We note, however, that as the result of this jump forward in the series, the intercalary month ends with an A day, just as February does, and that, therefore, for the rest of the intercalary year the series is exactly the same as it is in a normal year. If the jump had not been introduced, the last day of the month would have been G or H, and the Kalends of March would have been H or A, instead of B, and the relationship between the letters in the series and the dates of the months would have differed from the normal one for the major part of every intercalated year.

One fragment of *Ant. Mai.* contains the E and F letters from the end of the intercalary month, which mark *a.d. VI* and *a.d. V Kal. Mart.* On the right edge of the fragment, next to the E, is a large letter R, which must be the beginning of the word Regifugium, the festival which in normal years was held on February 24, *a.d. VI Kal. Mart.* If the Regifugium was listed in the intercalary month, we may assume that the Equirria, which came on *a.d. III Kal. Mart.* was also listed there. Thus we have the interesting situation that in the Republican calendar these festivals were recorded twice, once in February, and once in the intercalary month.

THE INTERPRETATION OF THE CONTENTS

The next step is to interpret the various elements in the calendar. Some of these are sufficiently clear. The dividing days, Kalends, Nones and Ides, and their use, are familiar from their constant occurrence in Latin literature and Roman documents. The full titles of many of the other named days, abbreviated in the calendar, also occur in the authors, and Varro gives most of the rest when, in his *De Lingua Latina* (6.12-26) under the general heading of *civilia vocabula dierum*, he lists

[26]

days *qui deorum causa . . . sunt instituti.* Macrobius (1.16.5-6) defines these days as *feriae stativae*, that is *feriae* which have fixed dates, as distinct from *feriae conceptivae* whose dates were set and announced (*conceptae*) annually by the priests or magistrates.

The meaning of the notes in small letters is made clear in many cases by information given by the authors. Sometimes they identify the god honored on a named day, often adding a reference to a place, in which case the day is probably the anniversary of the dedication of the god's temple in that location.[44] The learned notes of *Praen.* often explain the origin or character of certain rites. The notes on the anniversary days of the imperial household are self-explanatory.

The single letters attached to each day are not always so easy to understand. The first group is that of the nundinal letters. There is, as far as I know, no direct reference in the whole of Latin literature to these letters.[45] Ovid, however, must have had them in mind when, apropos of the types of days given in the calendar, he says *est quoque qui nono semper ab orbe redit* (*Fasti*, 1.54). Elsewhere in Latin literature we find plenty of references to an occasion which returned always in a cycle to the ninth day. It is known as *nundinae*, a plural form like *Kalendae*, the original meaning of which is "ninth day."[46] In ordinary usage, however, it came to mean "market day," or simply "market," because from time immemorial the Romans had held markets on these days. Since the A-H series seems designed to help one to keep track of this cycle of *nundinae*, modern scholars refer to them as the nundinal letters. There is no evidence that they were ever used to identify individual days. No Roman ever refers to a D or E day. Apparently they were simply a device for reckoning. It is assumed by modern students of the calendar that in any one year the *nundinae* were held regularly on days

[44] We can be sure that it is the dedication day when we are told so by an author, Ovid for instance. Otherwise it is a reasonable assumption. The same principle applies to the simple identification of the god without reference to a place, which may also identify a temple dedication day.

[45] Mommsen once thought he had found one but changed his mind (*RC*² 253 n. 49).

[46] For the derivation of the word, see Walde-Hoffmann, *Lateinisches Etymologisches Wörterbuch*³, vol. 2 (Heidelberg 1954) 188, s.v. *Nundina*.

[27]

marked by the same letter, but that, since the number of days in the year is not divisible by eight (the number of days from one *nundinae* to the next), in the following year the letter would change. In a year when the letter was E, for instance, the last *nundinae* of the year would fall on December 23. The ninth day thereafter (counting inclusively and remembering that December had only 29 days) would be January 2, a B day, so, for the next year, *nundinae* would come on B days.[47] In an intercalary year, if the *nundinae* were on an E day in January and February, the first *nundinae* of the intercalary month would fall on H, or A, and would so continue during the rest of the year, because of the skip in the series at the beginning of the intercalary month (see p. 26).

The second group of letters in the calendar consists of those which stand to the right of the nundinal letters on ordinary days and to the right of the name on named days. The clues to the meaning of most of these letters are provided by the notes in *Praen.*, the wording of which is reminiscent of the definitions of certain days given by various authors. Although these notes are sometimes interrupted by breaks in the stone of the inscription, the wording of what survives is sufficiently close to that of the passages in the authors to justify the assumption that both refer to the same thing, and therefore to justify the reconstruction of the notes on the basis of the passages. For example, in *Praen.*, although the left side of the top of the January column is missing, January 2 carries a note of which the last part of the lines read:

> . . . *llantur quod iis licet fari apud*
> . . . *s verbis lege agi non potest.*

Varro (*De L. L.* 6.29) defines *dies fasti* as those *per quos praetoribus omnia verba sine piaculo licet fari,* and elsewhere (*De L. L.* 6.53) as those *quibus verba certa legitima sine piaculo praetoribus licet fari.* Ovid (*Fasti* 1.48) says of the day: *fastus erit per quem lege licebit agi.* Macrobius tells us (1.16.14): *Fasti sunt quibus licet fari praetori tria verba solemnia "do dico addico."* Suetonius[48] offers: *Fasti dies sunt*

---

[47] For detailed discussions of *nundinae*, and the problems related to them, see Ch. 5 and App. 3.

[48] Quoted by Priscian (8.20 K.) from a lost work.

quibus ius fatur. From the occurrence of the words *licet fari* and *lege agi* in the inscription and the authors' definitions we conclude that the note in *Praen.* defined January 2 as one of the *dies fasti* and reconstruct it to read: [*Fasti dies appe*]*llantur, quod iis licet fari apud* [*magistratus populi Romani ea, sine quibu*]*s verbis lege agi non potest.* Since in other *Fasti,* which preserve the part of the January column missing in *Praen.,* January 2 is marked F, we also conclude that all days marked F are *dies fasti.* From the information given by the authors we find that *dies fasti* were those on which the legal process known as *lege agere* or *legis actio* might take place, in the course of which the praetor might pronounce the words *do, dico, addico,* without an expiatory sacrifice. As we shall see later, this definition means that on *dies fasti* citizens might initiate suits in civil law in the court of the *praetor urbanus.*

Having given this example of the method by which we can discover the meanings of most of the letters in this group, I shall postpone a detailed discussion of the evidence to later chapters. At this point I shall simply state the meanings of the rest of the letters, so as to provide the necessary technical vocabulary for further analysis of the calendar. The letter N stands for *dies nefasti,* which are the opposite of *dies fasti* because on them *legis actio* was not permitted. On *dies nefasti* there was also a ban on the activities which characterize days marked C, the *dies comitiales* when the *comitia,* the assemblies of Roman citizens, might be summoned to vote either on proposed legislation, in elections, or on the verdict in certain types of trials for criminal offences. The letters EN stand for *endotercisus,*[49] the archaic spelling of *intercisus.* The days so marked are defined as "split" because they were *nefasti* in the morning, while a sacrificial victim was being killed, and again in the evening, when the final offering of the victim was made, but in the intervening period they were *fasti.* The letters *Q.R.C.F.,* which occur only twice in the year, stand for *Quando Rex Comitiavit Fas.* The only *rex* in republican Rome was the *rex sacrorum* (or *sacrificulus*). Just what the verb *comitiare* means is not known (see p. 107n.), but whatever the action it

---

[49] This is the generally accepted form but recently Hermans has argued that it was *entercisus, MusHelv* 21 (1964) 173ff. See also W. Eisenhut, *RE,* Suppl. 10, 1168.

implies, when the *rex* performed it, the day, which had been *nefastus*, became *fastus*. A similar notation is attached to June 15, the letters *Q.ST.*(or *S.*)*D.F.* This is not preserved in *Praen.* but the ancient authors interpret it to mean *Quando Stercus* (or *Stercum*) *Delatum Fas.* On this day *stercus* was removed from the temple of Vesta, at which point the day, up to that time *nefastus*, became *fastus.*[50] These three days are called *dies fissi.* About two-thirds of the named days are characterized by a letter which is usually referred to in printed books as NP but actually looks like an N with an incomplete loop at the top of the right leg. This is probably an abbreviation of the type technically known as a ligature, in which two letters are combined to form one, in this case N and an archaic form of P. From the nature of the days to which it is attached, we must assume that this character had an important meaning, but no ancient definition of it has survived. Its meaning remains a problem which will be discussed later (see Chapter 4). Three named days are, in some of the *Fasti* but not all, marked FP. Again we have no ancient definition, and the meaning of the letters will be discussed in connection with these days (see Appendix 2, pp. 182f.). The named days themselves were *feriae stativae*, that is, stated days on which every year regularly certain religious ceremonies took place. The word *feriae* is usually translated "festival," although the connotation of the English word is not always appropriate to the Latin. *Feriae* will be discussed more fully in Chapter 4.

---

[50] *Stercus* is usually translated "dung," but the presence of dung in the holy of holies in the temple of Vesta is hard to explain. L. A. Holland, in *Janus and the Bridge* (*PMAAR* 21, Rome 1961) 320f., explains it as "trash," the remnants of offerings which had accumulated in the temple.

CHAPTER 2

THE CHARACTERS OF
THE DAYS IN THE CALENDAR OF THE
FIRST CENTURY B.C.

The description of the calendar given in the preceding chapter shows not only that it was a device for reckoning time, but also that it provided a Roman citizen with a good deal of useful information as to the characters of the various days, so that he could know ahead of time when he might pursue certain activities. This information is also apt to be useful to students of Roman history. For example, the fact that there are several periods in the year in which there are no *dies comitiales* can sometimes explain a delay in legislation or elections for which the ancient historians do not trouble to account. It is, therefore, important that we should be able to reconstruct the calendar of the republic as accurately as possible, with especial attention to the character of each day.

This reconstruction presents some problems. The republican pre-Julian calendar is known to us only in *Fasti Antiates Maiores*, whose fragments give us little more than half the year. Even if it were complete one would not unhesitatingly accept the evidence of a single document. Where the evidence of the Julian *Fasti* unanimously corroborates that of *Ant. Mai.*, we can accept it. Where the other *Fasti* differ from *Ant. Mai.*, we must try to explain the difference and determine which reading was correct for the republican period. Where there is a gap in *Ant. Mai.* we must try to establish what it probably read, remembering that the discovery of another inscription containing a republican calendar might prove us wrong. This last task is rendered more difficult by the fact that the Julian *Fasti* differ among themselves. Differences among all the *Fasti* occur most frequently in the material written in small letters, which suggests that these entries did not form part of the official calendar, but were inserted in each inscription ac-

[31]

cording to the taste or needs of the particular person who designed it.[1] In the following discussion I shall therefore confine myself to the material written in large letters, and especially to those letters which indicate the characters of the days. For the names of the individual *Fasti* and their abbreviations, see the list on pp. 187-90.

UNCERTAIN CHARACTERS

Of the 355 days in the republican year, the characters of 46 are uncertain. These days fall into two groups. Group 1 consists of 28 days which are marked NP in the Julian calendar, but which must have had different characters in the republican calendar. The evidence for 11 of these days is provided by *Ant. Mai.*, in which they are preserved with characters other than NP. The main reason for suspecting a change of character for those 17 days in this group which are not preserved in *Ant. Mai* is that, with 4 exceptions, they are not named days, whereas the other 49 NP days all have names. These exceptions are the Augustalia on October 12, established in honor of Augustus, the Kalends of August and the Nones of February and August. Since Kalends and Nones in other months are not NP days, except the Kalends of March, the latter come under suspicion. Furthermore, an explanation for a change of character is provided in the case of most of the 28 days by notes in the *Fasti* which explain that they were made *feriae* because they were the anniversaries of events connected with members of the imperial family. For a few of the days in this group no such explanation is given in the *Fasti*, but it has long been assumed that they also were *feriae* of the same type. In some cases this assumption has been confirmed by the discovery of *Fasti* with notations not previously known.[2]

The second group consists of 18 days whose characters are uncertain, not because any change can be suspected, but because the evidence of the different *Fasti* is in conflict, and must be weighed in order to determine the probable character in each case. Frequently the conflict is created by a single inscription

[1] On the nature of and reasons for these differences, see Degrassi, p. xxii.
[2] On Group 1 see *CIL* 1².1, p. 299; Wissowa, *RK*², 445f; Degrassi, pp. 368f.

which disagrees with several others. In some cases this is *Ant. Min.*, which was carelessly executed and is far less reliable than the other *Fasti*. I have not included in this group five named days which are marked N only in *Pinc.* or *Ven.*, because these *Fasti* never use NP at all, but only N.

The *Fasti* provide us with direct evidence for the character of each day by the character letters, but where there is disagreement they also provide indirect evidence which, while it is not always conclusive, often indicates a very probable solution. This evidence is derived from the study of the 309 days of the year whose characters are not in doubt. It has long been noted that the *dies fasti* occur regularly on the same dates of each month.[3] It is also true that days of other characters follow certain less obvious patterns within the month and over the year as a whole. Thus one can suggest the probable character of an uncertain day on the basis of its date, and the characters of the days before and after it.

The pattern of the days marked F(asti) or C(omitiales) can be seen most clearly in November, the only month in which there are no days of uncertain character and in which only the Ides (NP) is neither F nor C. Here the Kalends and the Nones and *dies postriduanus* (the following day) of each and *dies postriduanus* of the Ides (*a.d. XVII Kal. Dec.*), are all F. All other days are C. In the other months this pattern is changed only when a day has a character other than F or C. There is no certain case of a day which in November is F being C in any other month, or of one which is C in November being F in any other month.

The pattern followed by days marked N(efastus), NP, or EN(dotercisus) is not so precise, but it is possible to make some generalizations about it. There is no evidence that in the

---

[3] An apparent exception to this rule is found in the Julian *Fasti*. When Caesar added ten days to the year in order to bring it up to 365, he inserted one or two F days, near the end of each of the 29-day months, thus interrupting a sequence of C days. Macrobius gives the dates of the new days (1.14.9), and later explains that they were all *dies fasti* (1.14.12). In *Praen.* January 29 and April 26 are identified as days added by Caesar, and both are marked F. If they had not been F, no one could tell whether the new days were added at the end of the month, or inserted before it, and hence would not know whether these days would have been F in the pre-Julian calendar.

republican calendar any days other than named days were NP, although some named days were not NP. The Nones never were NP, and the Kalends only in March, but all the Ides were, and the majority of other named days. Of the 30 named days whose character is certainly NP,[4] only six precede the Ides, while 24 come later in the month. Of the five named days which are certainly N, four precede the Ides and only one comes later. Of the 42 unnamed days which were certainly marked N, 33 come before the Ides and only nine after the Ides. Thus, if it is uncertain whether a named day should be NP or N, we can say that the odds are slightly in favor of its being N if it comes in the first half of the month, and very much in favor of its being NP if it comes in the last half. It is also a peculiarity of N days that, unless they are named days, they normally occur in groups, or in conjunction with NP days. There are only two cases of an isolated N day interrupting a series of C days, September 12 and 15 (see Appendix 2).

THE DISTRIBUTION OF DAYS

A detailed statement of the evidence for the characters of the days which are in doubt is given in Appendix 2, with the reasons for my conclusions. Here I will simply summarize the results of these conclusions. They are also presented in a schematic reconstruction of the calendar of the late republic in Pl. 3, in which days discussed in the Appendix are marked by an asterisk.

The distribution of days over the year may be presented as follows. There are 195 C days, 58 N days, 49 NP days, 42 F days, 8 EN days, and 3 *dies fissi*, which are half N, half F. (The 3 named days which may be FP are included as F, see the note on February 21 in Appendix 2, pp. 182f.). The F and C days, as we have seen above (p. 33), are so distributed that theoretically a maximum of 5 F days and 23, or 25, C days would be possible in any one month. Actually this ideal is reached only in November, because in other months days of other characters are introduced. Unlike plain F days, the 3 named days which are F or FP, 4 of the 8 EN days, and the 3

---

[4] That is, 30 excluding the dividing days, among which all Ides and the Kalends of March are NP.

dies fissi come later in the month than *a.d. XVII Kal.* and also come on days which in other months are C. This is a point which will come up again in the discussion of the history of the calendar (see pp. 106f.). The minimum number of F days in any month is one (February, June, and July). February has six C days and April has seven. The other months have from 15 (July, December) to 23 (November).

N days present a more irregular pattern over the year, as well as from month to month. In three months there are none (January, August, November) while in both February and April there are 14. Not only do 46 of the 58 precede the Ides, but 52 come in the months from February through July, and only 6 in the whole rest of the year. The NP days also vary in frequency. Every month has at least one, the Ides, but June, September, and November have no others, while December has 6. There are, however, 24 in the first six months and 25 in the last. These results may be tabulated as follows:

	C	N	NP	F	EN	Fissi	Named days not K, N, or I
January	19	0	4	4	2		3
February	6	14	5	1	2		6 (1N, 1F)
March	18	1	6	4	1	1	4
April	7	14	5	3	0		5 (1F)
May	18	4	3	5	0	1	5 (3N)
June	16	10	1	1	0	1	2 (2N)
July	15	9	6	1	0		5
August	16	0	6	6	1		6 (1F)
September	21	2	1	5	0		0
October	21	1	4	4	1		3
November	23	0	1	5	0		0
December	15	3	7	3	1		6
Totals	195	58	49	42	8	3	45

I would have been very pleased if the total of *dies comitiales* had come to 193, because this would have suggested that the number of these days was supposed to match the number of centuries in the *comitia centuriata*. Although the count remains stubbornly at 195, I still suspect that originally there was some connection between the *dies comitiales* and the centuries.

CHAPTER 3

DIES COMITIALES AND DIES FASTI

THE COMITIA

We are now in a position to consider in more detail the various characters assigned to the days in the calendar, and the ways in which they influenced life in Rome in the first century B.C.

The largest group of days is made up of the *dies comitiales*. The explanation of their function requires a brief description of the *comitia* for which they were designated.[1] The most important *comitia* of the late republic were the assemblies of the citizens of Rome which were summoned to vote on various matters by magistrates who had the right to deal directly with the people (*ius cum populo agendi*). Before the *comitia* met, the auspices were taken by the magistrate. At the meeting the citizens voted on legislation in response to the demand (*rogatio*) of the presiding magistrate, on candidates for public office presented to them, and on the verdict in certain types of criminal trials (*iudicia populi*).[2]

There were two major assemblies, whose names were derived from the ways in which they were organized. In the *comitia centuriata* the people were arranged in groups called centuries, each of which cast a single corporate vote. Citizens were assigned to their centuries on the basis of their financial status (*census*), and the centuries voted in the descending order of wealth. This assembly elected consuls, praetors, and censors, and voted on the verdict in criminal trials which involved the *caput* (life or citizenship) of a citizen. In the first century, although the *comitia centuriata* had the right to vote on legislation, it very rarely did. It could be summoned by

[1] On *comitia* see Mommsen, *Staatsrecht*[3] 3.240-418; Liebenam, *RE* 4.1.679-715, s.v. *comitia*; G. W. Botsford, *RA*; L. R. Taylor, *Roman Voting Assemblies* (Ann Arbor 1966).

[2] For a recent discussion of the last type see W. Kunkel, *Untersuchungen zur Entwicklung des römischen Kriminalverfahrens in vorsullanischer Zeit* (*Bayer. Akad. der Wiss., Phil.-Hist. Kl., Abhandl.* n.f. 56, 1962).

[36]

consuls or praetors. If a tribune of the plebs wished to bring a man to trial before the *comitia centuriata*, he had to persuade a consul or a praetor to summon it for him.

In the *comitia tributa* the people were arranged in their 35 tribes, each of which cast a single vote. The tribes were geographical divisions of Roman territory, and a man belonged to the tribe in the area of which he lived or held property. The *comitia tributa* elected magistrates other than consuls, praetors, and censors, and voted on the verdict in criminal trials in which the penalty was a major fine. In the late republic it voted on almost all new legislation. It was summoned by the consuls and praetors. When the people in their tribal organization were summoned by a tribune of the plebs, who could not take the auspices, the assembly strictly speaking was not the *comitia tributa* but the *concilium plebis*, from which patricians were excluded.[3] For practical purposes, however, in the late republic the *concilium* was identical with the *comitia tributa,* except that it was not held under auspices, and could elect only tribunes of the plebs and plebeian aediles. Since the passing of the *Lex Hortensia* in 287 B.C. *plebiscita* (acts passed by the *concilium*) had been as binding on the whole people as *leges* passed by the *comitia*. An offshoot of the *comitia tributa* was an assembly composed of 17 of the 35 tribes, chosen by lot, which in the first century[4] elected members of the priestly colleges (pontifices, augurs, *quindecemviri sacris faciundis*, and *septemviri epulones*).

The *comitia curiata*, made up of *curiae* in which membership was hereditary, had originally been the only Roman assembly, but as the others developed, they took over most of its functions, until in the late republic it existed only in a vestigial form, in which thirty lictors represented the thirty *curiae* from which it derived its name. They were summoned by the *pontifex maximus* to vote on adoptions which involved the transfer of a man from one *gens* to another, and on wills of a certain type. They also voted on the *Lex Curiata* which annually confirmed the *imperium* of the newly elected chief magistrates, and they wit-

[3] Cf. L. R. Taylor, *op.cit.* (n. 1) 61f.
[4] Prior to the *Lex Domitia de sacerdotibus* of 104 B.C., it had elected only the *pontifex maximus,* for which purpose it originated during the third century.

nessed the inauguration of the *flamines maiores*, the priests of Jupiter, Mars, and Quirinus, and of the *rex sacrorum*. An assembly summoned by the *pontifex maximus* is called *calata*, from an archaic verb *calare*, "to summon," and as the meetings of the people summoned to hear the calendar announcements on the Kalends and Nones were described as *calata*, it may be that they were meetings of the *comitia curiata*.

The Romans had popular gatherings of another type, which were not *comitia*, although they are sometimes confused with them. A *contio* was a group of citizens summoned, without the taking of auspices,[5] by a magistrate who wished to address them, often on a subject on which they would later vote in the *comitia*. Only the magistrate who summoned them and those whom he invited up to the tribunal might speak. A magistrate of higher rank could, however, take the meeting away from him. The crowd had informal but vigorous ways of expressing its feelings on the subject under discussion, and the *contiones* frequently broke up in riots. *Comitia*, in which no speeches were allowed, were normally preceded by a *contio* which ended when the presiding magistrate ordered the crowd to separate into its voting groups.

DEFINITIONS OF *DIES COMITIALES*

In Chapter 1, I defined *dies comitiales* simply as those days on which the *comitia* might meet. The definitions given by the ancient authors are more technical, and are expressed in terms of the functions either of the magistrate or of the people. Macrobius (1.16.14), centering on the magistrate, says: *comitiales sunt quibus cum populo agi licet*, and then adds a further important detail: *et fastis quidem lege agi potest, cum populo non potest, comitialibus utrumque potest*. On *dies comitiales* the magistrate may deal with the people, and also, presumably when the *comitia* has not been called, action in civil

---

[5] The difference between *contio* and *comitia* is clearly stated by Gellius in an elucidation of a passage from Messalla: *"cum populo agere"* (the technical phrase for holding *comitia*) *est rogare quid populum, quod suffragiis suis aut iubeat aut vetet*, *"contionem" autem "habere"* *est verba facere ad populum sine ulla rogatione* (13.16.3). If the *contio* preceded the *comitia* for which auspices had been taken, perhaps, as Botsford says (*RA* 110), the auspices "extended to the *contio*," but I doubt it.

law (*lege agi*) is permitted, as on *dies fasti*. Ovid's definition (*Fasti* 1.53): *est quoque quo populum ius est includere saeptis*, contains a reference to the *Saepta*, the enclosures in which the voting units cast their ballots. *Fasti Praenestini* has a mutilated note for the first C day of the year, January 3, which reads: [*popul*]*us coire convocare*[6] *cogi potest ac lege . . . quem lege . . . lege agi non*. The first words describe the summoning of the people, and the latter part suggests that, like Macrobius' definition, it included a comment on *dies fasti*. Varro (*De L. L.* 6.29) gives us some further information: *Comitiales dicti, quod tum ut* ⟨*comitiis ad*⟩*esset*[7] *populus constitutum est ad suffragium ferendum, nisi si quae feriae conceptae essent propter quas non liceret ut Compitalia et Latinae*. According to this, the *dies comitiales* were so called because the people then attended the *comitia* to vote, unless certain religious celebrations which had no fixed date (*feriae conceptivae*) had been announced for days which were normally *comitiales*.[8] A brief definition given by Paulus (34 L.): *comitiales dies appellabant cum in comitio conveniebant,* is misleading because, like Varro's, it seems to imply that the *comitia* met on all *dies comitiales*, instead of on those for which a meeting had been set, which was certainly not the case in the late republic.[9]

RESTRICTIONS ON *DIES COMITIALES*

Varro's definition of *dies comitiales* tells us that *comitia* could not be held on these days if annual *feriae conceptivae*

---

[6] This must be a mistake for *convocari*, since the sense requires the passive infinitive. See Degrassi, p. 332.

[7] The MSS here read *ut esset populus*. It is obvious that the word from which Varro derived *comitialis* has fallen out. Degrassi, p. 332, accepts *ut* ⟨*in Comitio ad*⟩ *esset*, suggested by E. Vetter. I agree that *adesse* is the word used both in the summons to the *comitia* (Varro, *De L. L.* 6.91; Gellius, *N.A.* 15.27.4) and of attendance (Cicero, *pro Sestio* 109), but *in Comitio* seems improbable, because it does not fit the contemporary facts. If the *comitia curiata* still met there, the *centuriata* did not, because it could not meet inside the pomerium, and there is only one extant reference (Varro, *R.R.* 1.2.9) to the *tributa* or the *concilium plebis* meeting in the *comitium*.

[8] Varro here mentions only two of the *feriae conceptivae* which were annual, but there were several others, some of which he had described in 6.25f.

[9] For a discussion of the meetings of *comitia* in the early republic, see Ch. 6, pp. 104-8, 111.

happened to be scheduled then. *Comitia* could also be prevented, if special *feriae*, known as *imperativae*, were announced for *dies comitiales* by priests or magistrates. These could be rites intended to expiate prodigies,[10] which occurred in Rome with surprising frequency, or they might be *supplicationes*, days of prayer which were either thanksgivings to the gods for success[11] or prayers in times of danger (see p. 45).

Other occasions besides *feriae* could prevent the meeting of *comitia* on their own days. Macrobius quotes a statement from L. Julius Caesar's book on the auspices to the effect that on Roman *nundinae* it was impossible to hold *comitia*, and explains this by a reference to Granius Licinianus, who stated that *Lex Hortensia* (287 B.C.) had made *nundinae* into *dies fasti*[12] in order that people coming in from the country for the market might be able to settle law suits. Pliny (*N.H.* 18.12) and Festus (176 L.) mention the same restriction. How this came about, and what the character of *nundinae* had been previously will be discussed later (see pp. 103-6), but we have no

---

[10] An example of what such *feriae* could do is given by Livy, 34.55.1-5: *Principio anni, quo L. Cornelius Q. Minucius consules fuerunt, terrae motus ita crebri nuntiabantur, ut non rei tantum ipsius, sed feriarum quoque ob id indictarum homines taederet; nam neque senatus haberi neque res publica administrari poterat sacrificando expiandoque occupatis consulibus.* Finally the senate decreed that no one should report another earthquake on the day on which *feriae* had been set to expiate a previous one. The next year when the same prodigy occurred, there was no such effort to obviate the inconvenience: *terra dies duodequadraginta movit; per totidem dies feriae in sollicitudine ac metu fuere; in triduum eius rei causa supplicatio habita est* (Livy, 35.40.7). For *feriae* and earthquakes, cf. Suetonius, *Claud.* 22. On prodigies see L. Wulker, *Geschichtliche Entwicklung des Prodigiumswesen bei den Römern* (Leipzig 1903); R. Bloch, *Les prodiges dans l'antiquité classique* (Paris 1963).

[11] This type of *supplicatio* was often decreed in honor of a general who had won a victory. The number of days for the celebration increased steadily during the republic, until Caesar received 20 days for victories in Gaul (Caesar, *B.G.* 4.38.5; 7.90.8) and in 43 B.C. Cicero proposed a fifty-day *supplicatio* after the victory of Octavian, Hirtius, and Pansa over Antony (Cicero, *Phil.* 14.37). See L. Halkin, *La supplication d'action de grâce chez les Romains* (Liège 1953).

[12] 1.16.29f. *Julius Caesar sexto decimo Auspiciorum libro negat nundinis contionem advocari posse, id est cum populo agi, ideoque nundinis Romanorum haberi comitia non posse . . . lege Hortensia effectum ut (nundinae) fastae essent, uti rustici, qui nundinandi causa in urbem veniebant, lites componerent.*

reason to doubt that in the late republic the praetor could hold court on *nundinae* and assemblies could not meet. An exception to this rule probably prevented action at law also on *nundinae* if *feriae conceptivae* had been set for the same day.[13]

I do not know of any evidence that the use of *dies comitiales* was restricted during the celebration of the *Ludi*, but even if religious scruple did not so dictate, common sense would have done so. The majority of the citizen body attended the games and would have resented being called away from them. Moreover, consuls or praetors presided over the games, and could not have absented themselves. Politicians would have found attendance at the games desirable, for the crowd often expressed its opinions about political leaders at appropriate points during the dramatic performances, and a popular man might receive a very useful ovation when he entered the theater. The practice of *instauratio*, the repetition of games and *feriae* if some mistake had been made in ritual, also restricted *dies comitiales*.

There were two laws in effect in the first century B.C. which further limited the use of *dies comitiales*. The *Leges Aelia et Fufia* provided that no law might be presented to the *comitia* for a vote in the period between the announcement of the date for the *comitia* for elections and the actual day of the elections.[14] *Lex Caecilia Didia* required that a certain minimum period of time should elapse between the *promulgatio* of a law, and the *rogatio*, that is, between the day on which the magistrate who was proposing a law publicly announced its text and the day

[13] *Lites* were not permitted on *feriae*. See Cicero, *De Leg.* 2.19 and 29; Isidore, *De Nat. Rerum* 1.4, probably quoting Suetonius. Cicero (*De Div.* 1.102) says that in the formula for proclaiming *feriae* the order was given *ut litibus et iurgiis se abstinerent*. The rule probably derives from the general principle given by Macrobius (1.15.21) *feriis autem vim cuiquam fieri piaculare est*, although this did not prevent trials under public or criminal law from taking place on *feriae*.

[14] For a fuller discussion of these laws see Ch. 6, pp. 95ff. They contained other provisions which are frequently referred to in the ancient sources but the only direct evidence for this provision is the comment on Cicero *In Vatinium* 23 in the *Scholia Bobiensia* (148 Stangl): ⟨*De*⟩ *legibus dicit Aelia et Fufia, quae non sinebant prius aliqua de re ad populum ferri quam comitia haberentur ad designandos magistratus.* Dio (36.39) comments that, because the date of the elections had been announced in 67 B.C., a certain law could not be voted on.

on which he asked the *comitia* to vote on it. The period of time was twenty-five days, including both the day of the *promulgatio* and the *rogatio*, and was known as a *trinum nundinum*.[15] An attempt was made towards the end of the republic to increase the number of days on which *comitia* might be held. In 58 B.C. P. Clodius Pulcher, as tribune of the plebs, carried a law which apparently was intended to rescind the provisions of *Leges Aelia et Fufia*.[16] Among other details it provided that laws might be presented to the comitia on all *dies fasti*.[17] The question of whether this *Lex Clodia* remained in effect has been much debated,[18] but I know of no evidence that after 58 B.C. *comitia* ever met on *dies fasti* to vote on a law. Those legislative *comitia* whose dates are known come on *dies comitiales*.[19] Moreover, none of the definitions of *dies fasti*, all of which were written after 58 B.C., recognizes that it was possible to hold *comitia* on them, and their character was carefully preserved in the Julian *Fasti*. If Clodius' law was not actually repealed, it was certainly a dead letter as far as the calendar was concerned.

DIES COMITIALES AND THE SENATE

Although most of the rules dealing with *dies comitiales* prevent their use for *comitia*, for a few years at the end of the

[15] *Schol. Bob.* 140 Stangl: *Caecilia est autem et Didia quae iubebant in promulgandis legibus trinundinum tempus observari.* Cf. Cicero, *Phil.* 5.7.: *Ubi Lex Caecilia Didia, ubi promulgatio trinum nundinum.* Also Cicero, *De Domo* 41; *pro Sestio* 33; *Priscian,* 7.3.9. On the *trinum nundinum,* its length and its history, see App. 3.

[16] Cicero described this law, with perhaps some understandable exaggeration, as one *quae omnia iura religionum, auspiciorum, potestatum, omnis leges quae sunt de iure et de tempore legum rogandarum, una rogatione delevit.* We are concerned here with the *tempus legum rogandarum* (*pro Sestio* 56). For other evidence on this law see n. 17 below, and Cicero, *in Vat.* 18; *post red. in sen.* 11; *de har. resp.* 58; *in Pis.* 9; Asconius on *in Pis.* 9 (15 Stangl); Dio, 38.13.3.

[17] According to Cicero, what the law provided was *ut omnibus fastis diebus legem ferri liceret* (*pro Sestio* 33, cf. *De Prov. Cons.* 46). This does not mean that *dies fasti* became *dies comitiales,* or that the two types of day were assimilated. It means just what it says, that legislative *comitia* could meet on *dies fasti* as well as on *dies comitiales.* I mention this point because it has often been misstated in discussions of *Lex Clodia,* most recently by Astin, "Leges Aelia et Fufia," *Latomus* 23 (1964) 429.

[18] For recent bibliography see Ch. 6, n. 5.

[19] See list on page 58f.

[42]

republic these days could in turn prevent the meetings of the Senate. This rule is attributed to a *Lex Pupia*, probably passed in 61 B.C., but its exact nature is not clear, and, since it is of some importance in the complex history of the following decades, it will be useful to consider the evidence in some detail.[20] All the ancient references to the rule are related to the events of the years 57 to 49 B.C. In describing those of January, 57 B.C., Cicero (*Pro Sestio* 74) says: *consecuti dies pauci omnino Ianuario mense per quos senatum haberi liceret*. In the following year, in a letter (*Q.F.* 2.2.3) describing a senate meeting held *a.d. XVI Kal. Feb.* (January 15, Carmentalia NP) he gives the reason why the Senate cannot meet again: *consecuti sunt dies comitiales per quos senatus haberi non poterat*. In another letter reporting the same event he is more explicit: *senatus haberi ante K. Februarias per legem Pupiam, id quod scis, non potest, neque mense Febr. toto, nisi perfectis aut reiectis legationibus* (*Fam.* 1.4.1). These passages indicate that *Lex Pupia* forbade the Senate to meet during the long series of *dies comitiales* from January 16 to the end of the month, and that in February the reception of foreign embassies by the Senate took precedence over regular meetings. The latter provision seems to have come from a *Lex Gabinia*, and to conflict with *Lex Pupia*, for in 54 B.C. we hear (Cicero, *Q.F.* 2.12.3) that Appius Claudius is claiming that *Lex Pupia* does not forbid him to convene the Senate in February, and that *Lex Gabinia* requires him to do so for the embassies: *comitiali-*

[20] On *Lex Pupia* see P. Willems, *Le Sénat de la république romaine*, vol. 2 (Paris 1883) 151-156; R. Y. Tyrrell-L. C. Purser, *Correspondence of Cicero* (Dublin and London, 1st ed. 1890, 2nd ed. 1914) 3.298-301 (3².330-333); G. Rotondi, *LPPR* 399; A. O'Brien-Moore, *RE* Suppl. 6.702, s.v. *senatus*. The date of the law is uncertain. The consulship of M. Pupius Piso Frugi Calpurnianus in 61 B.C. provides an obvious explanation of its name. Mommsen dated it to the middle of the second century B.C., on the grounds that from this time until 91 B.C. there are no known instances of the senate meeting on a comitial day, and relatively few thereafter. (*Staatsrecht*³ 3.923). Lange (*RA* 2³.392) and Botsford (*RA* 425) date it in 71 B.C., in the praetorship of M. Pupius (cf. Broughton, *MRR* 2.121, who puts the praetorship in 72) on the grounds that it should have preceded *Lex Gabinia* of 67 B.C. Willems accepts 61 B.C., pointing to the several instances of senate meetings on comitial days in 63 B.C. After 61 no more are known until 52 B.C. On senate meetings, see also P. Stein, *Die Senatssitzungen der Ciceronischen Zeit (68-43)* (Diss. Münster 1930). For dates, see the list on pp. 55-58, below.

bus diebus qui Quirinalia (February 17) *sequuntur Appius interpretatur non impediri se lege Pupia quo minus habeat senatum et, quod Gabinia sanctum sit, etiam cogi ex Kal. Febr. usque ad Kal. Mart. legatis senatum cottidie dare.* The effect of convening the senate would apparently have been to prevent the *comitia* being held, for Cicero adds: *ita putantur detrudi comitia in mensem Martium,* which is doubtless what Appius Claudius was trying to achieve, in order to prevent the tribunes from bringing measures against Gabinius to the people. That his interpretation of the law was open to question is shown by Cicero's comment that the tribunes of the plebs intended to hold the *comitia* in spite of him: *sed tamen his comitialibus tribuni pl. de Gabinio se acturos esse dicunt.* There are other references to the conflict between senate meetings and *dies comitiales* which do not refer to *Lex Pupia.* A *senatus consultum* of 51 B.C. (Cicero, *ad. Fam.* 8.8.5) made special provision that, to deal with an urgent piece of business, the senate might meet on *dies comitiales* after the Kalends of March. It is odd that the *senatus consultum* itself is dated on a comitial day (September 29). Caesar implies that in the first five days of January, 49 B.C., the Senate could not meet on the two *dies comitiales,* January 3 and 4.[21] It did, however, meet on January 7, which is comitial, but this day may have been a *nundinae* and thus have become *dies fastus.*[22]

The exact terms of *Lex Pupia* are not clear. The only explicit references to it are related to January and February and it may have restricted Senate meetings only in these months, so that new legislation might be brought before the *comitia* promptly at the beginning of the year. There is no evidence that the *comitia* were forbidden by law to meet when the Senate did, but since both required the presence of magistrates, simultaneous meetings would have been inconvenient, if not impossible.[23] The only evidence that Senate meetings were restricted after

[21] *B.C.* 1.5.4 *itaque V primis diebus quibus haberi senatus potuit, qua ex die consulatum iniit Lentulus, biduo excepto comitiali, et de imperio Caesaris et de amplissimis viris, tribunis plebis, gravissime acerbissimeque decernitur.*

[22] Mommsen, *Staatsrecht*[3] 3.923. See below, p. 60 n. 54.

[23] Cf. the occasion when *comitia* are postponed in 63 B.C. to give the senate a chance to meet (Cicero, *pro Murena* 51).

February is the *senatus consultum* of 51 B.C. but it does not contain, as one would expect it to, any specific exemption from *Lex Pupia*. Mommsen (*Staatsrecht*³ 3.922f.) argued that *Lex Pupia* applied to the whole year, but that the Senate could exempt itself from the rule, if by so doing it did not interfere with scheduled *comitia*. Lange (*RA* 2³, 392f.) and Botsford (*RA* 425) interpret the law as forbidding Senate meetings only for days when the *comitia* actually met, and then only during the actual meeting. I am inclined to believe that *Lex Pupia* referred only to January and February, but that the *mos maiorum* dictated that the Senate should avoid comitial days throughout the year. That some principle did govern the choice of days for Senate meetings is clear from the item included in the book written by Varro at the request of Pompey when he was about to enter his first consulship (70 B.C.) and needed instructions on how to preside in the Senate; *quibus diebus habere senatum ius non sit* (Gellius, 14.7.9). There is however, no reference to a law, and earlier in the same passage *ius* seems to mean *mos maiorum* (14.7.4-5).

DIES COMITIALES AND POLITICS

The passages already cited from the ancient authors have indicated that, up to the fall of the republic, the rules relating to *dies comitiales* were no mere relics uncarthed from the past by antiquarians, but were in full force and had to be reckoned with. Of the twenty-seven meetings of the legislative and electoral *comitia* for which I have been able to find dates between the years 188 B.C. and 49 B.C. (see p. 58f.), not one comes on a day which is not *comitialis*. The rules by which the character of comitial days could be altered were used to advantage by politicians who wished to hamper their rivals' efforts.[24] Cicero (*Q.F.* 2.5.2) for example, in April, 56 B.C., praises the consul Lentulus for having eliminated *dies comitiales* by having the *Feriae Latinae* repeated and providing *supplicationes*, thus blocking some pernicious laws, especially one that the tribune C. Cato had promulgated. Cato was furious, and proclaimed in a *contio* that, if his days were taken

[24] Cf. L. R. Taylor, *Party Politics in the Age of Caesar* (Sather Classical Lectures 22, Berkeley 1949) 79f.

from him, he, presumably by his power of *obnuntiatio*, would in his turn prevent the holding of *comitia*, probably for elections (*Q.F.* 2.5.4). Considering that March with its 18 comitial days was passing and April has only 7, three of which come during *Ludi*, one can understand his rage. That this game could sometimes have embarrassing consequences can be seen in a letter from Caelius to Cicero in 50 B.C. (*Fam.* 8.11.1). He explains that Curio, fond as he is of Cicero, cannot vote for a *supplicatio* in honor of Cicero's victory in Cilicia, because if he did he would be thought to be playing into the hands of his opponents, who had already deprived him of all of his *dies comitiales* to date.

An interesting example of the unfortunate consequences of ignoring the rules is provided by Manilius, the tribune of 66 B.C. He entered office on the usual date, December 10, in 67 B.C., and on December 29 he carried a law which was promptly annulled by the senate the next day (Dio 36.42). The grounds for this action are made clear by Asconius' (57, 52 Stangl) comment on Cicero's reference to the law as one *in quo cum multa reprehensa sint tum inprimis celeritas actionis.* He explains that Manilius carried the law a few days after he had entered office and on the day of the Compitalia. In the first place, then, even if he had promulgated his law on the very day he entered office, he carried it before a *trinum nundinum* had elapsed, and thus had contravened *Lex Caecilia Didia*. The Compitalia was one of those *feriae conceptivae* which, when they came on comitial days, prevented the holding of *comitia* (see p. 39). Thus the senate had two good reasons for its action.[25]

DIES COMITIALES, COMITIA CURIATA AND CONTIONES

I know of no evidence that meetings of the *comitia curiata* were in any way limited by the characters of the days. The

[25] It may be this case Quintilian had in mind in the second part of his advice on how to attack the validity of a law: *aut enim de iure dubitari potest eius qui rogat, ut de P. Clodi, qui non rite creatus tribunus arguebatur; aut de ipsius rogationis, quod est varium, sive non trino forte nundino promulgata, sive non idoneo die* (2.4.35).

only dated meeting that I have been able to find came on *a.d. IX Kal. Sept.*, 69 B.C., which is a *dies intercisus*. It was the occasion of the inauguration of Cornelius Lentulus Niger as *flamen Martialis* (Macrobius, 3.13.11; cf. Broughton, *MRR* 2.135). Since the *comitia curiata* was concerned with matters very different from those which came before the other *comitia*, mainly matters of religion, I suggest that it would usually be held on days other than *comitiales*. If the *comitia calata* summoned for the announcement of the calendar was *curiata* (see p. 38) this suggestion would be supported, as it always met on Kalends and Nones, which are either F. or N.

L. Julius Caesar in his book on the auspices said that a *contio* cannot be held on Roman *nundinae*[26] (p. 40 n. 12). That this rule was not adhered to is sometimes deduced from a description of a *contio* given by Cicero (*Att.* 1.14.1): *tr. pl. Fufius in contionem producit Pompeium; res agebatur in Circo Flaminio et erat in eo ipso loco illo die nundinarum* πανήγυρις.[27] But the emphasis on the place and day suggests surprise at the crowd, and Cicero may have meant, not that this was a *nundinae*, but that the crowd was as big as if it had been. Mommsen thought it probable that *contiones* could be held only on *dies comitiales*, but the evidence which he cites refers only to the rule against *nundinae*.[28] As a matter of fact, the *contiones* whose dates we know were held on days of every character in the calendar, including NP, but I believe that they could not be held on *nundinae*, any more than *comitia* could, and for the same practical reasons (see pp. 105f.).

[26] Macrobius 1.16.29: *Caesar . . . negat nundinis contionem advocari posse, id est cum populo agi, ideoque nundinis Romanorum haberi comitia non posse.* The interpretation of these words is complicated by the definition of *contio* as *agere cum populo*, which properly applies only to *comitia*. (See note 5.) I am convinced that this is an interpolation by Macrobius, who felt that a definition would be helpful, but, characteristically, chose the wrong one. If the definition is omitted, the statement means that *contiones* cannot be called on *nundinae* and that *therefore* on Roman *nundinae comitia* cannot be held. The point is that *comitia* are preceded by *contiones*, and without a *contio* there cannot be *comitia*. Note the emphasis on Roman *nundinae*. The rule does not apply elsewhere. In the *Lex Coloniae Genetivae*, 81, we find the requirement *in contione palam luci nundinis in forum ius iurandum adigito* (*FIRA* 1.185).

[27] Mommsen, *Staatsrecht*[3] 1.199.

[28] *Loc.cit.*

DIES FASTI

The definition of *dies fasti* given in Chapter 1 was of necessity somewhat simplified, but we are now ready to examine the evidence in detail. First it should be noted that the adjective *fastus* is a technical term which is never used for any other purpose than to describe this group of days in the calendar.[29] The earliest statement about these days is Varro's. His enormous prestige must have led to its general adoption, for most of the later definitions show its influence. This has been unfortunate, because Varro had a particular purpose in composing his definition which compelled him to emphasize a minor aspect of the *dies fasti* at the expense of a complete picture.[30] In the section of his *De Lingua Latina* which concerns us here, he is discussing the origins of certain groups of Latin words, specifically words associated with periods of time, and the activities connected with them. In his definitions of *fasti* and later of *nefasti,* he is trying to demonstrate that these words are connected with the verb *fari,* "to speak." Thus he says (*De L. L.* 6.29): *dies fasti, per quos praetoribus omnia verba sine piaculo licet fari.* Shortly afterwards (6.30) he defines *dies nefasti* as those *per quos . . . nefas fari praetorem* "*do*" "*dico*" "*addico*". . . . This gives the impression that the *dies fasti* are characterized primarily by the words which the praetor may speak on them. He then explains, almost as an afterthought, that, *because* of this restriction on certain words, action at law, which requires the use of these words, is impossible on *dies nefasti*: *itaque non potest agi; necesse est aliquo ⟨eorum⟩ uti verbo, cum lege qui⟨d⟩ peragitur.* The same emphasis on the etymology is preserved in another passage (*De L. L.,* 6.53): *hinc fasti dies, quibus verba certa legitima sine piaculo praetoribus licet fari; at hoc nefasti quibus diebus ea fari ius non est, et, si fati sunt, piaculum faciunt.* Ovid

---

[29] The *Thesaurus Linguae Latinae* cites two examples, from late Latin, of *fastus* used with the negative as a synonym for *nefastus.* The masculine plural, *fasti,* is of course used freely as a noun.

[30] I am much indebted to the analysis of Varro's purpose presented by J. Paoli ("Les définitions Varroniennes des Jours fastes et néfastes," *Revue Historique de Droit français et étranger* [1952] 294-327), although I cannot accept his implication that Varro was attempting a deliberate falsification of the facts.

[48]

echoes Varro in his definition of *nefastus* (*Fasti* 1.47): *ille nefastus erit per quem tria verba silentur.* So does Macrobius: *Fasti sunt quibus licet fari praetori tria verba sollemnia do dico addico* (1.16.14). But in defining *dies fasti* Ovid says (*Fasti* 1.47) *fastus erit per quem lege licebit agi,* thus making their primary characteristic the possibility of action at law which Varro had mentioned only incidentally. Macrobius (1.16.14) does the same thing when he draws his distinction between *dies fasti* and *dies comitiales: comitiales sunt quibus cum populo agi licet, et fastis quidem lege agi potest, cum populo non potest, comitialibus utrumque potest.* This not only makes the action at law primary but gives us a second negative definition, that *comitia* (*agere cum populo*) could not be held on these days.[31] Caius, the jurist of the second century A.D., emphasizes the action at law in his definition of *dies nefastus: id est quo non licebat lege agere* (*Inst.* 4.29). Suetonius, in his *De Anno,* which is known only from quotations by other authors, produced an amusing compromise in his definition: *fasti dies sunt quibus ius fatur, id est dicitur,*[32] *ut nefasti quibus non dicitur* (Priscian, 8.20 Keil). He accepts Varro's etymology, but recognizes that in correct legal terminology the verb used of the praetor's pronouncement is always *dicere.*[33]

This survey of the evidence shows that the more inclusive and the technically correct description of the characteristic

---

[31] Cf. Livy, 1.19; *Idem* (Numa) *nefastos dies fastosque fecit quia aliquando nihil cum populo agi utile futurum erat.* This sentence is usually taken to mean that Numa established two main categories of days, *fasti* and *nefasti,* and that *comitiales* came under *fasti,* but the causal clause seems to me to indicate that Livy was defining the days on which *comitia* could not be held.

[32] *id est dicitur* is an implicit correction of Varro. Suetonius, like any Roman with legal experience, would have known that *fari* is never used in place of *dicere* in legal terminology. The same correction occurs in Isidore, *De Nat. Rerum* 1.4.

[33] For the definition of *dies fasti* in *Fasti Praen.,* see Ch. 1, p. 28f. A mutilated passage in Festus (162 L.) seems to have defined *nefastus* in terms of the praetor's three words. Paulus, in a section for which the part of Festus which he was excerpting does not exist, adds a note of cheer with the improbable statement: *fastis diebus iocunda fari licebat; nefastis quaedam non licebat fari* (83 L.). The best emendation for *iocunda* seems to be Huschke's *cuncta,* as a parallel for Varro's *omnia verba.*

activity of *dies fasti* is *lege agere,* if one is looking at it from the point of view of the man who brings the *legis actio,* or *ius dicere,* if one is thinking of the praetor. Varro, in his search for a derivation for *fasti,* has concentrated on one incident in the legal process, and introduced into the situation a verb which does not belong in the legal vocabulary at all. I have labored this point because Varro's concentration on the praetor's three words has sometimes led modern scholars to see in them the survival of a religious formula, and in the restriction on them a primitive tabu.[34] This can obscure the meaning that *dies fasti* had in the late Republic and lead to unjustified interpretations.

THE FUNCTION OF *DIES FASTI*

The history of the late republic gives the impression that the Romans spent most of their time in the law courts. As a result, a student who reads, for example, that on these days "civil and especially judicial business might be transacted without fear of divine displeasure"[35] will be surprised to discover that there were only 42 *dies fasti* in the year. The supply scarcely seems adequate to the demand. A closer analysis of the evidence, however, explains the situation. In the first place, we must remember that *dies comitiales* were also available for the *legis actio,* presumably if the *comitia* had not been convoked. *Nundinae* also were *dies fasti.* In the second place, the *legis actio,*[36] which was permitted on *dies fasti,* is part of the civil law which was administered by the *praetor urbanus qui inter cives ius dicit.*[37] Cases tried under criminal law in the first century B.C. were held in the *quaestiones perpetuae* (standing courts) presided over by their own officers, or more rarely before one of the *comitia.* They were not limited to *dies fasti,* and we find that

[34] For example P. Noailles, *Du droit sacré au droit civil* (Paris 1949) 285; K. Latte, *Römische Religionsgeschichte* (Munich 1960) 39; C. Peeters, *Fas en Nefas,* Een Semantische Studie (Utrecht 1945).

[35] Warde Fowler, *RF* 8.

[36] *legis actio* is the name of the process described by the verbal phrase *lege agere.*

[37] For descriptions of the *legis actio,* see A. H. J. Greenidge, *The Legal Procedure in Cicero's Time* (Oxford 1901) 49-78, 132-181; W. W. Buckland, *A Manual of Roman Private Law* (Cambridge 1939) 372-382; H. Lévy-Bruhl, *Recherches sur les actions de la loi* (Paris 1960) 102-130.

the great trials which figured so largely in the political history of the period took place on days of every type. In the third place, the *legis actio,* which had originally been the only form of procedure in civil law, had by the first century been largely replaced by a different form, the formulary procedure.[38] In the fourth place, only the part played by the praetor, known as *ius dicere,* was limited to *dies fasti.* This is the preliminary part of a civil case in which the praetor has to determine the *ius* or point of law involved. If he decides that there is a valid point, he pronounces it (*ius dicere*), and appoints a *iudex* or *iudices* (*iudices dare, iudicium dare* or *addicere*). After instruction as to the procedure to be followed, the *iudex* then takes over the case and brings in the verdict. The praetor may also, instead of appointing a *iudex,* hand the case on to another court, that of the *decemviri stlitibus iudicandis* or of the *centumviri.* Whichever course he follows, the part played by the praetor, and therefore the need for *dies fasti,* is comparatively small.

An interesting question connected with the small number of *dies fasti* is whether on these days the praetor was merely allowed to hold court, or obliged to do so. None of the ancient authors touches on this point, and modern opinions differ. I am inclined to think that there was an obligation, if only in custom, partly because otherwise the confusion would have been intolerable, partly also because in Cicero's day the *praetor urbanus* was not supposed to leave Rome for more than ten days at a time (Cicero, *Phil.* 2.31). This would allow him to absent himself during periods of *dies nefasti* or *comitiales,* but ensure that he would be back in Rome in time for the next *dies fasti.*

It is not possible to demonstrate that the rules about *dies fasti* were regularly observed in the late republic. The ancient historians were not as interested in civil law suits as they were in *comitia,* Senate meetings, and criminal trials, and they provide us with no dates by which to check whether or not trials under civil law came on *dies fasti.* On the other hand, the fact

[38] I am assuming that the formulary procedure was not restricted to *dies fasti.* This is a debated point and there is no clear evidence on it, but since the purpose of the formulary procedure was to break away from the inconvenience of the *legis actio,* I should suppose that when it was introduced it would have been exempted from the restriction.

that the *dies comitiales* were observed, and were a real factor in political life, indicates that the rules of the calendar were still in force. So too does the fact that the Julian calendar preserved the characters of the days.

THE RELATION OF *DIES FASTI* TO *DIES COMITIALES*

Modern authorities often state that *dies comitiales* are a sub-class of *dies fasti*, so that the latter name could correctly be applied to both groups. They sometimes even employ the term *dies fasti non comitiales* to refer to the smaller class. There is no ancient authority for this term and it crept into the literature by way of modern commentaries written in Latin (see Chapter 6, n. 8). As far as the period of the late republic is concerned, there is no evidence that the Romans thought of *dies fasti* and *dies comitiales* as anything but two perfectly distinct types of day. It does, however, seem to me highly probable that at an earlier date all these days were known simply as *dies fasti* and that subsequently they were divided into two groups in order to secure some time in which the *comitia* could not interfere with the praetor's court and vice versa. The evidence for the date at which this innovation took place, and the circumstances which led up to it will be discussed later in connection with the history of the calendar (see Chapter 6, pp. 106f., 111).

In the preceding discussion I have defined *dies fasti*, purely in terms of their function in the late republic, as those days on which *legis actio* was permitted. I have not considered the actual meaning of the word *fastus*, which must have been applied to calendar days in a much earlier period, when *dies comitiales* had not yet been separated out from the original body of *dies fasti*. This meaning is not easy to determine, because, as I have said, the word occurs in Latin literature only in connection with days of the calendar. It is generally agreed that it is an adjective formed from *fas*, and that its opposite *nefastus* comes from *nefas*. But this only pushes the problem back one step, leaving us to decide what *fas* and *nefas* mean. Varro's derivation from *fari* has failed to convince most modern scholars,[39] and indeed it would give a very limited scope to a word which covers a very wide area. Other derivations have been suggested, but for our purposes the etymology of the words is less important than the connotations which they had for the Romans of the historical period. If we consult the lexicons, we see that the phrase *fas est* is regularly used in connection with, or even as synonymous with, *ius est* or *licet*. To a Roman *fas* describes an action which is permitted or should be performed[40] and *nefas* is the opposite. *Quidquid non licet, nefas putare debemus* (Cicero, *Paradoxa* 3.25). But by whom is this permission granted or refused? Sometimes, when the action is a personal matter, the expression *fas mihi est* seems to imply what we would call a matter of conscience. Sometimes it refers to what is in accord with nature—*quod aut per naturam fas esset, aut per leges liceret* (Cicero, *Pro Milone* 43). *Nefas* can mean what is against nature, as in its use to describe a prodigy. But in matters which do not involve personal conscience or the laws of nature, such as what may or may not be done on certain days, we see that some one must have handed down rules. When we read that Aelius Gallus (Festus, 348 L.) said that to take legal action before the praetor on a *dies nefastus* was to act *contra voluntatem deorum*, we can say "Ah, yes, a religious tabu." But in a religious system which has no revealed code, such as the law of Moses, the will of the gods must be determined by man. In Rome it was determined by the colleges of priests, either the pontifices or the augurs.[41] Since the calendar was in the charge of the pontifices, it must have been they who determined the characters of the days. We can then give a very prosaic defi-

[39] Ernout-Meillet, *Dictionnaire étymologique de la langue Latine*[4], vol. 1 (Paris 1959) 217, *s.v. fas*; Walde-Hoffmann, *Lateinisches Etymologisches Wörterbuch*[3], vol. 1 (Heidelberg 1938) 458, *s.v. fas*; cf. C. Peeters, *op.cit.* (n. 34) and H. Fugier, *Recherches sur l'expression du sacré dans la langue latine* (Paris 1963) 127-152.

[40] K. Latte (*Römische Religionsgeschichte*, 38) says: "*Fas est* bedeutet dass man etwas tun kann, ohne religiose Bedenken zu haben, nicht etwa, dass man es tun muss." Theoretically, I think this is true, but in actual life, when one is faced with the necessity of acting, and one of two possible courses of action is *nefas*, the one which is *fas* must clearly be obligatory, not simply permitted.

[41] Cf. Cicero's description of the responsibilities of the priests, *De Leg.* 2.20f. and 30-34.

nition of *dies fastus* as a day which the *auctoritas pontificum* has opened to certain activities. All our evidence goes to show that these activities involved a public gathering before a magistrate, either in court, or, before *dies comitiales* were separated from *dies fasti*, in the *comitia*. There is no evidence that the character of *dies fasti* had anything to do with private business or affected the meeting of the Senate, which was in no sense a public gathering.

I would then define *dies fasti* as those days on which the pontifices permitted the *praetor urbanus* to hear *legis actiones*, and in the early period allowed magistrates to summon *comitia*. This is a somewhat narrower definition than that given by most modern authorities, who regard *dies fasti* and *comitiales* as days on which all secular activities were permitted, in contrast to *dies nefasti*, which were for religious matters. If my definition is correct, there must have been a reason why the pontifices imposed their rule. I believe that in this case, as in many other situations in Rome, the power of a priestly college was being used as an agent of the state to maintain order. Any one with any familiarity with Roman institutions will have realized that throughout their history the Roman authorities made a conscious effort to limit the occasions on which the people might gather in large numbers. This is amply proved by the fact that the citizens of Rome had no right of free assembly, and could not gather legally except at the summons of a magistrate. From the decree of the Senate in the case of the Bacchanalia[42] to Trajan's letter to Pliny about the fire company in Nicomedia,[43] we see how suspicious they were of the potential violence or subversiveness of any gathering, and when one considers how often even a legal *contio* turned into a howling mob, one must admit they had some justification. I would therefore interpret the original designation of certain days on which magistrates could deal with the people as an example of the effort to limit the opportunities for public gatherings which might lead to disorder.

[42] Livy, 39.14; *CIL* 1².2.581.
[43] Pliny, *Epist.* 10.33 and 34.

DATES OF SENATE MEETINGS
AND *COMITIA*

I have listed here all the senate meetings and *comitia* for which I have been able to find specific dates. Other probable dates of senate meetings for which the evidence does not seem to me conclusive will be found in P. Stein, *op. cit.*, below, note 49. There is a very full list of these dates in P. Willems, *Le Sénat de la république romaine*, 2.149-151, but it is inconveniently arranged. I have not included the dates on which consuls entered office, although normally there would have been a senate meeting that day. For these dates, see Broughton, *MRR* 2.637-639. I am very grateful to L. R. Taylor for her help in analyzing types of *comitia*. In dealing with dates, it is well to remember that in manuscripts they are painfully subject to scribal error.

SENATE

Year	Day	Character of Day	Evidence
210	*Id. Mart.* (March 15)	NP	Livy, 26.26.5
200	*Id. Mart.* (March 15)	NP	Livy, 31.5.2
195	*Id. Mart.* (March 15)	NP	Livy, 33.43.1
186	*Non. Oct.* (Oct. 7)	F	*Senatus Consultum de Bacchanalibus*, *CIL* 1².2.581; Dessau, 1.18
177	*Id. Mart.* (March 15)	NP	Livy, 41.8.4
	XVII Kal. April. (March 16)	F	Livy, 41.8.5
170	*VII Id. Oct.* (Oct. 9)	C	*Senatus Consultum de Thisbensibus*, *SIG*³ 646 I.
	pridie Id. Oct. (Oct. 14)	EN	*ibid.*, II. See below, n. 44
168	*Id. Mart.* (March 15)	NP	Livy, 44.19.1
	IX Kal. April. (March 24)	Q.R.C.F.	Livy, 44.20.2
	XV Kal. Oct. (Sept. 16)	C	Livy, 45.1.8
	XIV Kal. Oct. (Sept. 17)	C	Livy, 45.2.1
	VI Kal. Oct. (Sept. 25)	C	Livy, 45.2.3
165?	*III Non. Quinct.* (July 5)	NP	*Senatus Consultum*, Holleaux, *BCH* 48 (1924) 381-398. For year, see Broughton, *MRR* 1.438
165?	*IV Non. Mai.* (May 4)	C	*Senatus Consultum de Delphis*, *SIG*³ 612 c. For year see below, n. 45

Year	Day	Character of Day	Evidence
164?	Id. Interk. (Intercalary month 13)	NP	Senatus Consultum de Delo, SIG³ 664. For year see Broughton, MRR 1.440, n. 1
159	III Non. Mai. (May 5)	C	Senatus Consultum de Tiburtibus, CIL 1².2.586; Dessau 1.19
140?	Pr. Non. Quinct. (July 6)	N	Senatus Consultum de Narthacio, SIG³ 674. See Liticheff, BCH 6 (1882) 363-387; M. Holleaux, BCH 54 (1930) 9-11. For year of C. Hostilius' praetorship, see Broughton, MRR 1.480. For day see below, n. 46
135	V Id. Feb. (Feb. 9)	N	Senatus Consultum de Prienensibus, SIG³ 688
134	Id. Dec. (Dec. 13)	NP	Josephus, AJ 14.8.6, 145. For year, see Broughton, MRR 1.491 n. 2
126	VIII Id. Feb. (Feb. 6)	N	Josephus, AJ 13.9.2, 260-265. For year, see Broughton, MRR 1.509 n. 2
91	Id. Sept. (Sept. 13)	NP	Cicero, De Oratore 3.2
81	VI Kal. April. (March 27)	C	Senatus Consultum de Stratonicensibus, OGI 2.441, line 19. For day, see below, n. 47
78	XI Kal. Iun. (May 22)	N	Senatus Consultum de Aesclepiade, CIL 1².2.588
73	XVII Kal. Nov. (Oct. 16)	F	Senatus Consultum de Amphiarii Oropii Agris, SIG³ 747, lines 60f. See below, n. 48
66	Kal. Ian. (Jan. 1)	F	Dio, 36.42.2
65	Non. Feb. (Feb. 5)	N	Sallust, Cat. 18.7f.
63	Kal. Ian. (Jan. 1)	F	Cicero, Att. 2.1.3
	VIII Kal. Oct. (Sept. 23)	C	Suetonius, Aug. 94.5
	XII Kal. Nov. (Oct. 21)	C	Cicero, Cat. 1.7
	XI Kal. Nov. (Oct. 22)	C	Asconius, 4
	VII Id. Nov. (Nov. 7)?	C	See below, n. 49
	VI Id, Nov. (Nov. 8)?	C	See below, n. 49
	III Non. Dec. (Dec. 3)	N	Cicero, Cat. 3.8; 4.10
	pridie Non. Dec. (Dec. 4)	C	Cicero, Cat. 4.5, and 12
	Non. Dec. (Dec. 5)	F	Cicero, Att. 2.1.3
62	Kal. Ian. (Jan. 1)	F	Cicero, Fam. 5.2.8
	a.d. III Non. Ian. (Jan. 3)	C	ibid.
61	Id. Mai. (May 15)	NP	Cicero, Att. 1.16.9
	Kal. Dec. (Dec. 1)	N	Cicero, Att. 1.17.9
	a.d. IV Non. Dec. (Dec. 2)	N	ibid.
58	Kal. Ian. (Jan. 1)	NP	Cicero, Red. in Sen. 17. For character of day, see below, n. 50

Year	Day	Character of Day	Evidence
	Kal. Iun. (June 1)	N	Cicero, *Pro Sestio* 68
	a.d. III Id. Sext. (Aug. 11)	C	Asconius, 41
57	*Kal. Ian.* (Jan. 1)	F	Cicero, *Red. Quir.* 11; *Pro Sestio* 72
	a.d. IV Non. Ian. (Jan. 2)	F	Cicero, *Pro Sestio* 74. See below, n. 51
	Non. Sept. (Sept. 5)	F	Cicero, *Att.* 4.1.5
	a.d. VIII Id. Sept. (Sept. 6)	F	Cicero, *Att.* 4.1.6f. See below, n. 52
	Kal. Oct. (Oct. 1)	N	Cicero, *Att.* 4.2.4
	a.d. VI Non. Oct. (Oct. 2)	F	Cicero, *Att.* 4.2.5
	a.d. XVII Kal. Dec. (November 14)	F	Cicero, *Att.* 4.3.3
56	*Id. Ian.* (Jan. 13)	NP	Cicero, *Fam.* 1.2.1
	a.d. XVII Kal. Feb. (Jan. 14)	EN	*ibid.*
	a.d. XVI Kal. Feb. (Jan. 15)	NP	Cicero, *Fam.* 1.2.4; 1.4.1
	Kal. Feb. (Feb. 1)	N	Cicero, *Q.F.* 2.3.1
	VII Id. Feb. (Feb. 7)	N	*ibid.*, 2.3.2
	VI Id. Feb. (Feb. 8)	N	*ibid.*, 2.3.3.
	V Id. Feb. (Feb. 9)	N	*ibid.*, 2.2.3
	IV Id. Feb. (Feb. 10)	N	*ibid.*, 2.3.3
	Id. Feb. (Feb. 13)	NP	*ibid.*, 2.3.1
	Non. April (April 5)	N	*ibid.*, 2.6.1
	Id. Mai. (May 15)	NP	*ibid.*, 2.7.1
	XVII Kal. Jun. (May 16)	F	*ibid.*, 2.7.2
55	*III Id. Feb.* (Feb. 11)	N	*ibid.*, 2.8.3
54	*pridie Id. Feb.* (Feb. 12)	N	*ibid.*, 2.11.1
	Id. Feb. (Feb. 13)	NP	*ibid.*, 2.12.2
	Kal. Oct. (Oct. 1)	N	Cicero, *Att.* 4.17.4
52	*XIII Kal. Feb.* (Jan. 18)	C	Cicero, *Pro Milone* 27f.; Asconius, 29
	XII Kal. Feb. (Jan. 19)	C	Dio, 40.49.5
	III Kal. Mart. mense intercalario (intercalary month 26)	NP	Asconius, 31
	pridie Kal. Mart. mense intercalario (intercalary month 27)	C	Asconius, 39
51	*Id. Mai.* (May 15)	NP	Cicero, *Att.* 5.5.1
	Kal. Jun. (June 1)	N	Cicero, *Fam.* 8.1.2
	XI Kal. Sext. (July 22)	N	*ibid.*, 8.4.4
	Id. Sext. (Aug. 13)	NP	*ibid.*, 8.4.4; 8.9.2
	Kal. Sept. (Sept. 1)	F	*ibid.*, 8.9.2
	prid. Kal. Oct. (Sept. 29)	C	*ibid.*, 8.8.5
	Non. Oct. (Oct. 7)?	F	Cicero, *Att.* 5.21.2. See below, n. 53

[57]

Year	Day	Character of Day	Evidence
49	Kal. Ian. (Jan. 1)	F	Caesar, B.C. 1.5.4; Cicero, Phil. 2.51; Dio, 41.1.1
	IV Non. Ian. (Jan. 2)	F	Caesar, B.C. 1.5.4; Dio 41.2.2
	Non. Ian. (Jan. 5)	F	Caesar, B.C. 1.5.4
	VIII Id. Ian. (Jan. 6)	F	ibid.
	VII Id. Ian. (Jan. 7)	C	ibid. See below, n. 54
	Kal. April. (April 1)	F	Cicero, Att. 9.17.1
	IV Non. April. (April 2)	F	Cicero, Att. 9.17.1; Caesar, B.C. 1.32.2, and 1.33.3
	III Non. April. (April 3)	C	ibid.

COMITIA

Year	Day	Character of Day	Type of Comitia	Evidence
188	XII Kal. Mart. (Feb. 18)	C	centuriata (electoral)	Livy, 38.42.2
	XI Kal. Mart. (Feb. 19)	C	centuriata (electoral)	Livy, 38.42.3
179	VI Id. Mart. (March 10)	C	centuriata (electoral)	Livy, 40.59.4f.
	V Id. Mart. (March 11)	C	centuriata (electoral)	ibid.
	IV Id. Mart. (March 12)	C	centuriata (electoral)	ibid.
176	III Non. Sext. (Aug. 3)	C	centuriata (electoral)	Livy, 41.17.5
172	XII Kal. Mart. (Feb. 18)	C	centuriata (electoral)	Livy, 42.28.4
	XI Kal. Mart. (Feb. 19)	C	centuriata (electoral)	Livy, 40.28.5
170	V Kal. Feb. (Jan. 26)	C	centuriata (electoral)	Livy, 43.11.6
	III Kal. Feb. (Jan. 28)	C	centuriata (electoral)	Livy, 43.11.7
167	VIII Kal. Oct. (Sept. 23)	C	centuriata (judicial)	Livy, 43.16.12
	VII Kal. Oct. (Sept. 24)	C	centuriata (judicial)	ibid.
70	VI Kal. Sext. (July 27)	C	centuriata (electoral)	Pseudasconius, 21 (Stangl 212)
69	IX Kal. Sept. (Aug. 22)	EN	curiata	Macrobius, 3.13.11
67	pridie Kal. Ian. (Dec. 29)	NP	concilium pl. (legislative)	Asconius 57; Dio, 36.42.2. See below, n. 55
65	XVI Kal. Sext. (July 17)	C	concilium pl. (electoral)	Cicero, Att. 1.1.1

DIES COMITIALES AND DIES FASTI

Year	Day	Character of Day	Type of Comitia	Evidence
61	*VI Kal. Sext.* (July 27)	C	*centuriata* (electoral)	Cicero, *Att.* 1.16.13
59	*XV Kal. Nov.* (Oct. 18)	C	*centuriata* (electoral)	Cicero, *Att.* 2.20.6
58	[*III Non. Ian.*] (Jan. 3)	C	*concilium pl.* (legislative)	Cicero, *In Pis.* 8f. See below, n. 56
57	*VIII Kal. Feb.* (Jan. 23)	C	*concilium pl.* (legislative)	Cicero, *Pro Sest.* 75
	pridie Non. Sext. (Aug. 4)	C	*centuriata* (legislative)	Cicero, *Att.* 4.1.4
	XII Kal. Dec. (Nov. 19)	C	*tributa* (electoral)	Cicero, *Att.* 4.3.4f. On this and two following days, see below, n. 57
	XI Kal. Dec. (Nov. 20)	C	*tributa* (electoral)	
	IX Kal. Dec. (Nov. 21)	C	*tributa* (electoral)	
56	*XI Kal. Feb.* (Jan. 20)	C	*tributa* (electoral)	Cicero, *Q.F.* 2.2.2
54	*V Kal. Sext.* (July 28)	C	*centuriata* (electoral)	Cicero, *Att.* 4.15.8
52	*V Kal. Mart. mense intercalario* (intercalary month 24)	C	*centuriata* (electoral)	Asconius, 31
49	*V Id. Mart.* (March 11)	C	*tributa* (legislative)	CIL 1^2.2.600. See Broughton, *MRR* 2.258

[44] This section of the *senatus consultum* does not carry the usual opening statement that the presiding magistrates consulted the Senate on a certain day, but only records the date when the decree was written, and the senators who were present. I am not sure whether we can assume here, and in other *senatus consulta*, that the writing of the decree, which seems to have been done or witnessed by a small committee, always should be dated on the same day as the meeting at which the decree was voted. The Senate did not continue its meeting after sunset, and, in the case of a long meeting, the writing might be postponed. When Cicero delivered the Third Catilinarian oration to the people, it was almost nightfall, the Senate had been dismissed, but since the *senatus consultum* had not yet been written up, Cicero reported the decree from memory (*Cat.* 3.13).

[45] This *senatus consultum* has been dated, as in *SIG*[3] 612, in 189 B.C., on the assumption that the name of the magistrate in it was Sp. Postumius Albinus. M. Holleaux, after a close examination of the stone, reads the name as Octavius, and therefore lowers the date to, at the earliest, 165 B.C. when Cn. Octavius was consul.

[46] The date before the Nones is missing, but there is not room for more than προ[τεραι νω]νων.

[47] The number before the Kalends is missing, but the space seems to require this reading.

[48] This is the date on which the decree was written. See above, n. 44.

[49] Cicero delivered his First Catilinarian oration on one of these days, but which is uncertain. See P. Stein, *Die Senatssitzungen der Ciceronischen Zeit (68-43)* (Munster 1930) 13. In any case, both days are C.

[50] Ordinarily *Kal. Ian.* is F, but this year the Compitalia, which is *feriae conceptivae*, came on this day (Cicero, *In Pis.* 8), and changed it to NP.

[51] The text implies that a meeting was expected for this day, but it is possible that it was not held. See Cicero, *Att.* 4.2.4.

[52] Stein (*op.cit.* [n. 49] 34) puts this meeting on the 7th, which is C, because he takes *eo biduo* (*Att.* 4.1.6) to refer to the two days after the Nones. I think the phrase refers to September 4 when Cicero reached Rome, and to September 5, so that *postridie* (*Att.* 4.1.7) would be the 6th.

[53] The MS reading is: *quo autem die Cassi litterae victrices in senatu recitatae sunt, id est* (*idem*) *Nonis Octobribus, eodem meae tumultum nuntiantes.* This has been emended to *datae Nonis Octobribus,* or to *id est Nonis Decembribus.* The argument hinges on the length of time it would take for letters to reach Rome from Asia. The MS reading seems impossible, but which emendation is preferable, I cannot decide. In any case both Nones are F.

[54] Caesar, *B.C.* 1.5.4, says: *haec senatus consulto perscribuntur a.d. VII Id. Ian. itaque V primis diebus, quibus senatus haberi potuit, qua ex die consulatum iniit Lentulus, biduo excepto comitiali et de imperio et de amplissimis viris, tribunis plebis, gravissime acerbissimeque decernitur.* The senate met for the first five days of the year on which it could, omitting the two *dies comitiales,* January 3 and 4. It is odd that the Senate should not have met on the 3rd and 4th because they were *comitiales,* and then should meet on the 7th, which is also *comitialis.* The explanation may simply be that the situation demanded haste. It is also possible that the 7th was *nundinae* and therefore *dies fastus,* not *comitialis.* See Mommsen, *Staatsrecht*[3] 3.2.923.

[55] This day is normally C, but in 67 b.c. the Compitalia fell on December 29, and made it NP. For the effect of this on the law passed by Manilius, see Ch. 3, p. 46.

[56] I include this day because it is usually identified as the occasion of Clodius' first legislation in his year as tribune. I bracket it because I do not accept the date, for reasons discussed in App. 3, p. 205.

[57] On each of these three days, Milo managed to prevent the *comitia* from being held, but I include them here, as I have some others of which we know only that the date for them had been set, because they are evidence for the character of days on which *comitia* might be held. Also, Cicero's account of Milo's tactics is not only instructive but highly entertaining. For the date of the last day, I have accepted the reading given by D. R. Shackleton Bailey, in *Cicero's Letters to Atticus* (Cambridge 1965) 2.80 and 178.

[60]

CHAPTER 4

DIES NEFASTI AND NP

DIES NEFASTI

There are 58 days in the pre-Julian calendar which have the character letter N.[1] That these were *dies nefasti* is made certain by the brief but explicit statement in Paulus, derived from Verrius Flaccus: *Nefasti dies N littera notantur* (163 L.). The earliest explanation of this character is given by Varro, who lists these days under the heading of days instituted for the sake of men (*hominum causa instituti*) rather than for the gods.[2] He defines them as the opposite of *dies fasti*, because on them the praetor cannot say *do dico addico* and therefore *legis actio* is impossible. He adds that, if a praetor breaks this rule unintentionally, he may be freed of guilt by an expiatory sacrifice, but that, according to Quintus Mucius (presumably Scaevola, the famous pontifex), if he did it on purpose, he would be reckoned *impius* and would retain his guilt forever. In another passage Varro derives *nefasti* as he did *fasti*, from *fari*, explaining that on these days it is not *ius* to speak the three words.[3] Ovid (*Fasti* 1.47) echoes Varro's definition, as did Verrius Flaccus, to judge from a very mutilated passage in Festus,[4] and Macrobius (1.16.14) also speaks of the *tria verba sollennia*, and uses the verb *fari*. We also have definitions from two legal experts who use more technical terminology. Aelius Gallus, probably in

---

[1] See Ch. 2 and App. 2 for the exact number of these days.

[2] *De L. L.* 6.12: *Dicam prius qui deorum causa, tum qui hominum sunt instituti.* 6:27: *nunc iam qui hominum causa constituti videamus.* 6.30: *contrarii horum* (*dies fasti*) *vocantur dies nefasti, per quos dies nefas fari praetorem "do" "dico" "addico"; itaque non potest agi: necesse est aliquo ⟨eorum⟩ uti verbo cum lege qui⟨d⟩ peragitur. Quod si tum imprudens id verbum emisit ac quem manumisit, ille nihilo est liber, sed vitio, ut magistratus vitio creatus nihilo setius magistratus. Praetor qui tum fatus est, si imprudens fecit, piaculari hostia facta piatur; si prudens dixit, Quintus Mucius aiebat eum expiari ut impium non posse.*

[3] *De L. L.* 6.53: *ab hoc nefasti, quibus diebus ea fari ius non est et, si fati sunt, piaculum faciunt.*

[4] 162 L. For a discussion of this passage, see below p. 75f.

his book on the meaning of words pertaining to *ius*, listed, in connection with the meaning of *religiosus*, several acts which are to be avoided, and among them is *die nefasto apud praetorem lege agere*.[5] Gaius (*Inst.* 4.29) defines *dies nefastus* as one on which *non licebat lege agere*. Suetonius, who was at one time a practicing lawyer, spoke of *dies nefasti* as those on which *ius non dicitur*.[6]

All these definitions concentrate on the fact that on *dies nefasti* the *legis actiones* were forbidden, in contrast to *dies fasti*, but we can deduce another character of these days. Since *comitia* could be held only on *dies comitiales*, obviously they could not meet on *dies nefasti*, any more than they could on *dies fasti*. This explains the statement in Livy (1.19.7) that both *dies fasti* and *nefasti* were invented by King Numa *quia aliquando nihil cum populo agi utile futurum erat*, that is, because sometimes it would be convenient not to hold *comitia*.

To judge from the ancient evidence, the character *nefastus*, as it is used in the calendar of the republic, meant nothing more than that a *dies nefastus* was not *fastus* or *comitialis*. The adjective occurs very rarely in Latin literature of the republican period and then only in connection with the calendar, or in the technical vocabulary of priestly law.[7] In the empire, however, it was much more commonly used and the expression *dies nefastus* acquired a popular, non-technical meaning which has obscured its correct meaning in relation to the calendar. Gellius remarks twice (4.9.5; 5.17.1) that the unlearned and the *vulgus* most incorrectly apply the adjective *nefastus* to those days which are correctly called either *religiosi* or *atri*.[8] To

[5] Quoted by Festus, 348 L. For the full text, see below n. 11.
[6] Quoted by Priscian, 8.20 Keil.
[7] Aside from the passages quoted above, *nefastus* occurs once in the extant works of Cicero, in the archaic language which he adopts for his ideal laws, and in connection with a priest's decree: *quaeque augur iniusta nefasta vitiosa dira defixerit, inrita infectaque sunto* (*De Leg.* 2.21). Plautus uses the word once in an obvious pun on the character of days in the calendar when he says (*Poen.* 584) that certain *advocati* are not *nefasti* but pure *comitiales* because they spend more time in the *comitium* than the praetor does. I have not been able to find any other examples of *nefastus* in the literature of the republic, although of course *nefas* is common enough.
[8] Cf. Nonius (103 Lindsay): *atri dies dicuntur quos nunc nefastos aut posteros vocant*.

[62]

understand how this mistake could have arisen, we must consider the nature of the latter types of day, although they are never indicated in the *Fasti*,[9] and do not really belong in a discussion of the official calendar.

Gellius defines *dies religiosi* as those which are *tristi omine infames inpeditique, in quibus et res divinas facere et rem quampiam novam exordiri temperandum est* (4.9.5). They are days which have a bad reputation because of some evil omen, on which one should refrain from performing religious rites, and from beginning any new undertaking. As an example, he quotes Cicero (*Att.* 9.5.2) who describes as *religiosus* the *dies Alliensis*, July 18, the anniversary of the defeat of the Roman army by the Gauls in 390 B.C.[10] *Dies religiosi* are defined by Festus as those *quibus nisi quod necesse est, nefas habetur facere.*[11] When we investigate exactly what days are *religiosi* we find that most of them are the occasions of religious rites of the state which, because they have something mysterious or

[9] *Fasti Praenestini* had a note on the first *dies atri* of the year (January 2, 6, and 14) which must have explained their character, but the text is too damaged to give us any useful information. Degrassi and Mommsen both reconstruct the passages so as to define the days as *religiosi*, but I am inclined to think that they would have been called *atri*. January 14 is marked in several *Fasti* as *vitiosus ex senatus consulto*, and until the publication of *Fasti Verulani* in 1923 it was often stated that this was a synonym for *religiosus*. *Fasti Verulani*, however, identifies the day as the birthday of Antony, which, according to Dio (51.19.3), was decreed μιαρά after his death. The term *vitiosus* does not occur anywhere else as the character of a day, although μιαρά is fairly common among Greek writers of Roman history, usually as a translation of *religiosus*. The use of *vitiosus* may have been coined for use in Antony's case in order to avoid using *religiosus*, which might have seemed too complimentary.

[10] It was also the day of the earlier defeat of the Fabii at the Cremera. Cf. Livy, 6.1.11: *tum de diebus religiosis agitari coeptum, diemque a.d. XV Kal. Sextiles, duplici clade insignem, quo die ad Cremeram Fabii caesi, quo deinde ad Alliam cum exitio urbis foede pugnatum, a posteriore clade Alliensem appellarunt, †insignemque rei nullius publice privatimque agendae†fecerunt.* Also 6.28.6: *diem (Alliensem) contactum religione.*

[11] 348 L.: *Religiosus est non mod[ic]o deorum sanctitatem magni aestimans, sed etiam officiosus adversus homines. Dies autem religiosi, quibus nisi quod necesse est, nefas habetur facere: quales sunt sex et triginta atri qui appellantur et Alliensis, atque [h]i, quibus mundus patet. †esse† Gallus Aelius, quod homini ita facere non liceat, ut si id faciat, contra deorum voluntatem videatur facere. Quo in genere sunt haec: in aedem Bonae Deae virum introire; adversus †mysticiae† legem ad populum ferre; die nefasto apud praetorem lege agere.*

uncanny about them, have given the days their ominous character.[12] When Gellius says that res divinae should not be undertaken on dies religiosi, he must be thinking of private rites, for the festival of the Matralia took place on one (June 11), a sacrifice to Luna on another (August 24), and six temples were dedicated during the series of dies religiosi when the temple of Vesta was open.[13] Public religious rites obviously were not banned. On the other hand, public and private business was avoided. Paulus, or his source Verrius Flaccus, says that on the dies religiosi when the mundus was open,[14] one did not fight the enemy, enroll soldiers in the army, or hold comitia: ⟨non⟩ aliud quicquam in republica, nisi quod ultima necessitas admonebat, administrabatur (145 L.). Varro (quoted by Macrobius, 1.16.18) gave a similar list, adding that one should

[12] The days, other than the dies Alliensis, which are explicitly identified as religiosi are, first, the three on which the mundus was open, August 24, October 5, and November 8. (The mundus was an underground chamber in some way connected with the gods of the underground world and the dead. When it was open, the connection with the underworld was too close for comfort. (See Degrassi, p. 502; Kroll, RE 16.1.560-564.) For these see Festus 126 L., 144 L., and 348 L. Also religiosi are the days when the penus in the temple of Vesta was open (Festus 296 L.), probably June 7-15 (see Degrassi, pp. 466-471; Warde Fowler, RF 145-154; L. A. Holland, Janus and the Bridge [PMAAR 21, Rome 1961] 320f.). The days when the Salii moved the sacred shields (ancilia) are called religiosi by Livy (37.33.6). These are March 1, 9, 23 and October 19. (See Degrassi's commentary on these days for the evidence.) It is often said that there were two dies religiosi after the Feriae Latinae, the ceremony which the Latins celebrated jointly every spring on Mons Albanus, but the only evidence for this is Cicero's remark (Q.F. 2.4.2) that he has not been able to complete his daughter's betrothal because there were two such days after the Feriae. If these days were regularly religiosi, Cicero would have known it, and not have expected to complete the affair. But Cicero also says (Q.F. 2.5.2) that that year the Feriae Latinae were repeated, probably due to a real or pretended mistake in the ritual. It seems possible that the dies religiosi were the days between the first and second celebrations. There are other days in the year which are described as having the characteristics of dies religiosi, but are not explicitly identified as such. The dies parentales, February 13-21, fall in this group, and the Lemuria, May 9, 11, and 13.

[13] See Degrassi's commentary on June 11 and August 24, and for the dates of temple dedications see his indices, 5b (pp. 554-557), 5d (p. 557) and 8 (pp. 563f.); and the lists given by Wissowa, RK² 594-597, and by K. Latte, Römische Religionsgeschichte (Munich 1960) 415-418. In the latter, December 14 for the dedication of the temple of the Penates on the Velia is a mistake for October 14.

[14] On the mundus, see n. 12.

not start a voyage, or take a wife for the sake of having children. Cicero seems to have postponed his daughter's betrothal because of some *dies religiosi*.[15] In other words, these days were regarded as unlucky for any activity other than the conduct of the state cult.

Dies atri are defined by Varro as the days after the Kalends, Nones and Ides (the *dies postriduani*), which are called "black" because on them one began nothing new.[16] This not very illuminating statement is made clearer by Festus (or Verrius Flaccus) who lists these 36 days under the general heading of *dies religiosi* with the implication that *dies atri* also are unlucky.[17] They differ however from *dies religiosi* in that on them even the rites of the state cult in general are avoided. The statements of the ancient authors to this effect[18] are supported

[15] See n. 12.

[16] *De L. L.* 6.29: *Dies postridie Kalendas, Nonas, Idus appellati atri, quod per eos dies nihil novi inciperent.* The origin of the bad reputation of these days is attributed by tradition to the belief that the sacrifice which preceded the battle of the Allia took place on the day after the Ides of July. Therefore the pontifices decreed that no sacrifice should take place on this day of each month, and for good measure put the same rule on the days after the Kalends and Nones. See Macrobius, 1.16. 21-24, citing Gellius and Cassius Hemina; Livy, 6.1.11-12; Aulus Gellius, 5.17.1-2, citing Verrius Flaccus. A theory that *ater* here does not mean "black" is suggested by the comments of Varro (*De L. L.* 6.14) and Festus (304 L.) on the name of the festival of the Quinquatrus (March 19). They say that it is so called because it comes five days after the Ides, and cite as parallels the Tusculan custom of calling the sixth day after the Ides *sexatrus*, and the seventh *septimatrus*. If this is true, the correct form, a synonym for *dies postridianus*, may have been *dies atrus*, which was corrupted to *ater* with its implication of bad luck by the incorrigible Roman tendency to find dire meanings in innocent phenomena. It is also possible that *dies ater* originally referred only to the day after the full moon of the Ides, and meant the first day of the waning moon. It might then have been extended by analogy to the days after the Kalends and Nones. See J. Wackernagel, "Dies Ater," *Archiv für Religionswissenschaft* 22 (1923-1924) 215f. It seems to me, however, more probable that *dies atri* are simply the *dies postridiani* under a different name.

[17] See n. 11 for text.

[18] Livy, 6.1.12: *Quidam . . . etiam postridie Idus rebus divinis supersederi iussum, inde, ut postridie Kalendas quoque ac Nonas eadem religio esset, traditum putant.* Gellius, 5.17.2 (based on Verrius Flaccus): *Pontifices decreverunt nullum his diebus sacrificium recte futurum.* Macrobius, 1.16.25: *Fabius Maximus Servilianus pontifex in libro duodecimo negat oportere atro die parentare, quia tunc quoque Ianum Iovemque praefari necesse est.* Exceptions could be made. Gellius

[65]

by the fact that there is no record that any triumphs were held on these days, and I have not been able to find any temple that was dedicated on one of them.[19] The exception to the rule is provided by the *Ludi*, which spread over many *dies atri*. One might say that technically *dies atri* are a subclass of *dies religiosi*, and that not all of the latter are *atri*.

Gellius' opinion that it is incorrect to identify *dies religiosi* and *atri* with *dies nefasti* is confirmed by a glance at the characters of the days in the *Fasti*. Of the 36 *dies atri*, only 10 are *nefasti*, one is *endotercisus* and 25 are *fasti*. In contrast with the practice on *dies atri*, 19 triumphs are recorded for *dies nefasti*, and several foundations of temples. Although some *dies religiosi* are listed as *nefasti* in the calendar, many are not. The three days when the *mundus* was open are all *comitiales*, as is the *dies Alliensis*. If the *dies parentales* were *religiosi*, for which there is only indirect evidence, three of them are *comitiales* and the last, the Feralia, is *dies fastus*.

The conclusion seems to me clear that the *dies nefasti* of the calendar were not so called because of any belief that they were unlucky, but simply because, as is stated in some of the definitions, they were the opposite of *dies fasti*, and that the name was given them at the time when *dies fasti* included *dies comitiales*.[20] The name indicated simply that, according to the ruling of the pontifices, these days were not available for *legis actiones* or *comitia*. I would assume from its rarity in republican literature that, like *fastus* (see Chapter 3, p. 48) the word *nefastus* was originally part of the technical vocabulary of priests and was known to the public only in connection with the days of the calendar. In the Augustan age it was obviously picked up in literary circles to supply the oblique cases of the indeclinable

---

(4.6.10) reports an occasion when the college of pontifices decreed that the *feriae praecidaneae* might be held on a *dies ater*, and Livy (22.10.6) includes in the rules for a *ver sacrum* that, if a man performs his sacrifice on a *dies ater* unintentionally, it will still be valid.

[19] See Degrassi, *I.I.* 13.1, pp. 639f. for the dates of triumphs. The only *dies ater* in the list for the republican period, November 2, 54 B.C., is doubtful. Cicero in two different letters gives two different dates for Pomptinus' triumph. I would prefer November 3. Degrassi rejects August 14, 449 B.C., and reads *a.d. VII Kal. Sept.* instead of *a.d. [X]VII Kal. Sept.*, given in *CIL* 1.²1, p. 169. For references on temples, see n. 13.

[20] See above p. 52.

noun *nefas,* and as an adjective it acquired the connotations of *nefas.*[21] This development of the meaning would have been possible because the true character of *dies nefasti* must gradually have been forgotten, except by scholars, as the activities to which they were related became less common. The *legis actiones* lost much of their importance during the late republic, and the *comitia* dwindled rapidly under the principate. It would not be surprising if, under these circumstances, the association with *nefas* would lead to the belief that these days were unlucky, since there was no longer any other obvious explanation for their character in the calendar.

I have discussed the character of *dies nefasti* at some length because it is often stated by modern writers that activities were restricted on *dies nefasti* because they were days of religious observances.[22] In fact, it is sometimes said that all activities except those connected with religion were banned on these days.[23] There is however no ancient evidence that *dies nefasti*

[21] E.g. Horace, *Carm.* 1.35.35f. *quid intactum nefasti/ liquimus*? Here *nefasti* is used for the non-existent genitive of *nefas.* In *Carm.* 2.13.1 we find the first known use of *dies nefastus* in the sense of ill-omened: *Ille et nefasto te posuit die.* Considering the humorous tone of the first stanzas of this poem, I strongly suspect that Horace is here playing on *dies nefastus,* deliberately distorting the technical meaning in order to lead up to *nefas* in line 9. He may unintentionally have started the whole new interpretation of *nefastus* by his joke. More specific examples of the new usage are found in the suggestions made after the deaths of both Agrippinas that their birthdays should be listed among the *dies nefasti* (Suetonius, *Tib.* 53; Tacitus, *Ann.* 14.12.1), when, to judge from the case of Antony (see above n. 9), the correct word would have been *vitiosi,* not *nefasti.* In the *De Viris Illustribus* (23.7) it is said that the *dies Alliensis* was placed among the *dies nefasti,* although elsewhere it is always called *religiosus,* and its character in the *Fasti* is *comitialis.* It is worth noting that Vergil, who, according to his commentators, was an expert on religious matters, never uses the word *nefastus.* I cannot decide whether Livy (6.28.8f.) is using *nefasta* in the new sense, or is trying to give solemnity to his language by using a religious vocabulary (like Cicero, see above n. 7) when he says, referring to the site of the battle of the Allia: *locum insignem memoria cladis inritaturum se potius ad delendam memoriam dedecoris quam ut timorem faciat, ne qua terra sit nefasta victoriae suae.*

[22] E.g. Marquardt-Wissowa, *Römische Staatsverwaltung*[2] (Leipzig 1885) 291f.; Warde Fowler, *RF* 9; Wissowa, *RK*[2] 435; N. Turchi, *La Religione di Roma Antica* (Bologna 1939) 78; F. Bömer, *P. Ovidius Naso. Die Fasten* (Heidelberg 1957) 1.36.

[23] Warde Fowler says they were "unsuitable for worldly business." Turchi says they are "*quelli interamente dedicati al culto.*" The idea that

as a class had any more religious associations than *dies fasti* (see above, p. 61f.). If a *praetor urbanus* who accidentally held his court on a *dies nefastus* had to expiate his fault by a sacrifice, it was surely because he had broken pontifical law, not because he had broken a tabu by committing a secular act on a religious day. Except for the limitation on the praetor and the magistrates who had the right to summon the *comitia*, life in Rome pursued its normal course on *dies nefasti*. The Senate met, *contiones* were held, courts were open, except for the *legis actiones*, markets were busy.[24] We cannot explain these activities as simple neglect of religion in a sceptical age, because, as we have seen in the preceding chapter, the rule banning *comitia* on *dies nefasti* was regularly observed. In fact, if *dies nefasti* had ever been days of religious observance, it is very unlikely that they would ever have been confused with *dies atri* on which religious rites were avoided.

Dies nefasti have one peculiarity which I have not commented on, the fact that they occur in groups, irregularly distributed. Since this seems to be connected with their place in the historical development of the calendar, I shall postpone discussing it until later (see p. 116).

NP DAYS

We come now to the last major category of days in the calendar, the 49 which are marked NP. Unfortunately no ancient author mentions this character and we have no definition for it.[25] We can however discover a good deal about these days

---

there was a complete ban on work on these days has appealed to scholars who interpreted Roman religion on the basis of modern primitive religions with their periods of tabu. A look at the arrangement of *dies nefasti* in the calendar should convince anyone that agricultural work, at least, went on as usual. A farmer who stayed idle for 19 consecutive days in April, 9 in June and 15 in July would not have much of a crop.

[24] For senate meetings and *contiones*, see pp. 55-58, 47. When *nundinae* coincided with *dies nefasti*, the day became *fastus* and the praetor could preside over *legis actiones*. See pp. 85f.

[25] A badly mutilated passage in Festus is commonly emended to read as a definition of NP which would have come from Verrius Flaccus. Unfortunately the section of *Fasti Praenestini*, which would have contained his comment on the first NP day of the year, is lost. For a discussion of the passage in Festus, see below, pp. 75f. We may ask

simply from observation. In the first place, we note that, in the republican calendar, they are all named days: The Kalends of March, all the Ides, and 36 of the 45 days which have individual names.[26] The NP days obviously have in common the fact that religious rites are performed on them. The Kalends of March had been the New Year's Day of the calendar which preceded the pre-Julian, and was still observed with certain New Year ceremonies (see Chapter 6, p. 97). The Ides are all sacred to Jupiter, *feriae Jovi*.[27] The other named NP days are also *feriae*.[28] Religious rites and *feriae* are not, however, confined to days marked NP, or even to named days as a whole, but occur also on days of other characters. Thus we cannot define NP days simply as *feriae*, but will have to consider different types of *feriae* to see whether we can find one which coincides with what we know about NP days.

What are *feriae*? This is not an easy question to answer precisely.[29] The word occurs frequently in Latin prose, less fre-

---

why Varro and Macrobius, who explain all the other character letters, did not comment on NP. Merkel a long time ago made the astute suggestion that Varro in the *De Lingua Latina* was discussing normal terminology, and that, since the days marked NP were commonly referred to by their individual proper names, most of which he explains, he would have considered a discussion of NP irrelevant. (See *P. Ovidii Nasonis Fastorum Libri Sex* [Berlin 1841] xxxvii.) It is also possible that Varro was dodging the issue. To be consistent with his derivation of *fastus* from *fari* (see pp. 48-50) he had defined *dies nefasti* as those days on which the praetor might not speak. This is plausible for the majority of days marked N, but it would hardly do for the days which are the occasions of the major religious celebrations of the year. It would be like saying that weekdays are those on which the banks are open, and that Sundays are those on which they are not—true, but inadequate as a definition. If Varro had defined NP, he would have had to expand his definition of *nefasti* and sacrifice his etymology. As for Macrobius, if he found nothing in his sources about NP, the problem would not have occurred to him, as the calendars of his day no longer carried the character letters.

[26] For a discussion of the 9 named days which are not NP see below, pp. 76f.

[27] Macrobius, 1.15.15 and 21, confirmed by notations in the *Fasti*.

[28] Varro so describes many of them when he discusses their names (*De L. L.* 6.12-24), Macrobius cites the first three as examples of *feriae* (1.16.6.), and they are sometimes so identified in the *Fasti*.

[29] The best modern discussion of *feriae* is, in my opinion, the article by C. Jullian in D-S 2.1042-1066. See also O. E. Hartmann, *Ordo Judiciorum* (Göttingen 1859) 112-123; Wissowa, *RE* 6.2.2211-13, s.v. *Feriae*.

quently among the poets,[30] but no author defines it except by implication. Like *Kalendae, Nonae, Idus,* and *nundinae,* the form is plural, but is used of a single day. A common synonym for *feriae* is *dies feriatus.* The closest we can come to a definition of *feriae* is a definition of the synonym: *feriati dies in quibus res divina fit et abstinere homines a litibus oportet* (Isidore, *De Nat. Rerum* 1.4). The first part of this statement, that religious rites take place on *dies feriati,* is reminiscent of Servius' note on Vergil's allusion to *dies festi,* another expression which is commonly used as synonymous with *feriae* (see below, pp. 81ff.): *feriae enim operae deorum creditae sunt . . . feriae deorum causa instituuntur.* (Servius, *Georg.* 1.268). Varro discusses a long series of *feriae* under the heading of *dies deorum causa instituti* (*De L.L.* 6.12-26). Macrobius lists *feriae* under the heading of *dies festi* which he describes as *dis dicati* (1.16.2).

The second characteristic of *dies feriati* which Isidore mentions, abstention from civil lawsuits and quarrels, is referred to elsewhere. Cicero quotes, from the formula for the proclamation of *feriae,* an order to the people to observe this abstention: *ut litibus et iurgiis se abstinerent* (*De Div.* 1.102). In his ideal laws he provides: *feriis iurgia amovento,* and comments on this: *tum feriarum festorumque dierum ratio in liberis requietem litium habet et iurgiorum, in servis operum et laborum* (*De Leg.* 2.19 and 29). Elsewhere he describes *feriae* as *dies quieti* of the gods (*De Leg.* 2.55). Macrobius mentions that an act of physical violence committed on *feriae* is an offense which requires expiation: *feriis autem vim cuique fieri piaculare est* (1.15.21). It would seem that the ban on civil lawsuits and quarrels derives from a general ban on physical conflict, which

---

"Les Tabous des Feriae," by P. Braun (*L'Année Sociologique,* ser. 3 [1959] 49-125) is very rich in references both ancient and modern, but by limiting himself to a study of the tabus, the author does not take into account the full meaning of *feriae.* He takes as his *hypothèse de travail* the theory that "les tabous des *feriae* sont le moyen par lequel la tradition et la loi religieuse protègent un rêve collectif: le retour à l'âge d'or, transfiguration d'un passé réel."

[30] Since *feriae* is metrically a cretic it cannot be used in dactylic verse. Thus it never occurs in Ovid's *Fasti,* where it should have been used frequently. Instead, Ovid has to use *dies festi,* or the neuter *festum* as a noun.

[70]

might mar the peace of the day, for the *legis actio* involved an actual laying on of hands.

Another characteristic of *feriae*, and undoubtedly a most popular one, is the second point mentioned by Cicero, that such a day brings to the slave rest from toil and labor. Cicero seems curiously uninterested in the physical work of the free man, and seems to visualize his only occupation as that of the courts. We may, however, be sure that on *feriae* all men could take a holiday from labor, if only because *feriae* and *feriatus* are commonly used to describe holidays which have nothing to do with religious observances. For example, a schoolboy on vacation can be called *feriatus a studiis*.[31] The writers on agriculture list carefully work which should not be done on *feriae*,[32] although with good Roman practicality they also explain what may be done, and Pliny quotes a proverb to the effect that a poor farmer is one who does on ordinary days what he ought to do on *feriae* (*N.H.* 18.40). No writer talks about the work of city dwellers in detail, but Macrobius (1.16. 9-11) gives a sweeping pontifical rule that any work done on *feriae* defiles them: *adfirmabant autem sacerdotes pollui ferias si indictis conceptisque opus aliquod fieret*. The *rex sacrorum* and the *flamines* were not permitted to see work on *feriae* and used to proclaim that there should be none, and fined any one who disobeyed. Macrobius also quotes a more stringent ruling that anyone who worked on *feriae* unintentionally had to expiate himself with the sacrifice of a pig. The pontifex Scaevola said that an intentional infraction of the rule could not be expiated, but the more open-minded Umbro claimed that a man was not guilty if his work pertained to the gods, or was for the sake of the *sacra*, or was necessary for existence. Scaevola

[31] Trebonius, in a letter to Cicero, *Fam.* 12.16.2. Varro defined a truce as *belli feriae* (Gellius, 1.25.2), and Cicero asks about the god of Epicurus, who has no occupation, *deum sic feriatum volumus cessatione torpere?* (*De Nat. Deorum* 1.102). Plautus can say of a hungry man *venter gutturque resident esuriales ferias* (*Capt.* 468), and describe a sword which is not being used as *feriata* (*Mil.* 7).

[32] For rulings as to what might or might not be done on *feriae*, handed down by the pontifices, see Cato, *Agr.* 138; Columella, 2.21.2; Servius Auct., *Georg.* 1.270; Macrobius, 1.16.10, 11, 24, 25, 28. The argument between authorities cited by Macrobius is interestingly reminiscent of rabbinic debates as to what may be done on the Sabbath, especially in the conflict between rigidity and common sense.

was apparently forced into a corner by this and granted that one might do what, if it was not done, would be harmful. Servius gives us a slightly different and very vivid picture of how the rules were carried out in the city (*Georg.* 1.268). He says that, when the pontifices were going to sacrifice, they sent ahead of them their *calatores*, who, if they saw anywhere craftsmen sitting at their work, would stop them, so that they should not defile the eyes of the pontifices and the rites of the gods.[33] This seems to me a typical Roman compromise, and a sensible way of reducing the interruption of necessary labor. If a potter, a blacksmith, a shoemaker, or a fuller had had to stop work completely on every *feriae* in the year, he would never have earned a living, and the Roman householder would have found the shops empty of goods.

Feriae then seem to have shut down the civil courts, to have restricted certain types of work on the land, and to have offered a holiday to other workers, although the holiday was optional. The lazy, and those who were very punctilious in their attention to religion, probably took full advantage of the option. Others probably observed the holidays according to their individual taste. Some *feriae,* such as the Saturnalia, were very popular, others were hardly noticed (see below, pp. 78-81). A factor in their popularity may have been that on some of them, according to certain sumptuary laws, one was allowed to serve more expensive meals than usual.[34]

Although they are holidays, not all *feriae* are cheerful occasions. Livy frequently refers to special *feriae* ordered because some frightening prodigy has taken place, and these undoubtedly spread gloom through the city until the *pax deorum* had been properly restored.[35] A glimpse of the atmosphere at such times is given by Livy's description of what happened when a

[33] Cf. Festus 292 L.: †*Praeciamitatores*† *dicuntur qui flaminibus Diali, Quirinali, Martiali, antecedent⟨es⟩ exclamant feriis publicis, ut homines abstineant se opere, quia his opus facientem videre religiosum est.*
[34] Gellius, 2.24.
[35] Livy, 3.5.14: *caelum visum est ardere plurimo igni, portentaque alia aut observata oculis aut vanas exterritis ostentavere species. His avertendis terroribus in triduum feriae indictae, per quas omnia delubra pacem deum exposcentium virorum mulierumque turba implebantur.* It is interesting that Livy uses the word *feriae* only of the expiation of prodigies, except in the case of the *Feriae Latinae.*

series of earthquakes had lasted for thirty-eight days: *per toti-dem dies feriae in sollicitudine ac metu fuere* (35.40.7).

There are many different types of *feriae,* but they fall into two main classes, *publicae* and *privatae.*[36] The latter, with which we are not much concerned here, are the special religious observances traditional in a family, or those of an individual, such as the celebration of his birthday, or the mourning for his death. On these occasions the family, or the individual, is *feriatus,* but no one else is concerned. *Feriae publicae* are official *feriae* of the state, paid for by the state. They may be *stativae,* celebrated annually on the same date, *conceptivae,* proclaimed annually at the appropriate season, or *imperativae,* ordered specially by magistrates or priests because of some event, such as a prodigy, a disaster, or a victory.[37] *Feriae publicae* may also be performed on behalf of the whole people or on behalf of a subdivision of the people, such as those who live in a particular district.[38] Macrobius defines as *feriae publicae stativae* those which are *universi populi communes, certis et constitutis diebus ac mensibus et in fastis statis observationi-bus adnotatae, in quibus praecipue servantur Agonalia Carmentalia Lupercalia. Feriae* which come on fixed days and are designated with fixed notations in the *Fasti* can only be the named days of the calendar, as is indicated by the three examples which Macrobius gives.[39] What can we deduce further from his first words which explain *publicae* as meaning shared by the whole citizen body?

We have already noted that not all named days are marked NP. If the second part of Macrobius' definition applies to all the named days, it is reasonable to suppose that the first part applies to a special group among the named days, which can only be those marked NP. If we compare this with Festus' statement that *publica sacra* are those which are performed *publico sumptu pro populo* (see n. 38), we can define NP days as those

---

[36] Macrobius, 1.16.4-8; Festus, 282 L.; Cato, *Agr.* 140; Festus, 284 L., divides *sacra* as *publica* and *privata* in the same way.

[37] Varro's classification (*De L. L.* 6.25) is similar to that of Macrobius.

[38] Cf. Festus, 284 L.; *Publica sacra, quae publico sumptu pro populo fiunt, quaeque pro montibus, pagis, curis, sacellis.*

[39] Varro refers to them collectively as *dies statuti* (*De L. L.* 6.25).

named days on which *feriae* were celebrated at public expense for the benefit of the whole people, by the state. The rites would have been supervised by the *sacerdotes publici*, that is the priests who were in charge of the state cult, primarily the pontifices. Although these rites were *pro populo*, the participation of the people would not have been necessary for their correct and effective performance, as long as the priests or magistrates carried them out as representatives of the state. In fact some rites of the state cult, although not those of NP days, were carried out almost in secret.[40]

If we have arrived indirectly at an understanding of the character of NP days, we still have to consider the meaning of NP itself. It is generally assumed, I think correctly, that it is a ligature[41] combining N and P and that the N in the symbol means *nefastus*. NP days then, as *nefasti*, are closed to *legis actiones* and *comitia*. But what does the P stand for? It must in some way distinguish these days from ordinary *dies nefasti*. Since the sixteenth century, when the modern exploration of the calendar began as part of the new study of epigraphy, scholars have suggested a series of words beginning with P which could in some way modify *nefastus*. Popular suggestions have been *prior, parte* and *principio,* all of which were taken to mean that only part of the day was *nefastus*.[42] These words have now been rejected in general, for two reasons. The first is that a day which was *nefastus* at its beginning and end, and *fastus* in the middle was marked in the calendar as *endotercisus*, while those that began as *nefastus* and turned to *fas* had their own special notations, *Q.R.C.F.* and *Q.S.D.F.* Collectively they are called *dies fissi* (see pp. 29f.). There would seem to be no need for yet another notation for the same type. The second reason is that it would be very peculiar if the named days which are important *feriae* should have been less *nefasti* than a large

---

[40] Cf. S. Savage, *"Remotum a Notitia Vulgari," TAPA* 76 (1945) 157-165.

[41] A ligature, in the terminology of epigraphy and palaeography, is a combination of two or more letters written together in order to save space.

[42] This interpretation held the field until Mommsen argued against it (*RC²* [1859] 233). For the point of view before Mommsen's objection, see the discussions in R. Merkel, *op.cit.* (n. 25) xxxiv-xxxviii, and O. E. Hartmann, *Ordo Judiciorum* 1.38-58. The problem of NP has been most recently discussed by Degrassi, pp. 332f.

number of days with no religious associations. *Nefastus purus*, suggested by Huschke,[43] has been generally rejected.

Other suggestions have been made on the basis of a mutilated passage in Festus which, to judge from the parallel comment in Paulus' abridgment, defined *dies nefasti*, and may have contained the secret of what Verrius Flaccus said on the subject. In its present state the passage reads thus:[44]

ti dies nom...
aput quem l...
addico nep..
riores sunt q..
liberati sunt..
unt et in provin...
instituta fiunt..
et aedes sacrari so..

The early editors of Festus were content to keep the reading *nep. . .* in the third line, and to emend what follows as ⟨*nefasti p*⟩*riores* or ⟨*nefasti parte p*⟩*riore*. Mueller, in his edition of 1839, suggested (165) that instead of *nep. . .* the text should read: *N.P.* ⟨*qui nefasti poste*⟩*riores*.[45] Wissowa preferred to read NFP and interpret this as *nefas, feriae publicae*.[46] Lindsay, in his edition of 1930, accepted Mueller's reading. Neither Mueller nor Lindsay explained what they thought *posteriores* would mean, but presumably it would describe a day which was *nefastus* at the end, a character for which there is no other evidence. Recently J. Paoli (*REL* 28 [1950] 251-279) has argued for *nefasti posteriores*, interpreting the expression as the identification of *feriae* which were introduced or reorganized when the original Roman settlement was expanded to include the Quirinal Hill. The main objection to this theory, as far as it concerns the calendar itself, is that it gives NP a function quite

---

[43] *Das alte Römische Jahr*, 238.

[44] I quote the text here from p. 162 of Lindsay's edition in the Teubner series (Leipzig 1913). In his later edition of Festus, Lindsay has printed the passage with his emendations (*Glossaria Latina* IV [Paris 1930] 283).

[45] His reason for saying this was that it would have been contrary to the scribe's method of dividing words to have put the p of *priores* at the end of one line and all the rest of the word on the next line. See his supplementary note on p. 387.

[46] *RK*² 438, following a suggestion made by Soltau.

different from that of the other character letters, which all tell a citizen something which he will find useful in his daily life. A distinction between older and more recent *feriae* would be of purely antiquarian interest, with no immediate practical application, and I cannot see why it should have been included in the *Fasti*.

A very different interpretation of the passage in Festus was given by Mommsen, who read not *poste⟩riores* but *hila⟩riores*. He believed that NP was not a ligature of N and P, but a variant form of N used to distinguish joyful *feriae* from the *dies nefasti*, which he believed were *tristes et cum religione coniuncti*.[47] This theory as to the character of *dies nefasti* and NP days has been accepted by many scholars, but Wissowa rejected it, pointing out that many of the NP days could hardly be described as *hilariores*.[48] The preceding discussion of *dies nefasti* will have made clear why I cannot accept Mommsen's opinion as to their character.

The fragmentary character of the passage in Festus and the fact that the manuscript actually reads *nep.*, and not NP at all, lead me to feel that we would be wiser not to use this material as evidence for the meaning of NP. This leaves us with the entertaining, and probably impossible, task of trying to guess what Latin word beginning with p would make sense when combined with *nefastus*. I do not think that this can be done with any confidence in the result, but since so many others have ventured, it seems cowardly not to hazard at least a guess. I would suggest that Wissowa came closest to the mark and that NP stands for (*dies*) *nefasti publici*. This would inform the citizen body that these days are not only *nefasti* in the purely negative sense of ordinary *dies nefasti*, but have also the positive characteristic that they are the occasions of *feriae publicae pro populo*, and as such offer everyone a holiday.

If the theory that NP days are *feriae publicae stativae universi populi communes* is correct, it may explain the characters of certain named days which are not NP. There are nine of these: The Regifugium (February 24) N, the three Lemuria (May 9, 11, 13) N, the Vestalia (June 9) N, the Matralia

---

[47] *RC²* 233, note 12; *CIL* 1².1, pp. 289f.
[48] *RK²* 438.

(June 11) N,[49] the Feralia (February 21) F, and the two Vinalia (April 23 and August 19) F or FP. The N days must have been *feriae stativae* but not on behalf of the people as a whole. All that we know of the Lemuria indicates that its rites were carried out in individual homes by the *pater familias,* for the *manes* of the family. The Matralia was the peculiar celebration of mothers. We know practically nothing about the Regifugium, in spite of the many modern theories propounded about it, and it is quite possible, as Jullian has suggested, that it was "particulière au *rex sacrorum,* plutôt qu'un jour de fête publique."[50] The Vestalia was participated in only by women, for men could not even enter the temple. It is true that the bakers of Rome had chosen to hold their annual celebration on the Vestalia, but there had been no bakers in Rome until the second century (Pliny, *N.H.* 18.107), so that this must have been a popular addition to the official rites, and would not affect the character of the day in the calendar. The Feralia was the occasion of a purely family rite in honor of the dead, so that it is not surprising to find that it was not *feriae publicae,* although important enough to have been included in the calendar as a named day. Something of similar nature must have accounted for the character of the Vinalia, but what it may have been I cannot say.

A detailed discussion of the individual *feriae* of the NP days would provide the material for another book, but we may consider here how in general they affected the life of the city.[51]

[49] For my reason for assigning this character to the Matralia, see App. 2, p. 184.

[50] *Op.cit.* (n. 29) 1049, n. 1. He gives similar explanations for the Feralia (1048, n. 15), the Lemuria (1049, n. 8), and the Matralia (1049, n. 12), and comments with surprise on the character of the Vestalia, while accepting it. He suggests that the Vinalia were made private *feriae* by Augustus, but *Ant. Mai.* has disproved this theory.

[51] The ancient evidence on each day can be found in the *Commentarii Diurni* in Degrassi, which are fuller than the commentary in Mommsen's edition of the *Fasti* and have the new material. Much of the evidence is discussed in Warde Fowler's *Roman Festivals of the Period of the Republic,* but this book, while still very useful, is in many ways out of date. Frazer's edition of Ovid's *Fasti* covers only six months of the year, and is more concerned with comparative religion than with Roman institutions. A brief but useful list of festivals with much of the evidence is given in Marquardt-Wissowa, *Römische Staatsverwaltung,* 567-589. There is a great deal of useful information in Bömer, *P. Ovidius Naso*

They did not interrupt business affairs, for debts were commonly settled on the Ides (Cicero, *Att.* 10.5.3; 14.20.2; *Cat.* 1.14; Horace, *Epod.* 2.69). Schools were open on the Ides, for on this day pupils brought the schoolmasters their fees (Horace, *Serm.* 1.6.75). *Contiones* could be held on NP days,[52] and the Senate met then.[53] There was nothing to prevent criminal trials from being held on such days.[54] There is no evidence that the markets on *nundinae* were canceled or postponed when they coincided with NP days, as they often must have done. Some of the *feriae* on NP days were practically unknown to most people, as Varro points out in connection with the Furrinalia (*De L. L.* 6.19). On the other hand some of them were well known as the occasions of general public celebrations which remind one of our Christmas holiday season. The Saturnalia and the Quinquatrus, for example, were officially celebrated by religious rites on December 17 and March 19, but the festivities and holiday atmosphere connected with them lasted for several days.[55] The one feature which both well-known and obscure *feriae* must have had in common was the religious

---

(n. 22), but it is primarily an edition of the *Fasti*, not a study of the festivals. The best source book on Roman religion is still Wissowa's *Religion und Kultus der Römer*, but like all these books, except Degrassi's and Bömer's, it was published before the discovery of *Fasti Antiates Maiores*. There is a great need for a new study of the *feriae* which would incorporate new material, and replace that of Warde Fowler.

[52] E.g., Furrinalia (Cicero, *Att.* 2.21.2), Divalia (*Att.* 7.8.5), Parilia (Cicero, *Phil.* 14.16).

[53] For dates of Senate meetings see Ch. 3, pp. 55-58. There were frequent meetings on the Ides.

[54] This seems to be true of trials in the *quaestiones perpetuae* (cf. Greenidge, *The Legal Procedure in Cicero's Time* [Oxford 1901] 457) and of trials *de vi* (Cicero, *Pro Caelio* 1) and may have applied to *iudicia populi* as well as to the *quaestiones*. Examples of NP days on which trials were held are: *Id. Mart.* (Livy, 42.22.7); Equirria (Cicero, *Q.F.* 2.4.1): Quirinalia (Cicero, *Q.F.* 2.3.2); *Id. Sept.* (Cicero, *Quinct.* 29).

[55] For a discussion of the number of days included in the celebration of the Saturnalia, see Macrobius, 1.10.1-24. This passage offers an interesting example of how even a Roman can become confused in equating pre-Julian and Julian dates, and in explaining the effect of the addition of two days to the month of December. On the days attributed to the Quinquatrus see Varro, *De L. L.* 6.14 and Festus, 304 L., and compare Ovid, *Fasti* 3.809f.; Livy, 44.20.1: *legati ex Macedonia Quinquatribus ultimis adeo expectati venerunt.*

ceremony carried out *pro populo* under the supervision of the pontifices. The extent to which the *populus* participated in the celebration must have depended largely on the extent to which the rites, or the associations of the day, called attention to the occasion. No matter what caustic remarks Cicero makes about the Luperci (*Pro Caelio* 26), the descriptions of the Lupercalia make it clear that the people turned out in droves to watch them prancing practically naked around the forum. The Parilia, as the birthday of Rome, was a great occasion, even if its original connection with the flocks that once grazed on the site of Rome had been forgotten by most people.[56] The Liberalia was known to everyone because it was the day on which young men usually received the *toga virilis* which marked their coming of age.[57]

Some NP days were best known, however, for rites which had nothing to do with their real character but attracted more attention than their official state rites.[58] This is particularly true of the Ides. All owe their character to the fact that they are *feriae* for Jupiter, and marked by the *sacra Idulia*, but many of of them had become the occasion of other *feriae*. The Ides of March, for example, was the occasion of a sacrifice to a goddess called Anna Perenna, and a rowdy outing of the lower classes who went out to the banks of the Tiber and drank as many cups of wine as the years they hoped to live. The *feriae Annae Perennae* was accompanied by a sacrifice, but I doubt that it was *pro populo*. The Ides of May is a good example of a day with varied associations. On it, of course, the *sacra Idulia* were duly performed for Jupiter, but the best-known event of the day must have been the celebration of the

[56] The authors (see Degrassi, pp. 443ff.) speak of the pastoral celebration and of the anniversary, but I imagine that the people who lived in the city were mainly concerned with the latter, as are the *Fasti*. The bonfire which figures so largely in the descriptions of the ceremony must have been part of the rustic celebration. In a city so plagued by fires it would hardly have been permitted.

[57] Ovid, *Fasti* 3.771-790. Cf. Cicero, *Att.* 6.1.12: *Quinto togam puram Liberalibus cogitabam dare.* The *toga pura* could be assumed on other days. See Warde Fowler, *RF* 56, and Degrassi, p. 425.

[58] For the evidence for the celebrations referred to in this and the next paragraph see Degrassi's commentaries on the individual days, or Marquardt-Wissowa, *Römische Staatsverwaltung*: "Die Feiertage des römischen Kalenders," 567-589.

mercatores, who honored it because it was the anniversary of the dedication of the temple of Mercury, the patron of their guild. Because of the anniversary there must also have been a sacrifice to Mercury. The Ides of June must have been a lively day, for the flute players were *feriati*, held an *epulum* in the Capitoline temple, and roamed about the city drunk and wearing masks. The Ides of July was the anniversary of the battle of Lake Regillus, which was celebrated by an elaborate sacrifice, presumably to Castor and Pollux, to whose aid the Roman victory was attributed. It was also the occasion of a magnificent parade, the *transvectio equitum* which had been instituted by the censor Q. Fabius Maximus in 304 B.C. (Livy, 9.46.15; Dion. Hal., 6.13.4; Val. Max., 2.2.9). The Ides of August was a favorite day for the dedication of temples, of which the most famous was the temple of Diana on the Aventine. This was celebrated especially by slaves and women. On the Ides of October a chariot race was held on the Campus Martius and the winning horse was sacrificed to Mars. Its bleeding tail was taken to the Regia, while the inhabitants of two city districts battled for the possession of its head (Festus 190, 246 L.; Plut. *Q.R.* 97). The Ides of December saw a more sober celebration which would have attracted only local attention, and that of particular devotees of Tellus, for it was the dedication day of her temple, on which the aediles and *flaminicae* held a *lectisternium* for her and Ceres.

Other NP days besides the Ides had a double character. The rites of the Fordicidia performed for the people in their *curiae* must have been completely overshadowed by the *Ludi Ceriales* which were going on before and after it. The Quirinalia owned its popular name, *feriae stultorum,* to nothing connected with Quirinus, but to the fact that it was the day on which people who were so stupid as not to know which *curia* they belonged to could celebrate the Fornacalia, which they should have done earlier in their own *curia*. The Opalia and the Divalia on the 19th and 21st of December seem to have been swallowed up, as far as public attention goes, by the extended festivities of the Saturnalia.

We see then that the *feriae* of NP days affected the life of the city in different ways. Some of them affected everybody, and even turned normal customs upside down, as when, on the Saturnalia, masters waited on their slaves. Others would concern only those who had a particular devotion to the god whose day it was, or those who lived in the neighborhood in which its rites took place. These remind one of minor saints' days in Rome today, and the celebrations in honor of the titulars of particular churches, which are often accompanied by their own local *feste*. Others, like the sacrifice to Angerona on the Divalia and the *parentatio* to Acca Larentia on the Larentalia, were doubtless carried out in decent order by the priests, but did not interest the public.

Before we leave the subject of *feriae* we should touch on a matter of terminology which presents some problems. *Feriae* used in its primary sense seems to be a word which belongs to the technical vocabulary of religion, as we can see from the contexts in which it is used. In everyday speech it could be used simply to mean "holiday." There is, however, another expression used to describe days of religious observance which is often treated by ancient and modern writers as a synonym for *feriae*, and thus leads to confusion. This is *dies festus*, which with its opposite *dies profestus*, forms one of the alliterative phrases which are characteristic of colloquial Latin. The words occur throughout Latin literature. A few quotations will illustrate their use:

> festo die si quid prodegeris
> profesto egere liceat.
> > Plautus, *Aul.* 380f.

> . . . ut carpentis festis profestisque diebus . . . per urbem vectemur . . .
> > Livy, 34.3.9

> pauper Opimius argenti positi intus et auri
> qui Veientanum festis potare diebus
> Campana solitus trulla vappamque profestis.
> > Horace, *Serm.* 2.3.142-144

> . . . studium puerile fatiscit
> laeta nisi austeris varientur festa profestis.
> > Ausonius, 18. *Epist.* 22.10 b.

It is clear from the contexts in which the words are always used that *dies festi* are cheerful days, which should be enjoyed, and a glance at the definitions shows that this character was derived from their connection with religion. Macrobius (1.16.2) defines them as *dis dicati*, contrasting them with *dies profesti* which are granted to men for their private and public business (*hominibus ob administrandam rem privatam publicamque concessi*). Nonius (689 Lindsay) says that *festum* means *sollemniter laetum et feriatum*. Isidore (*De Nat. Rerum* 1.4) tells us: *profesti dies festis contrarii, id est sine religione. festi tantundem otii et religionis sunt.*

Obviously *dies festi* and *feriae* have much in common and their meanings overlap to a large extent. But each has a distinctive element which prevents them from being precisely synonymous. The essential connotation of *feriae* for the Roman was "day of rest" from his usual labors, but this might well be a day of mourning which he would never call *dies festus*. On the other hand the connotation of *dies festus* is the pleasure of the occasion, which may include *feriae* and may not.[59] For example the days of the *Ludi* are certainly *dies festi* (Cicero *pro Caelio* 1), but *ludi* are not *feriae*.[60]

It is my impression that the explanation for the confusion between *feriae* and *dies festus* is that, while the former is a technical word which was used by the layman with a broad derived meaning, *dies festus* and *profestus* were non-technical and be-

[59] The additional element of pleasure may be what Servius had in mind when he said (*Georg.* 1.268): *feriae deorum causa instituuntur, festi dies hominum quoque*. Dies festus clearly adds something to the concept of *feriae*. For example, Cicero in stating his ideal law (*De Leg.* 2.19) uses *feriae* alone, presumably in technical legal language, but when he interprets the law (*De Leg.* 2.29) he refers to the *ratio feriarum festorumque dierum*. Livy (22.1.19f.) describes the celebration of the Saturnalia in 217 B.C.: *per urbem Saturnalia diem ac noctem clamata, populusque eum diem festum habere ac servare in perpetuum iussus*. The day must already have been *feriae*, but it now becomes a *dies festus* also.

[60] Macrobius (1.16.2) lists *ludi* separately from *feriae*. Varro makes a careful distinction between *feriae* and *Ludi* which come on the same day (*De L. L.* 6.20): *Consualia dicta a Conso, quod tum feriae publicae ei deo et in Circo ad aram eius ab sacerdotibus ludi illi, quibus virgines Sabinae raptae*. When Augustus held the *Ludi Saeculares*, the official description of the rites included both *Ludi* and *feriae* (*CIL* 6.32323, line 39). The words (line 13) [*dili*]*genterque memineritis litibu*[*s*] must be part of the formula for the proclamation of *feriae* quoted by Cicero (see p. 70).

longed to the vocabulary of everyday speech.[61] It is, I think, impossible for us to determine just how these words are being used in any one passage in Latin literature, unless the context gives us a clue, because the Romans themselves used them loosely and probably could not have given a precise definition of them, unless they happened to be pontifices. A false sense of security is created in us when we read Macrobius' statement: *festis (diebus) insunt sacrificia epulae ludi feriae* (1.16.2), which suggests that *feriae* can be neatly docketed as a sub-class of *dies festi*, but one has only to read the earlier chapters of his *Saturnalia* to see that he uses the words quite interchangeably. He, or his source for the classification, has in fact tried to impose order where there is none, by forcing technical terms into the framework of a non-technical vocabulary.

As far as the official calendar is concerned it is easy to see why *feriae* are listed and *dies festi* are not. *Feriae* affected the character of a day officially, and *dies festi* did not.[62] It was therefore the responsibility of the pontifices to let men know when *feriae* came. Whether or not the public took the opportunity to enjoy a religious ceremony on a *dies festus* was its own business.

[61] Cf. Marquardt-Wissowa, *Römische Staatsverwaltung*, 293, n. 3: "Die Unterscheidung von *festi dies* (Feiertage) und *profesti dies* (Werktage) scheint nicht dem *ius sacrum*, sondern dem gewöhnlichen Leben anzugehören."

[62] A large number of *dies comitiales* come during the periods of the *Ludi* and in theory a magistrate could summon the *comitia* then, but he would be foolish to do so. See Ch. 3, p. 41. Cicero's comments on how Verres expected to postpone his trial shows a jury would not expect to have to serve during *Ludi* (*Verr.* 1.31).

CHAPTER 5

NUNDINAL LETTERS AND *NUNDINAE*

In Chapter 1 the letters, A-H, which recur regularly throughout the year in both the pre-Julian and Julian calendars, were identified as the so-called nundinal letters, by which the *nundinae* or ninth days could be reckoned (see pp. 27f.). The ancient authors tell us that originally these *nundinae* were the days on which Romans, who were then for the most part farmers, dropped their work on the land and came into the city to trade, to deal with their business affairs, including lawsuits, and to attend *comitia*.[1] In the first century, however, we find that *comitia* and *contiones* may not be held on *nundinae* because they had become *dies fasti* and private business had taken them over (see Chapter 3, pp. 40, 47).

In view of the nature of the *nundinae*, it is surprising to find that Macrobius classifies these days as *feriae* (1.16.5), but later he admits that there is a difference of opinion on this point and discusses the problem at some length (1.16.28-31).[2] He

---

[1] Varro, *De R. R.* 2. praef. 1-2; Dion. Hal., 7.58.3; Columella, 1. *praef.* 18; for the fullest detail we have Macrobius' citation (1.16.34-35) from Rutilius Rufus, the consul of 105 B.C. I suspect that Rutilius may here have been discussing the background of *Lex Caecilia Didia* of 98 B.C.: *Rutilius scribit Romanos instituisse nundinas, ut octo quidem diebus in agris rustici opus facerent, nono autem die intermisso rure ad mercatum legesque accipiendas Romam venirent et ut scita atque consulta frequentiore populo referrentur, quae trinundino die proposita a singulis atque universis facile noscebantur. unde etiam mos tractus ut leges trinundino die promulgarentur. ea re etiam candidatis usus fuit in comitium nundinis venire et in colle consistere unde coram possent ab universis videri. sed haec omnia neglegentius haberi coepta et post abolita, postquam internundino etiam ob multitudinem plebis frequentes adesse coeperunt.* On the early history of *nundinae*, see Ch. 6, pp. 103-6, and App. 3. For *nundinae* in general see M. Besnier, D-S 4.1.120-122; W. Kroll, *RE* 17.2.1467-1472. On related problems see M. P. Nilsson, *Primitive Time-Reckoning* (Lund 1920) 324-336; P. Huvelin, *Essai historique sur le droit des marchés et foires* (Paris 1897), to which I am much indebted for the illuminating discussion of the economic and social character of *nundinae* and their relation to markets in other cultures. I have found some interesting analogies in A. G. Dewey, *Peasant Marketing in Java* (Glencoe, Iowa, 1962).

[2] *quod autem nundinas ferias dixi potest argui, quia Titus de feriis*

[84]

cites three authorities, including Trebatius and the pontifices themselves, who argued that *nundinae* were not *feriae*, and Labeo, who claimed that they were. He cites the statement of L. Julius Caesar that *contiones* and *comitia* could not be held on *nundinae* (see Chapter 3, pp. 40, 47) as evidence that they were *feriae*, apparently not realizing that a negative restriction does not prove a positive character. He then tries to solve the problem by citing the statement of Granius Licinianus that *nundinae* were *feriae* inasmuch as on them the *flaminica* sacrificed a ram to Jupiter in the Regia, but that by *Lex Hortensia* (probably 287 B.C.) they had been made *dies fasti*, in order that *rustici* who had come to market could conduct lawsuits on these days also. From this Macrobius seems to conclude, although Granius does not say so, that prior to *Lex Hortensia nundinae* had been *feriae*, on which action at law was impossible. This is highly improbable, for the Twelve Tables provide for the possibility of legal action on *nundinae* (Gellius, 20.1.46-7; *FIRA* 1.33). The explanation of this confusion must, I think, lie in the varied meanings of the word *feriae*, discussed in Chapter 4 (see pp. 70f.). The pontifices in their ruling would naturally use it in its strict technical sense of a day of religious observance, whereas Labeo must have used it in the loose sense of "holiday," as apparently does Paulus (76 L.) when he refers to *nundinae* as *feriae sine die festo*, and as Macrobius elsewhere calls some of the days of the Saturnalia *feriatos . . . non festos* (1.11.50). Festus (176 L.) and

---

scribens nundinarum dies non inter ferias retulit sed tantum sollennes vocavit, et quod Iulius Modestus adfirmat Messala augure consulente pontifices, an nundinarum Romanorum Nonarumque dies feriis tenerentur, respondisse eos nundinas sibi ferias non videri, et quod Trebatius in libro primo Religionum ait nundinis magistratum posse manu mittere iudiciaque addicere. sed contra Iulius Caesar sexto decimo Auspiciorum libro negat nundinis contionem advocari posse, id est cum populo agi, ideoque nundinis Romanorum haberi comitia non posse. Cornelius etiam Labeo primo Fastorum libro nundinas ferias esse pronuntiat. causam vero huius varietatis apud Granium Licinianum libro secundo diligens lector inveniet. ait enim nundinas Iovis ferias esse, siquidem flaminica omnibus nundinis in regia Iovi arietem soleat immolare, sed lege Hortensia effectum ut fastae essent, uti rustici, qui nundinandi causa in urbem veniebant, lites componerent. nefasto enim die praetori fari non licebat. ergo qui ferias dicunt a mendacio vindicantur patrocinio vestustatis, qui contra sentiunt aestimatu aetatis quae legem secuta est vera depromunt.

Servius (*Georg.* 1.275) both classify *nundinae* as *dies feriati* which give the *rustici* an opportunity to go to the city to trade. To us perhaps a day on which so much business was transacted might not seem much of a holiday, but it certainly provided a break in the routine of work, and the gathering of people would give a gay air to the occasion. Schools were dismissed for the day, countrymen shaved and took a bath, probably by way of a treat at the public baths, while the city dwellers could entertain more lavishly than usual.[3]

The character of *nundinae* had a curious side-effect. As *dies fasti*, when they coincided with *dies comitiales*, they would prevent the holding of *comitia*, and probably this enabled the Senate to meet (see Chapter 3, p. 60 n. 54). When they coincided with *dies nefasti*, they would revoke the ban on *legis actio* so that the praetor could hold court. But what happened if they coincided with NP days? It seems improbable that they could change the character of *feriae stativae*. According to Cicero (*De Div.* 1.102; *De Leg.* 2.29), lawsuits could not be conducted on *feriae*, so we must assume that on such *nundinae* the praetor would not hear cases. There would, however, be nothing to prevent the market from functioning as usual, just as until recently the markets of modern Rome were open on Sundays. It would of course have been possible for the *nundinae* to have been postponed to the following day, but I know of no evidence that it was, and the classical world does not seem to have felt any impropriety in carrying on trade on a day of religious observance. In fact, it seems to have been considered an excellent time to turn an honest penny.

The column of nundinal letters prompts us to ask why the designers of the calendar felt it necessary to include a device for keeping track of an event which occurred regularly at such short intervals. The answer must lie in the function of the *nundinae* of the late republic, and in the uses of the nine-day period which they begin and end. The Roman market no longer concerned only the inhabitants of a small community whose farmers brought to town their produce to exchange it for the

---

[3] Varro, in Nonius, 316 L.; Seneca, *Ep.* 86.12; Athenaeus, 6.274 c.; Macrobius, 3.17.9. Cf. L. Halkin, "Le congé des nundines dans les écoles romaines," *Rev. Belge de Phil. et d'Histoire* 11 (1932) 121-130.

wares made by urban craftsmen. As Rome became the capital of Italy into which goods flowed from all over the world, her markets must have offered opportunities for merchants in all the smaller cities. They would have come to buy, but would also have found this a convenient time to negotiate deals with Roman businessmen, and with people from other towns. These days would also provide an opportunity for the exchange of information between political leaders in Rome and the men who were their liaison officers with all the important voters of the rest of Italy. Such men would come to Rome at irregular intervals, and would find the inclusion of the nundinal letters in the Roman calendars posted in their towns a great help in keeping track of the dates of Roman *nundinae*, which differed from those of markets in other places. One could plan a trip to the city and be sure one would not discover on arrival that one had just missed the *nundinae* and have to prolong one's doubtless expensive visit by several days.

For many residents of Rome there were other reasons why the nundinal letters would be useful. Since *nundinae* prevented the holding of *contiones* and *comitia,* the dates on which they would fall during the year would be an essential piece of information in the planning of political activities. The letters would also help to calculate another longer period of time which was politically important, the *trinum nundinum.* This had originally been the period which elapsed from one *nundinae* to the third one following, that is twenty-five days, if one follows the Roman habit of including the day from which one is reckoning. By the first century, and probably long before, the *trinum nundinum* had been dissociated from the actual *nundinae* and might be reckoned from any day in the A-H series to the third repetition of that day's letter.[4] The period was important politically because *Lex Caecilia Didia* of 98 B.C. (see Chapter 3, pp. 41f.) had enacted that it must elapse between the *promulgatio* of a law, that is its first presentation to the people, and its *rogatio* at the *comitia* summoned to vote on it.[5] The same

---

[4] See App. 3 for the evidence on which these statements are made.

[5] It is often said in the modern literature that candidates for public office were required to announce their candidacy at least a *trinum nundinum* before the elections. This would seem reasonable as a parallel to the period before legislative *comitia,* but there is no direct evidence for it.

[87]

period was required between the preliminary *contiones* and the final accusation before the *comitia* in the criminal trials before the people which were often major moves in political strategy. Because for purposes of dating days Roman months are broken into three parts of unequal lengths, and the days within each part numbered backward, it is not easy to calculate such periods in advance by the days of the month. It is much easier to run your eye down the column of nundinal letters until you come to the third repetition of the letter of the initial day, just as we use a modern calendar to locate the date of a day of the week months ahead.

It is also quite easy to learn to use the nundinal letters to calculate other periods of time which are not based on the nine-day system. Many Roman laws require actions to be taken within a number of days which is a multiple of ten. It does not take much experience to discover that all such numbers of days consist of a certain number of repetitions of a nundinal letter plus or minus either 1 or 3, if one counts inclusively. Twenty days, for example, is two repetitions plus three days, thirty is four minus three, sixty is seven plus three. If one's business required one to deal in these periods these combinations would soon become second nature.

With a little practice one could learn to do these calculations in one's mind, because in the Roman calendar the relation between the nundinal letters and the days of the year never changes, unlike the relation between the days of the week and the dates in our calendar. There are certain features of this relation which provide short cuts. For instance, because in the republican calendar there are always 25 days (a *trinum nundinum*) from the Nones of any month to the last day, the Nones, Ides, *a.d. X Kal.* and *pridie Kal.* of any month have the same letter, and the letter of the Kalends of the next month is the one following the letter of the Nones of the preceding month. If Roman schoolboys learned the letters of the Kalends and Nones of each month, as we learn mnemonic jingles

---

It might be derived from Macrobius 1.16.35 (see n. 1), and confirmed by Cicero's reference (*Fam.* 16.12.3) to Caesar's willingness to be present as a candidate for a *trinum nundinum*. The latter, however, refers to a very special case.

about the number of days in the month, their reckoning would have been greatly facilitated.

The methods of calculation which I have suggested above are of course applicable only to normal years. In the intercalary years there would be some inconveniences. Before the Kalends of the intercalary month either one or two nundinal letters were omitted, in order that the Kalends of March might fall on their normal B and the rest of the year thus follow the regular pattern (see Chapter 1, p. 26). This would mean that the letter which marked the *nundinae* for the year would change with the first *nundinae* of the intercalary month. Anyone who failed to anticipate this change might find his schedule upset, and indeed the whole community might be much inconvenienced if the pontifices suddenly decided to intercalate at short notice. One can see why in a constantly more complex economic and political society intercalation would become more of a nuisance than a help, and there would be an increasing tendency to omit it.

The usefulness of the nundinal letters in the republican calendar was greatly reduced in the Julian calendar, because, when one or two days were added to the 29-day months, the old *trinum nundinum* which ran from the Nones to the last day was destroyed. But the need for calculations based on the nine-day period rapidly disappeared too. Under the Empire the *comitia*, to whose activities the *trinum nundinum* was related, became less and less important while the seven-day planetary week gradually displaced the nundinal system.[6] The word *nundinae* lost all its association with the number nine and came to mean simply a market which might be held at any interval.

[6] It has in the past been assumed that this week, in which the days were named for the planets, began to be used in Rome in the second century A.D., but there is good reason to suppose that it was already familiar in the Augustan period. Three of the *Fasti* carry, as well as the eight letters of the nundinal series, another set of A to G. See Degrassi, p. 326, and "Un nuovo frammento del calendario romano e la settimana planetaria di sette giorni," *Scritti Vari di Antichità* (Rome 1962) 1.681-692. It is possible to see the seven-day week actually replacing the *nundinum* in some of the parapegmata (Degrassi, nos. 49-57), which list the days on which *nundinae* took place in different towns. Seven days are given, but eight towns. Originally they must have been scheduled for the eight-day period.

PART II

THE HISTORY OF THE
REPUBLICAN CALENDAR

CHAPTER 6

FROM THE FIRST TO THE FOURTH
CENTURY B.C.

METHOD

In the first part of this book I have discussed the calendar of
the first century B.C. and its functions, for which we have a
reasonably reliable body of evidence. It is now time to turn to
the calendar of the preceding centuries. In doing this I shall
follow a method which may prove trying to the reader, but
which I have found profitable. In writing the history of any
institution one usually begins at the beginning and works forward. I propose to begin at the end and work backwards. I
have chosen to do this because, if one is to begin at the beginning, one must know when it occurred, and this is exactly the
point which is uncertain in the case of the pre-Julian calendar.
The material presented in the *Fasti* in large letters, other than
the NP days added in the early years of the Empire (see p.
32), is usually assumed to represent the calendar as it was
originally framed in the regal period, complete with named
days, character letters and nundinal letters, which remained
unaltered throughout the period of the republic. This assumption is, however, based on no evidence at all, but on Mommsen's intuition. It was he who saw that the material written in
large letters in the *Fasti* is essentially identical in all the inscriptions, while the material in small letters varies considerably both in content and phraseology. He concluded from
this evidence that the names of the days, and the character and
nundinal letters, formed the original calendar which he dated in
the regal period, while the smaller writing represented additions
made later.[1] This conclusion is possible, but it carries with it an
implication which is difficult to accept, that is, that throughout
all the period of the republic, when every other Roman insti-

---

[1] For a detailed discussion of his arguments on the date, see App. 4,
pp. 207ff.

tution, and the whole of Roman society, changed and developed in a multitude of ways, the calendar which served these institutions remained static. A few scholars have expressed reservations about Mommsen's interpretation of the large letters, but the majority of those who have written about the calendar have accepted its contents as an indivisible unit, even when they have dated it in a period later than Mommsen did.[2]

It has therefore seemed to me that it might be profitable to review the evidence for the history of the calendar, working on the hypothesis that the large letters were not used in the *Fasti* to indicate the original elements in the calendar, a piece of information which would have had no practical use for a Roman citizen of the late republic, but that they represent the official calendar of the state, in which different items may have been introduced at different times as need arose.[3] In this review of the evidence, working backward from the calendar of the first century, I have found that many items which in relation to a static calendar appeared to contradict each other can be interpreted as belonging to different stages in a long development, and can be significantly related to events in the social and political history of the republic. There emerges a calendar which is not a fossil embedded in the structure of Rome, but is a part of the living organism of Roman society, adapted to the needs of the community as they changed.

THE FIRST AND SECOND CENTURIES

We have already seen that certain changes, not so much in the structure of the calendar as in its administration, took place during the first century.[4] Some of these are related to similar changes made in earlier periods. In 58 B.C., P. Clodius Pulcher, as tribune of the plebs, carried a law which, according to Cicero (*pro Sestio* 33) provided *ne auspicia valerent, ne quis obnuntiaret, ne quis legi intercederet, ut omnibus fastis diebus legem ferri liceret, ut lex Aelia lex Fufia ne valeret.* Discussion of these laws has usually concentrated on the first three clauses

---

[2] For a review of the history of this controversy, see App. 4.
[3] This was the point of view taken by O. E. Hartmann, for whose ideas see App. 4, p. 210.
[4] See pp. 41-46.

and the problems of the auspices,[5] but here we are concerned with the last two clauses. The provision that laws might be passed on all *dies fasti* was of course a contravention of the rule that *comitia* might meet only on *dies comitiales*, and Cicero says of Clodius *omnes leges quae sunt de iure et de tempore legum rogandarum una rogatione delevit* (*pro Sestio* 56). This presents us with the problem of determining what provision *de tempore legum rogandarum* had been made in *Lex Aelia* and *Lex Fufia* and was made invalid by *Lex Clodia*.

Lex Aelia and *Lex Fufia* date from the middle of the second century B.C., probably 150 B.C.[6] It seems clear that one item introduced then was that no new legislation could be presented to an assembly in the period between the announcement of the date of the *comitia* for elections and the actual holding of the elections.[7] McDonald, in a discussion of *Lex Clodia*, has concluded that *Lex Aelia* and *Lex Fufia* not only

[5] For the most recent discussions see W. F. McDonald, "Clodius and the Lex Aelia Fufia," *JRS* 19 (1929) 164-179; J. P. V. D. Balsdon, "Roman History 58-56 B.C.: Three Ciceronian Problems," *JRS* 47 (1957) 15-20; R. Gardner, *Cicero: the Speeches. Pro Sestio, In Vatinium* (Loeb Classical Library 1958) 309-322; L. R. Taylor, "Forerunners of the Gracchi," *JRS* 52 (1962) 19-27, esp. 22f.; G. V. Sumner, "Lex Aelia, Lex Fufia," *AJP* 84 (1963) 337-358; A. E. Astin, "Leges Aelia et Fufia," *Latomus* 23 (1964) 421-445. Cf. also J. Paoli, "Le notion de temps faste et celle de temps comitial," *REA* 56 (1954) 121-149, esp. 146.

[6] For the approximate date, 100 years before *Lex Clodia*, Cicero, *in Pisonem* 10. For the exact date, cf. L. R. Taylor, *op.cit.* (n. 5).

[7] This is deduced from the combination of the comment on Cicero, *In Vatinium* 23 in *Scholia Bobiensia* (148 Stangl), and Dio, 36.39. It is probable that, as Mommsen states (*Staatsrecht*[3] 3.1.376), the period referred to in *Leges Aelia et Fufia* was supposed to be a *trinum nundinum* (App. 3, pp. 194-206), but the evidence is weak. See Livy, 3.35.1: *comitia decemviris creandis in trinum nundinum indicta*, but there are at least ten cases in Livy in which elections are held *primo quoque tempore* or *primo die comitiali*, which suggests a shorter period. Cicero, *Fam.* 16.12.3, refers to the very exceptional circumstances of Caesar's candidacy for office in 49 B.C., and says nothing about the announcement of the date for elections. The period between the announcement of the date and the actual election may also have been much longer.

L. R. Taylor, in *Party Politics in the Age of Caesar* (Sather Classical Lectures 22, Berkeley 1949) 59f., says that after the elections were over no law could be voted on for another *trinum nundinum*, because *Lex Caecilia Didia* required this period between *promulgatio* and *rogatio*. But *Leges Aelia et Fufia*, as far as the evidence indicates, forbade only the *rogatio* before elections, not the *promulgatio*, so that a *rogatio* could take place soon after the election. Cf. Astin, *op.cit.* (n. 5) 438, for a different statement.

restricted legislation before the elections but, in order to achieve this, "forbade the holding of legislative assemblies on *dies fasti non comitiales*, among which was the period of three *nundinae* immediately before the *comitia consularia*."[8] This conclusion is, however, impossible, because it implies that previous to *Lex Aelia* and *Lex Fufia* the distinction between *dies fasti* and *dies comitiales* did not exist, whereas the provision of *Lex Hortensia*, 287 B.C., that *nundinae* were to be *dies fasti* and thus not available for *comitia* (see p. 40) shows that the distinction had existed long before the middle of the second century. A more plausible explanation of the provision in *Lex Aelia* and *Lex Fufia* in connection with *dies fasti* has been suggested by L. R. Taylor. She considers it possible that "before the time of the *Lex Aelia* and the *Lex Fufia* the *concilium plebis* had been permitted to meet on *dies fasti* as well as on the *dies comitiales* to which the *comitia* would have been restricted."[9] Since an assembly summoned by a tribune is, strictly speaking, a *concilium plebis*, not one of the *comitia* at all (see p. 37), it seems reasonable that originally the *concilium* should have functioned under rules different from those which applied to the *comitia*. It is also reasonable that, since *Lex Aelia* and *Lex Fufia* were designed to restrain the activities of the tribunes, they should also impose a limitation on the number of days available for those activities by ruling that the *concilium* could no longer meet on *dies fasti*. Like *Lex Clodia*, these laws would have had to specify that the limitation applied to all *dies fasti* in order to make sure that *nundinae* were included. Otherwise some hair-splitting tribune

---

[8] *Op.cit.* (n. 5) 176. The expression "period of three *nundinae*" is, of course, incorrect. It is like saying a "period of three Saturdays." In the middle of the second century, the period would have been described as a *trinum nundinum* (see App. 3, p. 199). The expression *dies fasti non comitiales*, which occurs throughout the modern literature, is also incorrect. It never occurs in the ancient authors. It came into modern usage from discussions of *Leges Aelia et Fufia* written in Latin, beginning, to the best of my knowledge, with that of Paulus Manutius, *De Legibus Romanis*, 1557 (reprinted in Graevius' *Thesaurus*, vol. 2.). It is, I believe, true that originally the days marked in the *Fasti* as *comitiales* were *fasti* (see p. 52), but once the category of *dies comitiales* had come into being, it was regarded as entirely separate from that of *dies fasti*. No ancient writer suggests that *dies comitiales* were a subdivision of *dies fasti*, as modern writers often do.

[9] *Op.cit.* (n. 5) 23, n. 24.

could have argued that *dies fasti* referred only to days so marked in the calendar. If in his law Clodius used the expression *legem ferri*, reported by Cicero, he was of course demanding far more than *Lex Aelia* and *Lex Fufia*, on this hypothesis, had taken away, for it would mean that all legislative assemblies could meet on *dies fasti*, not just the *concilium plebis*. One must however admit that any solution to the problem of *Lex Aelia* and *Lex Fufia* can only be tentative in the present state of the evidence.

A major change in the calendar is often attributed to the period of *Lex Aelia* and *Lex Fufia*, without, I believe, adequate evidence. Several modern authorities state that in 153 B.C. the beginning of the year was changed from March 1 to January 1.[10] It is certainly very probable that the calendar year originally began in March. Several ancient authors tell us so, pointing to the fact that the sequence of months whose names are formed from numbers is reckoned from March, and that typical New Year rites are celebrated in March.[11] The only evidence for dating the change to January in 153 B.C., however, is the fact that in this year the consuls began to enter office on the Kalends of January, as they always did thereafter.[12] But does this mean a change in the calendar year?

[10] Hartmann-Lange, *Der Römische Kalender* (Leipzig 1882) 24, cites J. J. Scaliger as the first modern authority for this idea. See Ginzel, 2.225-229, for a discussion. See also Warde Fowler, *RF* 5 (but note the apparent contradiction on p. 4.); M. P. Nilsson, "Studien zur Vorgeschichte des Weihnachtfestes," *Archiv für Religionswissenschaft* 19 (1916/1919) 68 and 91 (*Opuscula Selecta* I 232 and 254); N. Turchi, *La Religione di Roma Antica* (Bologna 1939) 78; Degrassi, pp. 315f. Mommsen believed that the calendar year began with March up to the time of Caesar's reform (*RC²* 103, 276ff.; *Staatsrecht³* 1.599f.) but the discovery of *Ant. Mai.* proved that the change had been made earlier. Carcopino (*Histoire Ancienne* [Paris 1936] III, Tome II, 991) follows Mommsen. Soltau (*RömChron* 41-45) attributed the change to *Lex Acilia* of 191 B.C., because he believed the *Fasti* of Fulvius began with January, while Bouché-Leclerq detected in it the influence of astrology and associated it with the discovery of the "Books of Numa" in 181 B.C. (*L'Astrologie Grecque* [1899] 189, n. 1). Cf. P. Boyancé, "Fulvius Nobilior et le Dieu ineffable," *RPh* 29 (1955) 172-192.

[11] Atta (quoted by Servius, *Georg.* 1.43), Varro, *De L. L.* 6.33 and Servius *Georg.* 1.43; Cicero, *De Leg.* 2.54; Ovid, *Fasti* 1.39-44, 3.135-152; Festus, 136 L.; Plutarch, *Q.R.* 19; Censorinus, *De Die Natali* 20; Macrobius, 1.12.5-7; Lydus, *De Mens.* 3.22 (61 Wuensch), 4.102 (141 Wuensch).

[12] Livy, *per.* 47; *Fasti Praen.*, January 1; Cassiodorus.

For centuries the consuls had entered office on a variety of different dates,[13] and there is no evidence that the calendar year had ever been adjusted to match the consular year. Such ancient authors as mention a date for the change from March to January assign it to Numa.[14] If the change had really taken place in 153 B.C. it could hardly have escaped the notice of ancient scholars, because the *Fasti* of Fulvius Nobilior (*cos.* 189 B.C.) would have begun with March.[15]

The modern belief that the beginning of the year was changed in 153 B.C. arises from the failure to recognize the fundamental difference between the calendar year and the consular year, and between their functions. The consular year defines the period during which a particular pair of consuls was in office. It can begin on any day of the calendar year and it may be shorter than a calendar year if the consuls leave office before their full term has expired.[16] The consular year is used to identify years in sequence. Lists of consuls from the beginning of the republic often accompany the calendar in the *Fasti*. When a Roman historian refers to an event prior to 153 B.C. as taking place at the beginning or end of the year, he is thinking in terms of the consular year. The calendar year, on the other hand, contains no variable elements, but is valid for any year. Its function is to provide dates within any one year, or dates which recur in a regular cycle. The dates of religious observances are determined by the calendar year, as are those of business transactions.[17] In treaties between Rome and other states periods of time were defined in terms of the calendar year.[18]

[13] For lists of the various dates see Mommsen, *RC*[2] 86-104; Leuze, *Die römische Jahrzählung* (Tübingen 1909) 335-375; Broughton, *MRR* 2.337f.

[14] Ovid, *Fasti* 1.39-44. Plutarch, *Numa* 18; Macrobius, 1.13.3; Lydus, *De Mens.* 4.102 (141 Wuensch).

[15] For Fulvius and his influence on the history of the calendar see pp. 123ff. W. Soltau points out, in *Prolegomena zu einer Römischen Chronologie* (Berlin 1886) 141, that if Fulvius in his commentary derived the name of January from Janus (*a deo principe*), as Varro's reference in his discussion of the names of the months suggests (*De L. L.* 6.33f.), then the year must have begun with January in Fulvius' day.

[16] Cf. Leuze, *Die römische Jahrzählung*, 337.

[17] Cf. Cato, *De Agr.* 146-150, on contracts.

[18] Cf. Leuze, *op.cit.* (n. 13) 383.

After 153 B.C. when the two types of year were synchronized, the distinction between them became academic, but Lydus (*De Mens.* 3.22 p. 61 Wuensch) refers to another method of classification. In discussing the dates on which different peoples begin their years, he says that the Romans had a priestly (ἱερατικὴ) beginning of the year in January and a traditional (πάτριος) one in March.[19] The word priestly must refer to the calendar year which was controlled by the pontifices, while Lydus connects the traditional beginning with the religious and popular celebrations of March.[20]

Lest we consider the Romans unnecessarily confused in their thinking about years, we should recall that in the United States we have, in addition to our calendar year, a fiscal year which begins in July, an academic year which begins in September, one religious year which begins on the first Sunday in Advent, another which begins on Roshoshonah, not to mention the lunar calendar privately observed by many Americans of Oriental origin, while the President's term of office begins on January 20th.[21]

In view of the evidence, I see no reason to believe that the beginning of the calendar year was changed in 153 B.C. It seems to me more probable that the republican calendar had always begun its year on the Kalends of January. The calendar which it supplanted must, however, have begun on the Kalends of March. The observances connected with that day and the whole month, many of which are clearly spring rites, survived both in strictly religious practice and as popular celebrations, and thus preserved the memory of the earlier opening of the year.

Why should the change from March to January have been made? In the older dispensation the year would begin with the spring month, March. The beginning of spring could be determined in a variety of ways: simply by the weather, by the

[19] He also refers to an ἀρχὴ πολιτικὴ or κυκλικὴ on September 1, which does not concern us here as he identifies it with the *indictio* of the empire. He seems to have been slightly confused as to some of his terms, for in 4.102 he describes the March New Year as πολιτικὴ.

[20] In the note on the Parilia (April 21) in *Praen.*, the words restored to read *principio an[ni pastoricii]* suggest yet another new year.

[21] For a similar variety of New Year's Days, see G. Megas, *Greek Calendar Customs* (Athens 1958) 16f.

[99]

time when the west wind began to blow, by the position of the sun in the signs of the zodiac, etc. The inventors of the pre-Julian calendar, however, seem to have wanted a more exact method of determining the relation of the calendar year to the sun. The easiest times at which to determine the progress of the solar year by simple observation are the spring and winter solstices. On these days the sun in its annual course rises at its northernmost or southernmost point on the horizon. All that one needs for a rough determination of the solstices is a fixed point from which one can regularly observe the horizon, and a landmark either on the horizon or between the horizon and the observation point by which to sight at the sun.[22] It would seem that the Romans decided to use the winter solstice as the check point by which they could see how their system was working and whether or not they should intercalate. Luckily for them Rome is admirably provided with the necessary facilities. The northeast end of the Capitoline Hill, where on the *arx* the rites of the Kalends and Ides were carried out, provides even today an unobstructed view of the horizon both to the east and to the west.[23] To the west over the long ridge of the Janiculum the crescent moon can be seen just after sunset. To the east, just before sunrise, the jagged outline of the mountains stands out black and clear against the sky, and provides a series of markers by which the exact point at which the sun comes up can be observed.[24] From this vantage point then, as the winter drew on and the days grew shorter and shorter, a watch would be kept until the sun rose over the mountains at a point just to the north of Tusculum, almost in line with the Sacra Via.[25] According to the date in the calendar on which this happened, the pontifices would know whether the calendar was running ahead of the solar year or behind it and how much, whether

[22] As in Athens Mount Lykabettos could serve as the landmark, according to Theophrastus (*De sign. pluv.* 1.4).

[23] The closest one can now get to the site of the Arx is either the top gallery of the Victor Emanuel Monument or the little garden behind Santa Maria in Aracoeli.

[24] Since one is not encouraged to climb the Victor Emanuel Monument before dawn, I have observed this from the roof of the American Academy in Rome, on the Janiculum.

[25] I am grateful to W. C. Michels, Professor of Physics, Bryn Mawr College, for calculating this point.

the intercalation system was functioning adequately or whether it needed correction by skipping intercalation for a year or by adding a month in what would have been an ordinary year.

At the beginning of the second century B.C. an action was taken in relation to the calendar the details of which are not clear. Macrobius in his discussion of intercalation (1.13.8-1.15.3) remarks on the variety of opinion as to when it was first introduced. After citing authors who suggest Romulus, Numa, and Servius Tullius as its originators, he continues: *Tuditanus refert Libro tertio Magistratuum decem viros, qui decem tabulis duas addiderunt, de intercalando populum rogasse. Cassius eosdem scribit auctores. Fulvius autem id egisse M'. Acilium*[26] *consulem dicit ab urbe condita anno quingentesimo sexagesimo secundo, inito mox bello Aetolico. Sed hoc arguit Varro, scribendo antiquissimam legem fuisse incisam in columna aerea a L. Pinario et Furio consulibus cui mensis*[27] *intercalaris adscribitur.* It is not clear just what Acilius (*cos.* 191 B.C.) really did. Macrobius obviously thinks that Fulvius meant that Acilius instituted intercalation, but it is probable that he, or his source, misinterpreted Fulvius' words. Even without Varro's reference to a law of 472 B.C. dated in the intercalary month,[28] common sense indicates that the Romans must have practiced intercalation centuries before Acilius' consulship, because even a lunar calendar requires intercalation, let alone the lunisolar cyclic calendar of the republic. Since Fulvius (*cos.* 189) was a contemporary of Acilius, he must have been aware of this. The words *id egisse M'. Acilium* may, however, refer back to the previous statement of Tuditanus and simply mean that Acilius, like the *decemviri*, introduced a law about intercalation with which of course Fulvius would have been familiar. This is the sense in which the passage has usually been interpreted[29] and the contents of

---

[26] The name is an almost certain emendation of the MSS, which read either *marcum* or *marcium*.

[27] The MSS read *mentio*, which, combined with *intercalaris*, can hardly be anything but a mistake for *mensis*.

[28] The reference to the intercalary month is often interpreted to mean that the law of 472 B.C. dealt with intercalation, but it seems obvious from the wording that the law was dated in an intercalary month. For the use of *adscribere* in dating see Cicero, *Att.* 3.23.1; *Q.F.* 3.1.8.

[29] Cf. Mommsen, *RC*[2] 40; Lange, *RA* 1[3].353; Ginzel, 2.270; Klebs,

the *Lex Acilia* have been deduced from the account of another event in the history of the calendar for which the sources give no date. Censorinus (*de D.N.* 20), Solinus (1.43), and Ammianus (26.1.12) all tell us that the difficulties in which intercalation had involved the Romans were increased when they handed over to the pontifices (or *sacerdotes*) the right to intercalate at their discretion, and the pontifices then used this right to oblige their friends who might for business or political reasons want a longer or a shorter year.[30] There is, however, no evidence that this transfer of authority had anything to do with *Lex Acilia*. It is possible that the connection was made by someone used to the regularity of the Julian calendar who attempted to explain the earlier confusion by putting the blame on an official scapegoat instead of on the system. One must, however, accept that in 191 B.C. something drastic needed to be done about the state of the calendar. Livy (37.4.4) records that in 190 B.C. an eclipse of the sun took place on *a.d. V Id. Quinct.*, which ought to be July 11. According to modern astronomers, however, the eclipse actually took place on what in our reckoning is March 14,[31] so that the calendar year was nearly four months ahead of the solar year. Such a majestic error must have been produced by constant failure to intercalate in the preceding years,[32] and would certainly justify instructions to the pontifices to remedy it as soon as possible. By 168 B.C. the error had been reduced, whether by the pontifices or not, to about two-and-a-half months, for the eclipse

RE 1.1.255; Rotondi, *LPPR* 273; Scullard, *Roman Politics 220-150 B.C.*, 28, n. 3.

[30] Cicero (*De Leg.* 2.29) attributes the invention of intercalation to Numa and its breakdown to the *neglegentia* of the pontifices. Macrobius (1.14.1) refers to the use which the pontifices made of intercalation, but does not mention any grant of authority to them.

[31] See the table of eclipses in Ginzel, 2.529, and his discussion of eclipses in relation to the Roman calendar, 2.210-218. Also De Sanctis, *Storia dei Romani* 4.1 (Turin 1923) 368f.; M. Holleaux, "Le Consul M. Fulvius et le siège de Samé," *BCH* 54 (1930) 1-41; P. Roussel, "Delphes et l'amphictionie après la guerre d'Aitolie," *BCH* 56 (1932) 1-36.

[32] It is possible that intercalation was avoided during part of the Second Punic War because it was regarded as unlucky. Cf. Macrobius, 1.14.1: *verum fuit tempus cum propter superstitionem intercalatio omnis omissa est*, and Ammianus, 26.1.7: (bissextum) *quod aliquotiens rei Romanae fuisse norat infaustum*. I know of no earlier evidence for this superstition in Rome, but it is a common one, even today.

observed on the night before the battle of Pydna, fought on *a.d. III Non. Sept.* (Livy 44.37-38) took place on June 21 by our reckoning.[33] Other discrepancies between the Roman calendar and the solar year occur from time to time until Caesar's reform,[34] when a year of 445 days was required to bring the calendar into line.[35] The pontifices at this time either could not or would not control the situation, perhaps from inefficiency, perhaps from the evil motives suggested by Censorinus. It is, however, possible, and certainly reasonable, to assume that *Lex Acilia* had ordered them to adjust the calendar.

THE THIRD CENTURY

If we turn back to the third century we find recorded a change in the calendar which has far-reaching implications. Macrobius in his discussion of the character of *nundinae* (see pp. 84ff.) quotes from Granius Licinianus, antiquarian of the Antonine period, the statement that *nundinae* are *feriae* to the extent that the *flaminica* sacrificed to Jupiter on these days, but that *Lex Hortensia* had provided that *nundinae* should be *dies fasti* in order that the country people who came to the city for the market might be able to settle their lawsuits then.[36] This *Lex Hortensia* is assigned by modern authorities to 287 B.C., when the dictator Q. Hortensius carried the famous Hortensian law which made *plebiscita* (acts passed by the plebs) binding on the whole people.[37] If then at this date *nundinae* became *dies fasti*, the question at once arises, what character had they had previously?

Our earliest evidence on this point comes from the Twelve

[33] The date given by Livy has been disputed by S. I. Oost, "The Roman Calendar in the Year of Pydna (168 B.C.)," *CP* 48 (1953) 217-230, but see Broughton, *MRR*, suppl., 48, citing for new evidence P. Charneux, "Rome et la confédération achaienne (automne 170)," *BCH* 81 (1957) 181-202.

[34] For a summary of the state of the calendar, see Ginzel, 2.268-273.

[35] Censorinus, *De Die Nat.* 20.8. Macrobius (1.14.3) says 443 days.

[36] 1.16.30: *ait enim nundinas Iovis ferias esse, siquidem flaminica omnibus nundinis in regia Iovi arietem soleat immolare, sed lege Hortensia effectum ut fastae essent, uti rustici, qui nundinandi causa in urbem veniebant, lites componerent. nefasto enim die praetori fari non licebat.* The last sentence is Macrobius' own comment. He assumes that *nundinae* had previously been *nefasti*, which is disproved by other evidence.

[37] For the evidence on Hortensius see Broughton, *MRR* 1.185.

Tables of the Law, in which it was stated that debtors should be brought before the praetor on *nundinae* (Gellius, 20.1.45-49). If already in the fifth century private law suits could be heard on *nundinae*, what, we may ask, had *Lex Hortensia* accomplished? We have seen (pp. 40, 47) that in the first century *contiones* and *comitia* could not be held on *nundinae*, but there is good evidence that this was not always so. Macrobius (1.16.34) gives us a clear statement from Rutilius Rufus (*cos.* 105 B.C.): *Rutilius scribit Romanos instituisse nundinas, ut octo³⁸ quidem diebus in agris rustici opus facerent, nono autem die intermisso rure ad mercatum legesque accipiendas Romam venirent et ut scita atque consulta frequentiore populo referrentur, quae trinundino die proposita a singulis atque universis facile noscebantur.* Dionysius (7.58.3), referring to events of the fifth century, comments that at that time the Romans conducted lawsuits and voted on public affairs on their market days which came every ninth day. Cassius Hemina (quoted by Macrobius, 1.16.33) and Varro (*R.R. 2. praef.* 1) say less specifically that *nundinae* were instituted so that the *rustici* might deal with *urbanae res.*³⁹ These statements, when combined, indicate that in the early period of the republic both private and public business could be conducted on *nundinae*, even if they came on *dies nefasti*, but that *Lex Hortensia*, by classifying *nundinae* as *dies fasti*, made them no longer available for *comitia*. In other words, before 287 B.C., as far as *nundinae* were concerned, the distinction between *dies fasti* and *dies comitiales* had not existed.⁴⁰

What was the motive behind Lex Hortensia? Pliny⁴¹ and

---

³⁸ I cannot believe that Rutilius himself said *octo* for the correct *septem*. Either Macrobius or his source must have used a text which read VII, and, not being used to thinking in terms of *nundinae*, read it as VIII.

³⁹ Cf. Columella, *R. R.* 1. *praef.* 18, who paraphrases Varro.

⁴⁰ Botsford, *RA* 471, accepts the evidence of Rutilius and Dionysius that before 287 B.C. *comitia* were held on *nundinae*. Mommsen (*Staatsr.*³ 3.1.373) says that *Lex Hortensia* forbade *comitia* on *nundinae*, but in a note rejects the evidence of Rutilius and Dionysius about the practice of the *Urzeit*. Lange (*RA* 2³.114) proposed that up to 287 B.C. the *concilium plebis* had been allowed to meet on *nundinae*, but that *Lex Hortensia*, by making *nundinae dies fasti*, restricted it to *dies comitiales* like the *comitia*. Degrassi (p. 325) follows Mommsen.

⁴¹ *N.H.* 18.13: *ideo comitia nundinis habere non licebat, ne plebs rustica avocaretur.*

Festus[42] imply that *comitia* were banned on *nundinae* in order to prevent the assemblies from interfering with the business of the market. Why had the separation of these activities become desirable? It has been suggested that the pressure of increasing commerce brought about the change, and there is much to be said for this idea.[43] In the early days of the republic before Rome had to cope with the vast affairs of empire, her citizens lived either in the city or within easy walking distance. It would have been highly practical to set aside one day in nine for a "town meeting" on which all business matters could be attended to so that work on the land was not interrupted too frequently. The market would naturally grow up in connection with the meeting.[44] By the beginning of the third century the Roman markets must, however, have been serving a larger population and a larger area, and the *nundinae* must have provided the opportunity for a more sophisticated type of business than the simple farmers' market of the past. The business men of Rome may have wanted to eliminate the distraction of the *comitia*.

On the other hand the new arrangement would prevent the market from interfering with the *comitia*. It would also tend to limit the number of citizens attending the *comitia* to those who were seriously interested in the business to be presented, or to those whom the political leaders in Rome had summoned to the city to cast their votes for or against a particular issue. Since something of a holiday mood seems to have pervaded *nundinae, comitia* held on these days may not always have been as orderly as would seem desirable, and the *contiones* which preceded the *comitia* may have been more difficult to control than they would be on other days.

There may also have been a more specific political motive.

---

[42] 176 L.: *nundinas feriatum diem esse voluerunt antiqui ut rustici convenirent mercandi vendendique causa, eumque nefastum, ne ⟨si⟩ liceret cum populo agi interpellarentur nundinatores. Nefastum* is an error either in the text or on the part of Festus.

[43] P. Huvelin, *Essai Historique sur le droit des marchés et foires* (Paris 1897) 90.

[44] Huvelin (*loc.cit.*, n. 43) argues that markets and fairs normally attach themselves to gatherings which bring together customers for the merchants, rather than the market days giving an opportunity for an assembly.

The new classification of *nundinae* has been seen as an attempt to balance the concession made to the plebs in the matters of plebiscites by reducing the number of days on which the *comitia tributa* could meet.[45] If, however, the *concilium plebis* continued to meet on *dies fasti* until the middle of the second century (see page 96) this provision of the *Lex Hortensia* would actually have worked to the advantage of the plebs, by limiting the days available for *comitia* summoned by consuls and praetors, while leaving a much greater number of days free for the *concilium* summoned by the tribunes. In this case both provisions of *Lex Hortensia* would be to the advantage of the plebs, rather than one compensating for the other.

THE FOURTH CENTURY

However much doubt there may be as to the motives which inspired the *Lex Hortensia de nundinis,* or the details of the law in relation to the *concilium plebis,* I think there can be no doubt that in the early republic *nundinae* served as both *dies fasti* and *dies comitiales.* If in the case of *nundinae* the two types of day were not separated until 287 B.C., we must consider the possibility that in the calendar itself all those days which after 287 B.C. were marked either *fasti* or *comitiales* had had, before 287 B.C., only one character. I myself believe that they were *dies fasti* and that the character *comitialis* was introduced into the calendar by Lex Hortensia.

The first piece of evidence for this belief is the fact that in the first century B.C. *comitia* could not be held on *dies fasti,* but that the praetor could hold court on *dies comitiales* on which the *comitia* were not actually meeting. In the second place, the pattern of days in the calendar of the first century suggests that the *dies comitiales* were superimposed on an originally much larger group of *dies fasti.* There were in the first century five days in the month which could be *fasti,* but never *comitiales*: the Kalends, the Nones and the three *dies postriduani* (see page 33). The *dies intercisi* and *dies fissi,* however, which are part *fasti* and part *nefasti* (see page 29f.) fall, with one exception, on days which in other months are

45 Botsford and Lange in passages cited in n. 40.

normally *comitiales,* and so do the three named days which are marked F or FP (see page 34f.). This suggests that at some time all the days which later were marked *comitiales* had been *dies fasti*[46] and that, when the category *comitialis* was introduced, a few days in each month were deliberately reserved for the exclusive use of the praetor's court, and remained *fasti*. But days which were only partly *fasti*, or named days which were *feriae* even if they were *fasti*, that is the *dies intercisi* and *dies fissi*, the Feralia and the two Vinalia, would have retained their original characters. They survive as exceptions to the pattern, like islands of F along a coastline which had been submerged by the rising flood of C.[47]

Another minor piece of evidence suggests that in the early republic there was no distinction between *dies fasti* and *dies comitiales*. Macrobius (1.16.22-24), citing as his sources the *Annales* of Gellius and the *Historiae* of Cassius Hemina, reports a decree of the pontifices made in the year 389 B.C.: *pontificesque statuisse postridie omnes kalendas nonas idus atros dies habendos ut hi dies neque proeliares neque puri neque comitiales essent.*[48] This implies that, until the *dies postriduani* were thus declared *dies atri*, some of them, at least, would have been available for *comitia*. But none of them in the calendar of the first century are *comitiales*. One might question whether the actual words of the decree are correctly quoted here, and whether either of the annalists of the second century B.C. could possibly have found it in pontifical records.

---

[46] This has been convincingly argued by J. Paoli (*op.cit.* n. 5), to whom I am deeply indebted. I do not, however, agree with his implication that the *dies comitiales* were introduced in the second century (*op.cit.* 148, cf. 147 n. 2). The division between *dies fasti* and *dies comitiales* was attributed to *Lex Hortensia* by P. E. Huschke, *Das alte römische Jahr und seine Tage* (Breslau 1869) 283.

[47] J. Paoli (*op.cit.* [n. 5] 123-145) argues that the *dies fissi* marked *Q.R.C.F.* are also evidence that, when this character was first used, *dies comitiales* as a class did not yet exist. He interprets *comitiavit* as "entered the comitium" and considers the king's entrance as the beginning of the *fas* period. On the basis of Paulus, 311 L., I am much inclined to agree with him, but hesitate because of the uncertainty in the reading in Varro, *De L. L.* 6.31.

[48] On *dies atri* see pp. 62-66. For versions of the episode in which the wording of the decree is not so explicit, see Gellius, 5.17, quoting Verrius Flaccus, and Livy, 6.1.12.

On the other hand, if either of them had invented the decree, it is improbable that they would have slipped in a phrase which implied that these days had in the fourth century a character other than that with which they were familiar in the calendar of their own period.

One might argue that the distinction between *dies fasti* and *dies comitiales* would be a prerequisite for the classification of *nundinae* as *dies fasti*, and that therefore it must have been introduced before *Lex Hortensia*. This is possible, but I believe that at the earliest the introduction must have taken place very shortly before 287 B.C., after the last years of the fourth century. This belief is based on my interpretation of a major episode in the history of the calendar which took place not later than 304 B.C., the publication of the *Fasti* by Cn. Flavius. This man was the son of a freedman, and, according to one tradition, a *scriba* of Appius Claudius Caecus. In 304 B.C. he became curule aedile. Either while he was still a *scriba* or during his office, he published the *Ius Flavianum*, an account of the legal procedures known as *legis actiones*, together with a calendar.[49]

[49] For his career see Broughton, *MRR* 1.168; Münzer, *RE* 6.2.2526f. The problems connected with the *ius Flavianum* are not pertinent to this discussion, and I shall not go into them, although the connection between the calendar and the *legis actiones* is obvious. On the calendar: Cicero, *Att.* 6.1.8.: *E quibus (libris) unum* ἱστορικὸν *requiris de Cn. Flavio, Anni filio. Ille vero ante decemviros non fuit quippe qui aedilis curulis fuerit, qui magistratus multis annis post decemviros institutus est. Quid ergo profecit quod protulit fastos? Occultatam putant quodam tempore istam tabulam, ut dies agendi peterentur a paucis. Nec vero pauci sunt auctores Cn. Flavium scribam fastos protulisse actionesque composuisse, ne me hoc vel potius Africanum (is enim loquitur) commentum putes. Pro Murena 25: Posset agi lege necne pauci quondam sciebant; fastos enim volgo non habebant. Erant in magna potentia qui consulebantur; a quibus etiam dies tamquam a Chaldaeis petebatur. Inventus est scriba quidam, Cn. Flavius, qui cornicum oculos confixerit et singulis diebus ediscendis fastos populo proposuerit et ab ipsis his cautis iuris consultis eorum sapientiam compilarit.* Livy, 9.46.5: *civile ius, repositum in penetralibus pontificum, evolgavit fastosque circa forum in albo proposuit, ut quando lege agi posset sciretur.* Valerius Maximus, 2.5.2: *Ius civile per multa saecula inter sacra caerimoniasque deorum immortalium abditum solisque pontificibus notum Cn. Flavius, libertino patre genitus et scriba, cum ingenti nobilitatis indignatione factus aedilis curulis, vulgavit ac fastos paene toto foro exposuit.* Pliny, *N.H.* 33.17: *Hic namque publicatis diebus fastis, quos populus a paucis principum cotidie petebat, tantam gratiam plebei adeptus est (libertino patre alioqui genitus et ipse*

The ancient sources which mention Flavius' *Fasti* (see n. 49) state clearly in general terms what he did and why he did it, but they are not specific as to the details which would enable us to understand exactly what part Flavius played in the development of the calendar. This lack of detail has led to some controversy, even in antiquity, and leaves the problem still open to interpretation. The sources say that Flavius posted in the Forum a calendar which contained the *dies fasti* because at that time very few people knew on what days legal action in the praetor's court was permitted, but had to obtain this information from the *pauci principum* who did know. As Cicero says (*pro Murena* 25), *fastos enim volgo non habebant.* This situation presented Cicero with a puzzle, because he believed that the calendar had been published in the fifth century by the *decemviri*. He discusses the point in a letter to Atticus (*Att.* 6.1.8 see n. 49) in answer to a query which Atticus had raised about a passage, now unfortunately lost, in the *De Re Publica.* Cicero had apparently put into the mouth of Scipio a reference to Flavius' publication of the calendar. Atticus must have objected to this on the grounds that Flavius' action would have been useless because he lived long after the *decemviri.* Atticus' objection is deduced from Cicero's answer. He says: certainly Flavius was later than the *decemviri*, but what he did was useful because, so it is believed, that table had been hidden so that the *dies agendi* (*dies fasti*) were not generally known. His implication that the calendar had been published by the *decemviri* has been accepted by many modern scholars,[50] but his explanation that it was concealed has

---

scriba Appi Caeci cuius hortatu exceperat eos dies consultando adsidue sagaci ingenio promulgaratque) *ut aedilis curulis crearetur* etc. Macrobius, 1.15.9: *priscis ergo temporibus antequam fasti a Cn. Flavio scriba invitis patribus in omnium notitiam proderentur, pontifici minori haec provincia delegabatur ut novae lunae primum observaret aspectum visamque regi sacrificulo nuntiaret.* Gellius (7.9) quotes verbatim from Calpurnius Piso an account of Flavius' election and his behavior as aedile, and the account of his *Fasti* may go back to the same source.

[50] See Ideler, *Handbuch der mathematischen und technischen Chronologie* (Berlin 1825-1826) 2.66f.; De Sanctis, *Storia dei Romani*, 1² (Florence 1956) 258f. (1¹ [Turin 1907] 265f.); Mommsen, *RC*² 30-33; *CIL* 1².1, p. 283; Wissowa, *RE* 6.2.2016; F. Bömer, *P. Ovidius Naso. Die Fasten*, 1.43; Degrassi, p. xx.

not. Thus Atticus' question *quid profecit quod protulit fastos* still remains. Even if the pontifices had tried to keep the character of the days secret, what, asks the modern scholar, would have prevented the Romans from noting for a few years the days on which the praetor held court, and then listing these *dies fasti*? Why did they wait for Flavius to discover and publish the information?

Various answers have been proposed. For example, Mommsen maintained that Flavius simply included in his compilation of the *legis actiones* a copy of the decemviral calendar.[51] De Sanctis presented a similar explanation when he stated that Flavius published in contemporary form material contained in the XII Tables in archaic and incomprehensible orthography.[52] Hartmann believed that the reason why people in the fourth century could not be sure of the characters of the days was that the pontifices had been in the habit of juggling the calendar by intercalating a day occasionally in order to avoid the unlucky coincidence of *nundinae* with the Kalends of January or with any Nones.[53] This would, of course, upset the sequence of days. In order to prevent this, Flavius published his calendar, which the pontifices could not reject without revealing what they had been up to. Beloch produced a much more radical theory when he stated that Flavius actually invented the pre-Julian calendar to replace a lunar calendar based on the observation of the crescent moon.[54] None of these modern theories explains satisfactorily the unanimous opinion of the ancient sources that up until Flavius' publication of the calendar the *dies fasti* had not been known to the public. They either discount parts of the evidence or introduce new complications. This is inevitable as long as one assumes that the character of each day had been fixed in the pre-Julian calendar from the time it was introduced.

If, however, we can abandon this assumption, a simpler explanation of Flavius' achievement becomes possible. If, before Flavius, the Romans had a calendar and yet did not know

[51] *RC*[2] 210. [52] *Storia dei Romani*, 2[1].63ff.
[53] Hartmann-Lange, *Der Römische Kalender*, 110-131. On this superstition about *nundinae* see App. 1, pp. 164-67.
[54] "Die Sonnenfinsternis des Ennius und der Vorjulianische Kalender," *Hermes* 57 (1922) 119-133; *Griechische Geschichte* (1927) 4.2.256-271.

the characters of the days, it would seem obvious that the characters were not included in the calendar, but could be different each year. The published calendar would thus have contained only part of the information which was announced each month on the Nones by the *rex sacrorum*, that is, the *feriae*,[55] which included the Ides, and the Kalends and Nones (see pp. 19ff.). What Flavius must have done was to insert in this framework all the other days of the year with a fixed character for each day.

If this explanation can be accepted, we may turn back for a moment to the question of the date at which the distinction between *dies fasti* and *dies comitiales* was introduced. We have seen that the *terminus ante quem* must be 287 B.C. when the *nundinae* were classified as *dies fasti*. We have also considered the possibility that the distinction did not exist in the early republic but that *dies fasti* were available for *comitia* and a *dies comitialis* simply became so temporarily when it was the occasion of a meeting of the *comitia*. Now the ancient sources make it clear that the purpose of Flavius' calendar was to let ordinary citizens know on what days legal action was permissible. All that was needed to accomplish this was to list all such days as *dies fasti*, including all those that were later listed as *dies comitiales*. If one of these days was to be used for *comitia*, notice would in any case have to be given long enough ahead of time to prevent any serious inconvenience. The demand that *comitia* should be restricted to specific days of their own would have arisen not from the need for orderly administration of private law, but from the need for orderly procedure in public law and politics. It therefore seems probable that Flavius' calendar marked 237 days as *fasti* and that subsequently, as part of the constitutional changes represented by *Lex Hortensia*, 195 of these days were listed in a new permanent category as *dies comitiales*, while the *nundinae* were allotted to the *dies fasti*.

If Flavius' calendar contained 237 days marked F, how were

[55] This would not be like the *Fasti* with which later Romans were familiar, but would resemble the Greek sacred calendars, although these contain also a mass of material relating to details of sacrifices. Cf. S. Dow, "The Athenian Calendar of Sacrifices," *Historia* 9 (1960) 270-293, with bibliography.

the other days of the year marked? In order to answer this question we have to consider how, according to the theory I have proposed, the calendar would have been administered before Flavius, and what information about the days would have been public knowledge. The calendar of the *decemviri*, probably posted in the Forum, would have listed the named days, Kalends, Nones, Ides, Agonalia, Carmentalia, etc. If it was on a bronze table,[56] like the XII Tables, economy would dictate that no further information would be included but would be provided orally each month when the *rex sacrorum* announced the *feriae*. We can reconstruct a formula which he might have used from the words spoken by the praetor when he proclaimed the date of the Compitalia which were *feriae conceptivae*: *dienoni populo Romano Quiritibus Compitalia erunt. quando concepta fuerint, nefas.*[57] In announcing *feriae stativae universi populi communes* (see p. 73) the *rex* would give the date, use the words *populo Romano Quiritibus* and conclude with *nefas*. This would mean that the day would be *feriae* for the whole people and, as a separate item, that there would be no *comitia* and no praetor's court. If the *feriae* were not *universi populi communes* he would substitute the appropriate group for *populo Romano Quiritibus* but would end with *nefas*, unless it was one of the *feriae* which were *dies fasti*, in which case he would either simply omit *nefas* or substitute *fas*. Thus, although the characters of the days which were *feriae* may not have been marked in the calendar, they would have been common knowledge ever since the monthly announcements began. It seems probable that on this occasion the *rex* would also announce those days of the month which, although not *feriae*, were to be *nefasti*. These, of course, could be different every year. Since they were not written down in the *Fasti*, but only announced orally once, obviously it would be difficult to remember them. People who had not attended the meeting would have to get the information secondhand, and

---

[56] Dionysius says (10.57.7) the XII Tables were engraved on a bronze stele, as was the *Lex Pinaria Furia* of 472 B.C. (Macrobius, 1.13.21), which would be far more consistent with Roman custom than Pomponius' statement that they were on ivory (*Dig.* 1.2.2.4).

[57] The formula is quoted by Gellius, 10.24.3, to illustrate the use of the old form *dienoni*.

the pontifices could always later in the month, if need arose, change their memory of what the *rex* had said.

When Flavius came to assign a fixed character to each day, he was thus faced with two types of *dies nefasti*, those on which there were *feriae* and those on which there were not. It was necessary to distinguish between them because, while the plain *dies nefasti* had only the negative quality of being closed to certain activities, most of those which were *feriae* had also the positive quality of being, at least to some extent, holidays for the people.[58] I would suggest that in order to make this distinction clear to those who could now consult the published calendar instead of going to hear the *rex*, Flavius invented for the *feriae stativae universi populi communes* the mark NP which combined the N of *nefastus* with the P which may have stood for *publici* (see pp. 74ff.). The other *dies nefasti* he would have simply marked N. The *dies intercisi* and *dies fissi* (see pp. 29f.) would in the past all have been announced by the *rex*. They would, therefore, have recurred regularly every year, their characters would have been known, and Flavius would have assigned them their traditional characters in abbreviated form.

There is one other element in the calendar which must be considered in this connection, the column of nundinal letters. The fact that the seventh letter in the series is G proves that they cannot have appeared in the calendar of the fourth century in the form in which they occur in even the earliest *Fasti, Ant. Mai.* In the early Latin alphabet, taken over from the Greek via the Etruscan, the seventh letter was the Greek zeta, and the sound of G was not distinguished from that of C, which did duty for both.[59] G was substituted for Z in the sequence of the alphabet by Spurius Carvilius, a teacher of the mid third century.[60] This however does not mean that nundinal letters of

[58] Cf. S. Dow, "The Law Codes of Athens," *Proc. Mass. Hist. Soc.* 71 (1953-1959) 14: "stated in the lowest terms, such lists told people when they would get a dinner with meat."

[59] Cf. Mommsen, *RC*² 253; Sontheimer, *RE* 16.1.66; Degrassi, p. 381. On the Latin alphabet see D. Diringer, *The Alphabet* (New York 1948) 533-538.

[60] Plutarch, *Q.R.* 54 and 59; cf. Varro, *De L. L.* 5.64. On Carvilius see Goetz, *RE* 3.2.1629. The invention of the letter is sometimes attributed to Appius Claudius Caecus, on somewhat inadequate grounds (Schanz-

the earlier alphabet may not have occurred in the calendar of the fourth century.

A fact which might have some bearing on the date at which nundinal letters were first used in the calendar is that here, instead of numerals, letters are used to identify days in a series. I know of no other example of this usage in Latin. In Greek the practice began in the Ionian cities of Asia Minor in the latter half of the sixth century,[61] was known but not common in fifth century Athens and became widespread in the Hellenistic period.[62] If then the Romans adopted the device from the Greeks, it would be slightly more probable that they would have done so in the third century rather than in the fourth.[63] They may, however, have invented it independently, for a practical motive for using letters instead of numerals is obvious. It is easier and quicker to carve or paint eight single letters than the eighteen letters contained in the numerals I-VIII. A column of single letters also is more regular and neater in appearance than a column of numerals of varying widths.[64]

Perhaps the best way to approach the problem of when the nundinal letters would first have been used in the calendar is to ask when would they first be useful. Since it is not difficult to keep track of a nine-day cycle, the chief functions of the letters must have been to identify the individual days which intervened between *feriae*, so that it would be easier to deter-

---

Hosius, *Römische Literaturgeschichte* [Munich 1927] 1⁴.42). It certainly occurs earlier than the middle of the third century in inscriptions, but may have been used as an alternative to C, without having as yet been given a place in the alphabet.

[61] L. H. Jeffery, *The Local Scripts of Archaic Greece* (Oxford 1961) 327.

[62] M. N. Tod, "The Alphabetic Numeral System in Attica," *BSA* 45 (1950) 132.

[63] One might argue that the Ionian use of letters could have come to Rome earlier through contact with Ionian colonies such as Velia or Massilia. One might even conjure up the figure of Hermodorus of Ephesus who is said to have assisted the *decemviri* in drawing up their laws (Strabo, 16.642; Pliny, *N.H.* 34.21; cf. Münzer *RE* 8.1.859-861), and suggest that he taught them this useful device.

[64] When numerals are used to give dates in the *Fasti* they are usually small, and are inserted unobtrusively between the nundinal column and the character letters, as in *Ven.* and *Praen.* For the disagreeably ragged effect when they are on the same scale as the other columns, see *Ant. Min.* (Degrassi, pp. 208-210).

mine when *nundinae* coincided with *dies nefasti*. If I am right in thinking that in the calendar of the fourth century only *feriae* had as yet fixed characters, there would have been little point to listing the nundinal letters in the calendar.

The other important function of the nundinal letters was to facilitate the calculation of the *trinum nundinum* (see pp. 87f.) but this function would not develop until the *trinum nundinum* had become an independent unit of time, no longer determined by actual *nundinae*. This must have happened at some time between the codification of the XII Tables and the passage of *Lex Hortensia* in 287 B.C., probably during the fourth century. (See App. 3, pp. 199ff.) On the basis of these considerations I would conclude that the nundinal letters might have formed part of the pre-Flavian calendar, but that more probably they were introduced by Flavius in connection with the assignment of characters to individual days.

In a period when only named days listed in the calendar had fixed characters, who would have had the authority to decide whether the other days were to be *fasti* or *nefasti*, and on what basis would the decision have been made? As far as we know the ultimate authority for the organization of the calendar and its administration throughout the republic rested with the college of pontifices. Since the ancient sources refer to the *principes* or *pauci principum* (see p. 108 n. 49) from whom the people had to inquire the character of a day, the pontifices must have communicated their decision to a few leading men, perhaps the magistrates. Certainly the praetor, after the office was created in 367 B.C., would have been vitally concerned to know when he could hold court. But even if magistrates were informed, the decision would rest with the pontifices. It seems probable that this situation may have caused some friction between pontifices and praetors, for there was a rule that a praetor who unintentionally held court on a *dies nefastus* could expiate his error, but one who did it intentionally could not (see p. 61). This rule suggests that at some period a praetor, without a list of *dies fasti*, could in all honesty make a mistake, but a praetor who resented pontifical interference with his court might defy the authority of the college and have to be disciplined.

[115]

As to the basis on which the pontifices might have decided that a day other than *feriae* should be *nefastus*, the only evidence is provided by the pattern of days in the calendar of the late republic. We have seen (p. 34) that in this pattern the *dies nefasti* are not distributed over the year as the other days are, but occur in large blocks. If Flavius was responsible for this rather inconvenient system it seems reasonable to suppose that he was following a pattern to which Romans were accustomed. This means that the pontifices also had arranged for blocks of *dies nefasti*. What practical purpose would this have served? We noted (p. 67 n. 23) that in the first century these days occur at seasons when, if the calendar was functioning properly, agricultural work would be particularly pressing.[65] I would suggest therefore that at an earlier period the pontifices had habitually declared a moratorium on urban activities such as lawsuits and *comitia* at times when farmers should not be distracted from their work.[66] The *nundinae* of course would not have been interfered with, and would have provided opportunity for any absolutely essential business. The times for such blocks of *dies nefasti* would have been determined originally not by calendar dates, but by necessity, depending on whether the spring came early or late, or when the harvest was ready, and they would have lasted until the pressure of work was over. The fact that in Flavius' calendar *dies nefasti* could be assigned to fixed dates and defined periods, never swallowing up a whole month, reflects the way in which, by the end of the fourth century, the center of interest in Rome had shifted from the agricultural problems of a comparatively small market-town to those of a constantly expanding urban state.

[65] This is true in the first six months. The absence of *dies nefasti* in the last half of the year is odd. It ignores the vintage, the autumn ploughing and sowing, and the olive harvest.

[66] For a survival of this idea see Ulpian (*Dig.* 2.12.1): *ne quis messium vindemiarumque tempore adversarium cogat ad iudicium venire, oratione Divi Marci exprimitur quia occupati circa rem rusticam in forum compellendi non sunt.* Aristotle remarks that Peisistratus went on circuit so that farmers should not have to leave their work in order to attend to law suits in the city (*Ath. Pol.* 16:5). For an example of conflict between agriculture and politics see L. R. Taylor, "Was Tiberius Gracchus' Last Assembly Electoral or Legislative?" *Athenaeum* 41 (1963) 51-69.

In order to have created a demand that days should have fixed characters, however, the pontifices must have done more than order blocks of *dies nefasti* at more or less the same time every year. They must also have exercised their rights arbitrarily over individual days at short notice. One would perhaps not be unfair if one suspected that they sometimes did this from personal or political motives, but it would have been easy and natural for the pontifices to have persuaded themselves that they would be acting in the best interests of the state, or upholding the *mos maiorum*, if they occasionally used their power to interfere in private or public affairs by imposing an unexpected ban on the court and the *comitia*.

The most surprising thing about the calendar of Flavius is that it was accepted. If the pontifices made any effort to suppress it, the effort was so ineffectual that it was not recorded. We may ask what developments in the fourth century made it possible that the son of a freedman could encroach with impunity on the authority not only of the pontifices but on that of the whole body of the patricians from which the college was made up. Several factors come into play in the situation. This is the century which saw the end of patrician domination and it is possible that with the rise of the plebeians the power of the pontifices was temporarily diminished. Furthermore, the institution of the praetorship in 367 B.C. must soon have led to an increased efficiency in the administration of private law which would have accentuated the need for a fixed court schedule. Up to 367 B.C. presiding over lawsuits between private citizens would have been only one of the many duties of the consuls, but it was the primary function of the praetor, who during his year of office would undoubtedly be on his mettle to uphold the dignity and value of the new magistracy. An increasing group of ex-praetors discussing the problems of the court and resenting the difficulties imposed upon them by the pontifices might well have voiced a demand for a more practical calendar. Another factor which would have increased the need to fix the characters of days permanently must have been the expansion of Roman territory. Between 387 and 318 B.C. ten new tribes were organized, and by the end of the fourth century Roman citizens were living as far south as the Volturnus river.[67] For these people it would be maddening to undertake several days' journey to Rome and then discover that they could not attend to their business because a series of *dies nefasti* had begun. The more complicated the organization of the Roman state became and the wider its territories grew, the greater would be the need for a calendar whose details would be known to the whole citizen body. It is probable that all classes of society would feel the need, and even patrician magistrates who by instinct would be reluctant to curb the pontifices would recognize the necessity of doing so. It is even possible that the pontifices, eventually almost always magistrates themselves and responsible citizens, saw the problem and cooperated in what later partisan accounts represented as a rebellion against their authority.

It is very tempting to indulge in speculations about this whole episode. How did Flavius become involved in the situation in the first place? Did that great innovator, Appius Claudius Caecus, suggest to him that he should undertake the job? Did Claudius' first praetorship precede Flavius' publication? Did his experience in that office exasperate him so much that he rallied public opinion behind the new calendar? He was not a pontifex himself.[68] Was he on bad terms with the college after his high-handed reorganization of the cult of the Ara Maxima, and was he therefore willing to spite them? But for all these questions there is no evidence on which to build even a theory.

[67] L. R. Taylor, *The Voting Districts of the Roman Republic* (*PMAAR* 20, Rome 1960) 47-56.
[68] See his elogium, *I.I.* 13.3. no. 79.

CHAPTER 7

THE FIFTH CENTURY B.C.

THE INTRODUCTION OF THE
PRE-JULIAN CALENDAR

When we turn back in time from the period of Flavius we find that the ancient authors tell us almost nothing about the calendar of the fourth and fifth centuries, but a great deal about the calendars of Romulus and Numa, most of which is confused and difficult to interpret. Three brief references indicate that the *decemviri*, in the middle of the fifth century, took some action in relation to the calendar, while all the others concern the Kings. In order to evaluate this material it will be necessary to consider it in some detail, but before doing this we should consider what the calendar itself can tell us about its early history. As I have pointed out before (see pp. 16f.), the character of the pre-Julian calendar demonstrates that it was derived from an earlier lunisolar calendar based on lunar months determined by actual observation of the moon, but that it has been completely divorced from any relation to the moon.[1] The number of days in the year, and the observances of the Kalends, Nones, and Ides prove the first point, while the 31-day months and the intercalation of a period considerably less than a lunar month prove the second. The structure of the calendar also shows a pattern which suggests a carefully thought-out plan rather than a casual growth. There are, including the dividing days, 81 named days in the year; with two exceptions[2] they are always separated from each other, within each month, by a

---

[1] A lunisolar calendar can be modified into a conventionalized form in which months of 29 and 30 days alternate. By occasional intercalation of a day or two such months can be kept not too far from the actual phases of the moon. It is possible that the Romans modified their lunar calendar in this way, but I doubt it, not because no ancient author mentions it, but because I think such a plan might have been regular enough to satisfy them without the more drastic changes involved in the pre-Julian calendar. The invention of the latter would seem to me to be inspired by exasperation with the uncertainties inherent in a real lunar month.

[2] The Terminalia and Regifugium are on the 23rd and 24th of Feb-

single day, or by an odd number of days. Of the 45 named days which are not dividing days, only one, the Poplifugia of July 5, precedes the Nones. In every month except February and the intercalary month, the Nones are so located that the rest of the month is a *trinum nundinum*. The first of these elements in the pattern looks as though it were intended to avoid the possibility of two *feriae* ever falling on successive days, which might produce an undue interruption of work.[3] The second suggests that, after the pre-Julian calendar had been introduced as well as before, people were expected to get their information about the month's activities from the announcement made by the *rex* on the Nones.[4] The third element in the pattern is a great help in calculating *nundinae* and nundinal periods, as anyone who has tried it can testify. It must have been devised for this purpose, because otherwise it would have been much simpler to have assigned the Nones and Ides to the same dates in both the long and the short months.[5]

The method of intercalation in the pre-Julian calendar tells us that its designers *intended* to produce a cyclic calendar which could be kept in approximately correct relation to the seasons by regular intercalation in alternate years.[6] I say intended, because unfortunately they did not know enough astronomy to see the practical defects in an excellent theory. They did at least avoid the nuisance of intercalating or omitting a day, or a couple of days, in order to stay in phase with the moon, as was sometimes necessary in the Greek calendar.[7]

---

ruary, the second Equirria is on the day before the Ides of March. Since all named days except the Regifugium and the second Equirria come on odd days, the number of days between the last named day of each month and the Kalends of the next is, with these two exceptions, always even.

[3] Cf. Mommsen, *RC*[2] 244.

[4] On this announcement see Ch. 1, pp. 19f.; Ch. 6, pp. 111f.

[5] The variation in dates for the Nones has been taken as perpetuating the variation in length of time between the crescent moon and the first quarter (see Ch. 1, p. 13, p. 21; Ch. 7, pp. 130ff.). I think it more likely that the Nones were assigned to the 5th or 7th day of the month, whichever would produce the desired *trinum nundinum*, after it had been decided to have 29- and 31-day months. Conversely 30-day months may have been excluded because then the Nones, as first day of the *trinum nundinum*, would fall on the 6th and the Ides on the 14th, and it would not be possible to separate named days by an odd number of days.

[6] On this method of intercalation see Ch. 1, pp. 16ff., and App. 1.

[7] Cicero, *Verr.* 2.2.129.

So much the calendar can tell us. It cannot tell us when the Romans broke away from their old calendar, or why. The importance of the answers to these questions is emphasized if we remember that no other people in the ancient world completely abandoned the use of lunar months in their calendars.[8] To find the answers we must turn to the ancient authors who deal with the history of the calendar. The fullest accounts are given by Plutarch (*Numa* 18f.), Censorinus (*De Die Natali* 20) and Macrobius (1.12.1-14.15) (see pp. 147, 150ff., 153-59). They differ in details and report differences among their sources, but they all arrive at the same end result. Each begins with the year devised by Romulus. According to Plutarch this began with March and consisted of 360 days, with months which varied from less than 20 to more than 35 days. Numa, noting that the lunar and solar years differ by eleven days, attempted to adjust his calendar to the solar year by intercalating 22 days every other year.[9] He also shifted the beginning of the

---

[8] The Egyptians had a system of 30-day months supplemented by five days to make a year of 365 days, which they used as a civil calendar concurrently with lunar calendars. (See R. A. Parker, *The Calendars of Ancient Egypt* [*Studies in Ancient Oriental Civilization*, no. 26] Chicago 1950). Similarly the Athenians, at some time in the first half of the fifth century, took to dating documents according to the days in the term of office of each prytany, which had no relation to the lunar month, but they also used dates of the lunar months in the festival calendar which served the purposes of everyday life. (For a useful bibliography of recent work on the Athenian calendars see P. A. Clement's review of B. D. Meritt's *The Athenian Year* in *AJA* 69 [1965] 192-196.) Beloch refused to believe in a date earlier than Flavius for the pre-Julian calendar. "Und sollen wir denn glauben, dass ein Kalender, der auf den Mond keine Rücksicht nahm, in Rom schon zu einer Zeit eingeführt worden ist, wo in der ganzen übrigen Welt, von Aegypten abgesehen, noch kein Mensch an ein reines Sonnenjahr dachte?" (*Griechische Geschichte* [Berlin 1927] 4.2.257). In extolling the Egyptian calendar J. H. Breasted remarked: "It is extraordinary that the Greeks never possessed the intellectual emancipation to reject the moon entirely from their calendar and to adopt a conventional month dictated by social needs." (*Time and its Mysteries* [James Arthur Foundation Lectures, New York University] New York 1936, p. 63.) Even De Sanctis would have hesitated to date the pre-Julian calendar at 450 B.C. (*Storia dei Romani* 2[1] [Turin 1907] 520 n. 2) if it had not been for the evidence of Ennius' eclipse, for which see below, p. 126.

[9] Plutarch's statement is not clear, but I think he must mean that Numa gave up Romulus' year and adopted a lunar year of 354 days, although he omits to mention this step. The intercalation he describes added to 360 days would be far too big.

year to January. Plutarch adds the remark that some say Numa added January and February to what had been a ten-month year. According to both Censorinus and Macrobius, the year of Romulus had 304 days divided into ten months,[10] March to December, of which six had 30 days and four had 31. Censorinus admits that Licinius Macer and Fenestella claim that the Roman year had had twelve months from the beginning, but he prefers the account given by Junius Gracchanus, Fulvius, Varro, Suetonius, and others. He then explains that Numa, according to Fulvius, but Tarquin, according to Junius, added 51 days to the year, bringing it up to 355, and then, by subtracting one day from each of the 30-day months and adding the six thus obtained to the 51, was able to create two new months of 29 and 28 days, which he called January and February and placed at the beginning of the year.[11] Macrobius' version is only slightly different. He says that Numa first made a year of 354 days in which January and February both had 28 days, but he soon added one day to January so that the number of days in the year, and in each month except one, should be uneven, because long before Pythagoras he divined the power of uneven numbers.

The year of Numa then, according to these accounts, was identical with the ordinary (not intercalary) pre-Julian year. Unlike Plutarch, Censorinus attributes the first use of intercalation to an undated period later than Numa, without identifying its inventor. Macrobius in his main discussion (1.13.8-15) says that after the Romans, following Numa's system, had calculated their year according to the moon, they were forced to adopt an intercalary month. Although he adds that they derived their method from the Greeks,[12] what he describes is actually the pre-Julian intercalation. In a later passage he reports (1.13.20) that Licinius Macer attributed

[10] The ten-month year is also referred to by Ovid, *Fasti* 1.27f.; Gellius, 3.16.16; Solinus, 1.35; Servius, *Georg.* 1.43; Lydus, *De Mens.* 1.16 (9 Wuensch).

[11] Ovid (*Fasti* 1.43f.) says the same thing.

[12] He says that the Greeks intercalated ninety days every eight years, as do Geminus (*Isagoge* 8.29-31) and Censorinus (*De Die Nat.* 18), but, like Solinus (1.42), he seems to have thought that the three months thus obtained were added all together at the end of the period, instead of being intercalated in three different years.

the first use of intercalation to Romulus, Valerius Antias to Numa, and Junius Gracchanus to Servius Tullius. Cicero also credits Numa with inventing intercalation (*De Leg.* 2.29), as does Livy (1.19.6).[13]

We see then that the great majority of our sources, beginning with Fulvius Nobilior (*cos.* 189) (quoted by Censorinus), consider Numa the inventor of the twelve month year, and those who mention its months always include ones of 31 days which are impossible in a lunar calendar. Opinion is divided as to who invented Roman intercalation, but the only type the authors seem to know of is that used in the pre-Julian calendar. In other words, the tradition leaves no place in Roman history for a true lunar calendar, in spite of the fact that some of the authors recognize that the beginning of a Roman month was originally determined by the appearance of the crescent moon (Varro, *De L. L.* 6.28; Macrobius, 1.13.8; 1.15.5). The tradition obviously presents an impossible sequence of events. One cannot, however, lightly dismiss a tradition so well attested without trying to explain how it came into existence. In this case luckily the explanation is not far to seek. The source of the confusion is the magnification of Numa and his learning. However the picture of the wise Numa, the father of Roman religion, may have originated,[14] it certainly was embellished by the popular belief that he was a disciple of Pythagoras.[15] This

[13] Livy's statement presents difficulties: *Atque omnium primum ad cursus lunae in duodecim menses discribit annum; quem quia tricenos dies singulis mensibus luna non explet desuntque dies solido anno qui solstitiali circumagitur orbe, intercalariis mensibus interponendis ita dispensavit ut vicesimo anno ad metam eandem solis unde orsi essent plenis omnium annorum spatiis dies congruerent.* In the Oxford text Conway has added *sex* between *desuntque* and *dies*, but, as J. S. Reid pointed out in his review (*JRS* 5 [1915] 144), if any number should be read here it should be *undecim*. The rest of the passage seems to attribute to Numa the invention of the 19-year intercalary cycle which was devised by Meton, the Greek astronomer of the fifth century, but see Mommsen *RC*² 44 n. 60.

[14] See K. R. Prowse, "Numa and the Pythagoreans," *Greece and Rome*, s.2,11 (1964) 36-42; R. M. Ogilvie, *A Commentary on Livy Books 1-5* (Oxford 1965) 88-91.

[15] The belief is denied by Cicero (*De Re Pub.* 2.28; *Tusc. Disp.* 4.3), Livy (1.18), Dionysius (2.59), and Plutarch (*Num.* 18), indirectly criticized by Macrobius (1.13.5), but upheld by Ovid (*Met.* 15.4-481; *Fasti* 3.153).

belief manifested itself dramatically in 181 B.C.[16] Two huge boxes were dug up in a field below the Janiculum. Inscribed on them in Latin and Greek letters were statements that in one was buried Numa Pompilius, and in the other were his books. When they were opened there was no trace of Numa, but there were the books, some on pontifical law in Latin, some on philosophy in Greek. After the discoverer of this trove and many of his friends had read the books, the *praetor urbanus* heard of them, seized them, read them, and decided that they should be burned as subversive of religion. Although the owner appealed for help to the tribunes, the senate upheld the praetor and the books were formally burned in the comitium. The philosophy contained in the books was identified by Cassius Hemina, Calpurnius Piso, and Valerius Antias as Pythagorean, while later writers argued on grounds of chronology that this would be impossible. However that may be, the supposed connection with Pythagoras must have led to Numa's being associated with the pre-Julian calendar. Censorinus tells us (20.4) that Fulvius said that Numa made a year of 355 days instead of one of 354. He adds, without quoting Fulvius, that the extra day was the result either of ignorance, or, as he himself believes, of the superstition which considers uneven numbers lucky. The importance of uneven numbers was of course a well-known and important Pythagorean doctrine. Macrobius makes the connection clear when he says that Numa added a day to the lunar year *in honorem imparis numeri, secretum hoc et ante Pythagoram parturiente natura*. The fact that he takes the trouble to point out that Numa had anticipated Pythagoras shows that he was deliberately contradicting the idea that Numa had been influenced by Pythagoras in his determination of length of the year.

It is not difficult, I think, to see how the connection between Numa and the 355-day year came about. Censorinus quotes it from Fulvius Nobilior, the author of the first recorded commentary on the Roman calendar.[17] Fulvius was consul in 189 B.C.,

[16] I give here Livy's account of the episode (40.29.9-14). It is described also by Pliny (*N.H.* 13.84-87), and Valerius Maximus (1.1.12). They cite as sources Calpurnius Piso, Cassius Hemina, Sempronius Tuditanus, and Valerius Antias.

[17] For his career in this period, see Broughton, *MRR*, for 189-187 B.C.

when he took charge of the war in Aetolia which he carried on as pro-consul in 188 and 187 B.C. Subsequently he built the temple of Hercules and the Muses in which he placed his *Fasti*.[18] Since he does not appear to have held any further offices which would have taken him away from Rome, he was probably there when the "Books of Numa" were found. Even if he was not himself a Pythagorean, as has been suggested,[19] it seems very probable that the connection between Numa and Pythagoras would have given him an answer to the question which is still a puzzle—why did the pre-Julian calendar have 355 days instead of 354? If Numa was a Pythagorean, he must have liked odd numbers. Ergo, *he* must have invented this peculiar year.

It would seem then that in their enthusiasm for Numa the Romans telescoped the history of their calendar, thus squeezing out the period of the lunar year and almost obliterating the traces of the introduction of the pre-Julian year. It is our problem to determine a possible and probable date at which the introduction could actually have taken place. As to possibility, the date cannot be later than the end of the fifth century,

---

For his commentary see Macrobius, 1.12.16: *Fulvius Nobilior in fastis quos in aede Herculis Musarum posuit* etc. I give his work priority as it seems probable that the Cincius who wrote *Fasti* was not the annalist who was a contemporary of Fulvius, but the later antiquarian. Cf. Schanz-Hosius, *Römische Literaturgeschichte* 1⁴ (Munich 1927) 174f. In "Zur Frage von dem Alter des vorcäsarischen Kalenders" (*Opuscula Selecta* 2, 979-988) 984, Nilsson has suggested that it was not this Fulvius but his son, Quintus, who wrote the commentary on the *Fasti*. The son was consul in 153 B.C. when the consuls first entered office on January 1. Nilsson attributes this innovation to an interest in the calendar on the part of Quintus. There were, however, practical reasons for the change, and indeed I doubt that anything as important as the consular term of office would be tampered with because of the scholarly whim of an individual.

[18] Whether the *Fasti* was in the form of a book, or of an inscription, painted on the wall of the temple like *Fasti Ant. Mai.*, with notes like *Fasti Praen.*, is an open question. A calendar with its black and red letters would certainly make a striking decoration for the temple, and would impress the public with Fulvius' erudition. But I do not know why Fulvius could not have written his commentary in book form, and then decided to present it in calendar form on the temple wall. I like to think that he inspired Verrius Flaccus with the idea for *Fasti Praen.*

[19] Cf. P. Boyancé, "Fulvius Nobilior et le dieu ineffable," *RPh* 29 (1955) 172-192.

if we are to believe Cicero's statement (*De Re Pub.* 1.25) that Ennius and the *annales maximi* recorded an eclipse of the sun which took place on the Nones of June in about the 350th year after the founding of the city. There were several eclipses in the period 410-390 B.C., and the one described by Ennius is usually identified as having occurred, according to our calendar, on June 21, 400 B.C.[20] For our purposes the actual year is irrelevant. The important thing is that it was observed on the Nones. Since a solar eclipse can take place only when the moon is between the earth and the sun, that is at the conjunction, it must always precede the appearance of the crescent moon, which in a lunar calendar marks the beginning of the month. If the Romans had not already broken from the lunar calendar and started using the pre-Julian calendar, this eclipse would have taken place before the Kalends of June, not on the Nones.

When we look for a probable date we have again to consider the character of the pre-Julian calendar and to stress again the importance of the fact that in it the Romans had broken away from dependence on the moon. Such a break cannot be attributed to an early period, but demands a date as late as is consistent with the evidence.[21] With this in mind we can turn to the evidence which associates the *decemviri* of 450 B.C. with the calendar.[22] As we have seen (p. 109) Cicero implies (*Att.* 6.1.8) that the *decemviri* published the *Fasti*, but that their edition disappeared, so that Flavius' edition was necessary. This alone, however, is not conclusive evidence for the introduction of the pre-Julian year, for the *Fasti* of the *decemviri* could, for all Cicero tells us, have been based on the lunar year.[23] A more vital reference is embedded in Macrobius' at-

[20] Ginzel, 2.211-216. Cf. O. Leuze, *Die römische Jahrzählung* (Tübingen 1909) 377.

[21] See n. 8.

[22] I presented some arguments for dating the pre-Julian calendar to the period of the *decemviri* in my paper "The 'Calendar of Numa' and the Pre-Julian Calendar," *TAPA* 80 (1949) 320-346 (see App. 4). Some of them I still consider valid, and repeat here. Others I now reject, partly on the grounds of new archaeological evidence, mainly because after sixteen years' more work, I know a good deal more about the Roman calendar and calendars in general.

[23] If, as I have suggested above (see p. 111), the pre-Flavian calendar

tempt to identify the inventor of Roman intercalation: *Tudita-nus refert Libro tertio Magistratuum decem viros qui decem tabulis duas addiderunt de intercalando populum rogasse. Cassius eosdem scribit auctores* (1.13.21).[24] Thus Sempronius Tuditanus (*cos.* 129 B.C.) and Cassius Hemina, the annalist of the middle of the second century, both stated that the second board of *decemviri* brought before the people a bill on the subject of intercalation. Macrobius apparently cites this as evidence for the date at which Romans first used intercalation, but he himself proceeds to point out that they were doing so before the *decemviri*: *sed hoc arguit Varro scribendo antiquissimam legem fuisse incisam in columna aerea a L. Pinario et Furio consulibus, cui mensis intercalaris adscribitur.*[25] But Macrobius and Varro to the contrary, the fact that in 472 B.C. a law was dated in an intercalary month does not prove that the pre-Julian method of intercalation was already in use, for the lunar calendar also requires an intercalary month. It does, however, prove that the *lex de intercalando* of the *decemviri* can only have introduced some change in an already existing method. Since the most striking feature of the pre-Julian year, and the one which most directly affected the life of every Roman, was its unique type of intercalation, it seems reasonable that a law introducing the new calendar should be described as *de intercalando*.

I would therefore conclude that the period of the *decemviri* provides us with a date which is possible, inasmuch as it is earlier than Ennius' eclipse, and probable, inasmuch as it is the latest date before the eclipse for which there is any evidence. Moreover the period itself is more probable than most. It is always difficult to persuade people to accept a change in their

---

contained only named days, one could not tell by looking at it what sort of year it was based on.

[24] Unless there is some statement to the contrary the phrase *populum rogasse* implies that the proposed bill was voted into law. I take *auctores* to mean *auctores legis*, the sponsors of the law. Macrobius is probably paraphrasing Cassius, or quoting him from a later source, for in the republic the man who proposes a law is usually called *lator*, while *auctor* is used of the supporters of the law. Cf. L. R. Taylor, "Magistrates of 55 B.C. in Cicero's *Pro Plancio* and Catullus 52," *Athenaeum* 42 (1964) 14-16.

[25] On this passage see Ch. 6, nn. 27 and 28.

calendar, even when it may be highly desirable for practical reasons. Ptolemy Euergetes III in 238 B.C. decreed that the Egyptians should adopt the leap-year system which Caesar finally put into effect, but his subjects paid not the slightest attention.[26] The English rioted when they finally had to join the rest of Europe in using the Gregorian calendar. A change can be brought about by a person with absolute authority, such as Caesar or the Pope, or it can take place in a time of many changes when people are less inclined than usual to mind breaking with the past, such as the French Revolution with its short-lived calendar, or the Russian Revolution, which abandoned the Orthodox calendar. The middle of the fifth century in Rome seems to fit the latter situation. No matter what version one adopts of the history of the early republic, no one can deny that it was a period of marked change, a time of new ideas when people were prepared to accept new institutions. One institution which the new republic must have come to need very soon was a regular calendar by which the length of a magistrate's term could be exactly determined,[27] so that there would be no argument as to the day on which he had to leave office. If, as seems probable,[28] the consuls exchanged the *fasces* and the presidency of the Senate from month to month, it would have been very desirable to know ahead of time how many days each month would have. If debt was as serious a problem in this period as the sources suggest, both debtors and creditors would have found a precise calendar very useful.

One other passage suggests that the *decemviri* altered the year, but it is too obscure to be used as anything but secondary evidence. Ovid, like other writers, tells us that Numa added January and February to the ten-month year of Romulus, putting them at the beginning of the year (*Fasti* 1.43f.), but

[26] Ginzel, 1.196-200. Actually, the decree ordered that every four years an extra day, after the five epagomenal days and before the new year, should be the occasion of a festival, but this amounts to the same thing as the Julian leap year.
[27] On this point, cf. W. K. Pritchett, "The Athenian Lunar Month," *CP* 54 (1959) 154. He speaks of the advantage of 36 hours of advance notice, but certainly the longer the better.
[28] L. R. Taylor and T. R. S. Broughton, "The Order of the Two Consuls' Names in the Yearly Lists," *MAAR* 19 (1949) 1-14.

subsequently he makes the puzzling statement that January was in the past the first month, and February used to be the last:

> primus, ut est, Jani mensis et ante fuit;
> qui sequitur Ianum, veteris fuit ultimus anni.
>
> (*Fasti* 2.48f.)

He then adds:

> postmodo creduntur spatio distantia longo
> tempora bis quini continuasse viri.
>
> (*Fasti* 2.53f.)

This appears to mean that the *decemviri* joined periods which had been separated by a long space, that is, they shifted February from its position as twelfth month to follow January as the second month. Although this statement has sometimes been taken literally, it seems to me wildly improbable. I believe that Ovid is here misinterpreting one of his sources. I have already given my reasons for supposing that the change of the beginning of the year from March to January took place when the pre-Julian calendar was introduced (see pp. 97ff.). If this is correct, Ovid may well have found somewhere, perhaps in Cassius Hemina or Sempronius Tuditanus, the statement that, before the *decemviri*, the year had ended with February. Since he believed that Numa had made January the first month, he could only assume that the *decemviri* had moved February from twelfth to second place, while his source had meant that the *decemviri* moved the end of the year from February to December.[29]

To summarize the results of the foregoing discussion, I would suggest that a calendar containing only named days (see p. 111) was published by the *decemviri*, and that they also passed a law introducing the pre-Julian year. It is possible that the *decemviri* of 451 B.C. published the calendar as part of the XII Tables, since there was in antiquity a strong tradition that a code of laws should contain a calendar,[30] and that, as Ma-

---

[29] If his source was Cassius or Sempronius, or an intermediary, this statement could have occurred in an explanation of why intercalation, in which they were interested, took place in February. This would not have required any reference to January which might have cleared up Ovid's confusion.

[30] A. K. Michels, *op.cit.* (n. 22) 338.

crobius says, the *decemviri* of the next year passed the law. If the calendar contained only named days, later generations, used to the form invented by Flavius, might not have recognized a genuine calendar, which would account for the belief, mentioned by Cicero, that it had been suppressed. On the other hand, it is equally possible that it was the *decemviri* of 450 B.C. who, in connection with their law, made public in writing a list of named days which had previously been kept by the pontifices as the basis for the monthly announcement of the *feriae* made by the *rex*. In this case the more technical details of the actual dates of the various rites, and the principles on which they were assigned would be the business, if not the secret, of the pontifices, and would be recorded in the *libri pontificum* as the basis of the monthly announcement according to the new style, after the pre-Julian year had been adopted.

THE *FERIALE* OF THE FIFTH CENTURY

I have suggested earlier that, before Flavius published his calendar in which every day of the year was listed, the calendar known to the public contained only named days. Assuming that this hypothesis is correct, we must now consider whether the list of named days remained the same throughout the period of the republic, before and after the introduction of the pre-Julian year, or whether it developed gradually, as I have suggested happened in the case of the other elements in the calendar.

Many of the named days must have been present in the old lunar calendar. Among these must have been the Kalends and the Ides, which were determined by the phases of the moon. The Nones are less certain, depending on the meaning of the word *Nonae*. It is generally held by both ancient[31] and modern scholars that *Nonae* is the feminine plural of the adjective *nonus*, and that the word was formed on the analogy of *Kalendae* to identify the ninth day before the Ides. The ancient authors also give the alternative explanation that it is derived from *novus*, and is connected with the new moon.[32] The objection to this is, of course, that the Nones can have had

[31] Varro, *De L. L.* 6.28; Festus, 176 L.; Macrobius 1.15.13.
[32] Varro, Festus, and Macrobius. Also Plutarch, *R.Q.* 24.

nothing to do with the new moon, if the Kalends were determined by the crescent moon. Modern scholars have disagreed as to whether the Nones originally marked the first quarter of the moon,[33] or simply the ninth day before the Ides, as a form of *nundinae*.[34] It seems to me very probable that the meeting at which the *rex* announced the *feriae* for the month did take place originally on the day of the first quarter. A practical reason for this is that it is very easy to tell by looking at the moon that it will reach the first quarter at its next appearance,[35] and therefore anyone who had not happened to hear the announcement on the Kalends would still be able to know when he had better hie himself into the city if he wanted to be at the meeting next day. On the other hand it seems to me very improbable that this day was called *Nonae* as long as

[33] The only ancient authorities for this are Dionysius (16.3.2) and Lydus (*De Mens.* 3.10, 45 Wuensch). Dionysius is explicit: τὰς νουμηνίας οἱ Ῥωμαῖοι καλάνδας καλοῦσι, τὰς δὲ διχοτόμους Νόνας, τὰς δὲ πανσελήνους Εἰδούς. This passage is one of the excerpts preserved in the Ambrosian MS, so that its context is unknown. It follows an explanation of why Appius Claudius was called Caecus, which suggests the possibility that Dionysius was discussing the calendar of Flavius, who was associated with Appius Claudius. Some modern supporters of the theory are: Ideler, *Handbuch der mathematischen und technischen Chronologie* (Berlin 1825-1826) 2.39f.; Mommsen, *RC*[2] 16; Warde Fowler, *RF* 7; Ginzel, 2.173.; W. Sontheimer, *RE* 16.1.62-64; J. Bayet, *Histoire politique et psychologique de la religion Romaine* (Paris 1957) 89; E. Bickermann, *Einleitung in die Altertumswissenschaft* (ed. A. Gercke–E. Norden, Leipzig-Berlin 1933) 3.5.17, and *Chronologie* (Leipzig 1963) 25; Degrassi, p. 323.

[34] W. Soltau, *RömChron* 131-134, supports this theory in a short review of the argument; he is followed by M. P. Nilsson, *Primitive Time-Reckoning* (Lund 1920) 167; A. H. Salonius, "Zur Römischen Datierung," *AnnAcadScientFenn* 15 (1921-1922) no. 10, 11-13; W. Kubitschek, *Grundriss der Antiken Zeitrechnung* (Munich 1928) 134; W. Ehlers, *RE* 17.1.846-849.

[35] Nilsson states that the Nones are secondary in the Roman calendar, which he believes originally divided the months only by the crescent and full moon (*op.cit.* [n. 34] 167). He bases this on his observation that primitive peoples very rarely note the quarters of the moon in their calendars and gives as the reason: "The shape of the moon on the 8th or 22nd day differs very little from that of the previous and the following days, and does not constitute a turning point like the full moon." (171). The first part of the argument can be reversed. If the Romans observed the first quarter they were not so primitive as scholars persist in making them. As to the second, on the basis of my own observation, I simply do not agree. The straight edge of the semicircle of the first quarter is unmistakable. See Ch. 1, p. 13, and n. 14.

the Romans were using actual observation to determine the Kalends and the Ides. This is because the period between the first quarter and the full moon varies, from month to month, from 6.5 days to a fraction more than 8 (see Chapter 1, p. 13), so that it would be impossible to assume that the day of the first quarter would always be the ninth day before the Ides. The name *Nonae* could be used only when the lunar month had been abandoned and the Ides had been assigned to a fixed day in each month. In the pre-Julian calendar the Nones are, except in February, the first day of the *trinum nundinum* which ends on the last day of the month. I would suggest that the name was invented when the pre-Julian calendar was introduced, in order to distinguish this new "ninth day," which was fixed to a date, from the already familiar "ninth day," *nundinae*, which revolved through the years.

The 45 other named days, referred to collectively as the *feriale*, present a problem which is not easy to attack and, I think, probably impossible to solve in our present state of knowledge. One would like to know the history of each of the *feriae*, when it originated and received its name, when it was included in the calendar, whether it was already in the calendar before 450 B.C. or came in later. One approach to these questions is to ask for what reason a named day would appear in the *Fasti*. Mommsen's answer, which has been generally accepted,[36] was that the *feriae* recorded in the inscriptions in large letters constitute the oldest *feriale* of the Romans, while later additions to the *Fasti* were recorded in small letters. He dated this *feriale* early in the regal period, on the grounds that there was no valid evidence that any of its *feriae* originated later, and that many cults which are reported to have originated after the reign of Numa have no days named for them. Mommsen seems to have derived his date in the reign of Numa from the fact that the cult at the Tigillum Sororium, which tradition assigns to the reign of Tullus Hostilius, is not included in the *feriale*. Later scholars, while accepting Mommsen's theory in general, have dated the *feriale* towards the end of the regal period, basing their arguments on the fact that no day has a name relating it to the cult of Juppiter Optimus Maximus, whose

---

[36] For details see App. 4, pp. 207ff.

temple on the Capitoline Hill was completed and dedicated in the first year of the Republic. There are, of course, two obvious weaknesses in this method of dating the *feriale*. In the first place, we have no evidence for the date at which many of the *feriae* were established which would justify us arguing that they should be dated either early or late. In the second place, there is no reason to assume that all cults of a god[37] would have days named in their honor, especially when the day on which the cult is celebrated, like that of Juppiter Optimus Maximus, happened to be the Ides, or one of the Kalends, which already had their own names.

Mommsen's theory that named days were included in the *feriale* on the basis of their antiquity was, as I have pointed out (see p. 93), an intuitive assumption which, unlike many of his intuitions, has not been confirmed by new evidence. Since throughout this book, I have worked on a different assumption, that the material written in large letters in the *Fasti* comprises not the oldest but the most important elements in the calendar, I cannot now avail myself of Mommsen's theory in discussing the history of the *feriale*, but must propose some other theory consistent with my own assumption.

At this point it is helpful to turn the problem upside down, not to ask, on what basis a named day had been included in the *feriale*, as we see it in the first century B.C., but to ask what types of day had been excluded. All days which have no official religious character are excluded, even if popular superstition had conferred upon them commemorative names, like the *dies Alliensis*,[38] or the *dies Cannensis*. Among days of official religious character, obviously *feriae conceptivae*, whose dates vary from year to year, are automatically excluded. *Ludi*, the games which extended over several days, are not listed. The *feriale* does not include days on which were celebrated

---

[37] I am here distinguishing between the god identified only by his own name, e.g. Jupiter, and the special cults in which he appears with a title, e.g. Juppiter Optimus Maximus, Juppiter Stator, Juppiter Feretrius, Juppiter Fulgur etc. The named days are identified as *feriae* for the god, not for the individual cults. If a cult is celebrated on a named day, perhaps because it is the anniversary of the dedication of the temple, the fact is noted in small letters, as in Fasti *Ant. Mai.* the Ides of September carries the note *Iovi O. M.*

[38] See Degrassi, on July 18.

[133]

certain rites which have no specific name, such as those on which the *mundus* was open,[39] the *ancilia* were moved,[40] or the Vestals went to the Argei.[41] It ignores *dies religiosi* and the existence of rites which were celebrated on the Kalends, Nones, and Ides, such as the sacrifice of the October horse on the Ides of October, the *epulum Jovis* on the Ides of September, or the festival which gave the adjective *Caprotinae* to the Nones of July. Rites which coincide with other named days are omitted from the *feriale*, like the Septimontium, which comes on the Agonium of December 11, or the Juturnalia on the Carmentalia of January 11. When rites extend over several days, they are not indicated in the *feriale*, for example, the *parentatio* which begins on the Ides of February and ends on the Feralia, February 21, or the days on which the temple of Vesta was open, June 7 to June 15.[42]

As we look at these days which are not in the *feriale*, we see more clearly the characteristics of those which are. They have a religious character, they have fixed dates, they are single days, they have their own names. If more than one rite occurs on the same day, only one can give its name to the day.[43] A rite which makes the day NP (*universi populi communis*) takes precedence over one which does not, as in the case of the Agonium of December 11 which takes precedence over the Septimontium, which was for the *montani* only.[44] In the naming of days, the Kalends, Nones, and Ides take precedence over

[39] August 24, October 5, and November 8. See Degrassi.
[40] See Degrassi on March 1.
[41] March 16 and 17, see Degrassi, and on the Argei, L. A. Holland, *Janus and the Bridge (PMAAR* 21, Rome 1961) Appendix A: *Vestals, Argei and the Island Legend.*
[42] For these rites see Degrassi on the days cited.
[43] Exceptions to this rule are the Agonium of December 11, and the Liberalia (March 17), also called Agonium. On December 11, *Fasti Ost.* reads AG. IND, and *Fasti Amit.* AG. IN. On March 17 LIB. AG (or AGON or AGO) occurs in *Fasti Caer., Verul.,* and *Vat.* These double names may be required in order to distinguish between the different Agonia, although they do not occur with the other two on January 9 and May 21. On December 21 in *Fasti Ost.* the first letters of the name DIVALIA are missing, and only an N is preserved. Degrassi reconstructs this as [DIV(alia)A]N(geronae), but it is not clear why the name of the goddess should have been given.
[44] See Degrassi on December 11.

any rites which may be performed on them, although the rites may give them popular nicknames not recorded in the *feriale*, like the *Kalendae Fabariae* of June. Finally, the names of the days in the *feriale* are all single words.

These, then, are the characteristic features of the days listed in the *feriale*. We cannot however argue, *post hoc propter hoc*, that the days were so listed *because* they had these characteristics. We can only say that without these characteristics they would not have been listed. A calendar serves a practical purpose, and we must consider what purpose is accomplished by listing such days. The predominance of days with a religious character may suggest that the *feriale* was designed to remind people of their religious obligations, and their opportunities for a holiday, but we must remember that a great many other religious days were not included, and that conversely some of those which were included had ceased, certainly by the time of the late republic, to have any religious significance for the majority of Romans. It seems more probable that the real purpose of listing all the named days (i.e., both the *feriae* and the dividing days) is the fundamental purpose of any calendar —to enable people to organize their lives in relation to regularly recurring events. It is obvious that the dividing days provided fixed points in time by which activities could be planned, but the other named days could be used in the same way. We often find Cicero referring to days by name instead of by date,[45] although never for business matters, nor in official language. We may assume that in informal conversation and among the less educated classes this practice was more common, as in the Middle Ages saints' days were used instead of dates. One simple reason for this would be that in conversation it is much easier to say *"Quirinalia"* than *"ante diem duodecimum Kalendas Martias."* Livy's occasional use of named days for dates (e.g. 26.27.1; 30.36.8; 40.2.1; 44.20.1)

---

[45] E.g. Lupercalia (*Q.F.* 2.12.4); Quirinalia (*Q.F.* 2.3.2; 2.12.3); Feralia (*Att.* 8.14.1); Terminalia (*Att.* 6.1.1; *Phil.* 12.24); Liberalia (*Att.* 6.1.12; 9.9.4; 14.14.2; 14.10.1; *Fam.* 12.25.1); Quinquatrus (*Att.* 9.11.2; 9.13.2; *Fam.* 12.25.1); Parilia (*Att.* 2.8.2; 4.10.2; *Phil.* 14.14); Cerialia (*Att.* 2.12.2; 2.12.4); Saturnalia (*Att.* 5.20.1; 5.20.5; 13.52.1; *Cat.* 3.10). In some cases he names the day because of its associations or to introduce a joke, but often simply for identification.

indicates that he found them in his sources, and that even in writing the practice was usual in earlier periods.[46]

If we accept the idea that the purpose of recording the named days in the calendar was to provide a frame of reference for individual or communal activities, we can form some idea of how the man (the *rex*, the *pontifex maximus*?) who was first charged with drawing up the written calendar might have proceeded. First he would note down the Kalends, Nones (or first quarter day) and Ides. Using these as his framework, he would then insert all the other important single days which could be written in easily because their names were single words. (He would, of course, have to leave out such days if they were *feriae conceptivae*.) He would now have produced a list which would be easy for other people to memorize and to recite, as we recite the names of the months or the days of the week if we are trying to calculate a future date. Groups of days such as the *Ludi* could not be included in the list because individual named days often occur during the Ludi, and the simultaneous events would make it difficult to recite the list. In a written calendar one can have two entries for one day which one can take in at a glance, but one cannot pronounce two words simultaneously. I would guess that the memorization of the list would be a part of a Roman's education, just as he must have had to face the appalling task of memorizing the lists of consuls. The fact that people could memorize the list of names would not obviate the need for the announcement made by the *rex*. Macrobius says (1.15.12) that the *rex* told the people the *causae feriarum* and *quid esset eo mense faciendum*. While I would not necessarily take Macrobius' word for this, it stands to reason that the *rex* did not simply say "Such and such *feriae* will be on such and such a day." He certainly had to remind his hearers of the nature of the ritual to be performed, the time, the equipment needed (milk, wine, pig, lamb, ox?), the costume (plain toga, or will wreaths be worn?), where the procession will form, etc.[47]

[46] If this is correct, the dates in many records must have been changed into the other form. In the *Fasti Triumphales*, for instance, triumphs are often recorded on the dates of *feriae* but the Quirinalia and Terminalia are the only ones identified.

[47] Members of academic faculties will remember their need for in-

A list of the named days would provide the basic element on which the rest of the calendar might grow. If *feriae conceptivae* became *stativae*, they could be added. As the Romans became more literate and less dependent on memory, the habit of adding other useful material to the written *Fasti* would develop. Matters of practical importance for everyone would be put in large letters, as we find the nundinal letters and the characters of the days, and the official calendar would take the shape with which we are familiar.

The foregoing discussion has given a possible explanation of the purpose of the *feriale* which may have determined the days which were listed, and cleared the way for a consideration of the problems involved in trying to trace the history of the individual days. The first problem, of course, is raised by the fact that we really know very little about the rites performed on most of the *feriae*, so that we often cannot be sure what their purpose may have been, or to what type of religious ceremony they belonged, and therefore cannot guess what their history may have been. Thus we are forced to think first in generalizations. We can reasonably assume that in a small community supported by agriculture and frequently in conflict with its neighbors, as Rome must have been in her early days, the most important religious rites of the community must have been those that guaranteed good crops and growing flocks. The occasions for these would have been determined by the seasons. Next in importance, after the food supply was secured, would be the rites on which depended the security of the city and its citizens from dangers external and internal. The gods who give success in war must be invoked when the citizens take up arms. The gods who can grant the internal stability and continued existence of the city must be conciliated at all times, in every activity, while those who threaten human life, the gods of the underworld, and the dead, must be propitiated at the seasons when their power is greatest. Rites of these types which develop in answer to universal human needs would probably have been brought to Rome by the first settlers as

---

struction in annual ceremonies in which they have taken part for most of their lives.

part of their heritage from their old homes, and would be the oldest stratum in the state cult of the city, although in the hands of later generations and a mixed population they would have been modified and acquired Roman features.

A different type of rite would be represented by those connected with cults which grew up on Roman soil. The hills, the springs and brooks, the groves, had their own deities. The great gods of the Latins or the Sabines revealed themselves in Rome in special forms which required new cults, and the Romans in need brought to Rome strange gods to be worshipped in new ways.

How would these developments affect the history of the calendar and its *feriale*? The basic pattern of the calendar would be provided obviously by the rites connected with seasonal activities. Ploughing, sowing, cultivating, reaping, the breeding of flocks, their shift from winter to summer pasture, the vintage, the olive harvest, come at the same season every year. In a land of small independent communities war is seasonal too. A prudent man hopes to avoid fighting on his own territory until his harvest is in. The best way to injure his neighbors is to ravage their crops before the harvest, but too late for a second planting. The rites of agriculture and war would then follow the seasons in sequence, giving a pattern to the year. On the other hand, exactly because they follow the seasons, they will not always fall on the same day, or even in the same month. A long, cold winter, and a late spring may postpone the *feriae* designed to protect the growing crops, but, if the food supply runs low, they may prompt raids on the neighbors and speed up the rites of war. For these reasons, although the agricultural rites determined the pattern of the religious life of early Rome, they could not provide a regular calendar until the pattern of life changed. If, for example, the Robigalia was thought of as the immediate means of protecting the corn in the fields of Rome, and was performed for the immediate benefit of farmers living within easy walking distance of the city, it could not be celebrated until the corn in those fields was in the right state. As long as this situation prevailed, *feriae* of this type could not be assigned to fixed days of a particular month.

But the pattern of life did change. The city grew, the urban population increased, with increased trade local agriculture would become less vital, the distinction between city folk and the *rustici* became more pronounced, and finally the citizen body began to spread over a much wider area. With all these changes, many of the rites which had been thought of as the efficacious means whereby the crops were made to grow for each farmer could be regarded as formal petitions made annually to the gods on behalf of the whole state. Although they would still come at the same general time of the year as they always had, they could now be given a regular date not determined by the weather in Rome, and could be incorporated in the *feriale*. Other rites, however, remained always intimately connected with the seasons, and remained therefore *feriae conceptivae*, celebrated as they had been from time immemorial on the appropriate day on the farms and great estates, and in the city on behalf of all Romans everywhere.

The tendency towards formalization in the religion of the state, which would result inevitably from the growing complexity of the state, would affect the rites of war too. As Rome's territory increased, so did her military enterprises. The security of the city and its possessions would be guaranteed by regular annual ceremonies, not by ones performed as needed for particular raids or campaigns.

While lunar observation was still being used in Rome those *feriae* which were now associated only with the seasons, not with specific activities, could be assigned to particular days dated in relation to the phases of the moon. For example, the Agonium might always come four days after the first quarter of the January moon, and the Lupercalia two days after the full moon of February. Varro's explanation that the Quinquatrus is so called because it is the fifth day after the Ides of March (*De L. L.* 6.14) suggests that such a method of dating was familiar to the Romans for days, other than the Nones, which were announced for a certain number of days after the Kalends (Varro, *De L. L.* 6.27). It would, however, be difficult to date the *feriae* by reckoning backward from the dividing day, in the Roman method with which we are familiar, until the number of days in the months and the actual dates of the

[139]

Nones and Ides in each month had been fixed in a regular scheme.[48]

We can then postulate that the sequence of many Roman *feriae* had actually been determined before the city was founded, when they were celebrated in the places from which the first Romans came. Some which grew up in the city and its environs would have been fitted into the sequence, if they were related to the seasons. Others might have acquired a fixed date at the time of their origin, if they were related to civic routine rather than the seasons. But here again we can in most cases talk only in general terms, because in the majority of cases we cannot be perfectly sure to which category any particular *feriae* belong. I would guess that the oldest *feriae* were those determined by the seasons, but that they were also the ones which acquired fixed dates the latest. The mere fact that a named day is listed in the *feriale* does not, in my opinion, guarantee that it belongs to an early period.

On the other hand, we can take into consideration the fact that styles change in religion as in other matters. In a simple or poor society it is natural to honor the gods by actions, rituals, and sacrifices which cost little, and to celebrate the holy day by some entertainment in which the worshippers participate. One can, for instance, imagine that originally the mules were raced at the Consualia[49] by the farmers who owned them. A richer society will build the god a temple and make him expensive gifts, one with more leisure will invent more prolonged rites which offer more sophisticated amusement for men as well as gods. Already in the sixth century the Romans were building temples, and may have begun to hold the votive games which later developed into the annual *Ludi*, dedicated to Jupiter. As time went on the *Ludi* took in more and more days, and added theatrical performances to the earlier horse races. By the late third century new *ludi* were established in honor of other gods. Other rituals proliferated, such as *supplicationes*

[48] The Athenians seem to have been able to use a backward count for the last ten days of the month, even when the exact length of the month was uncertain, but it must have been very inconvenient. I would guess the Romans adopted the backward count either when or after they adopted the pre-Julian calendar.

[49] Festus, 135 L.

FIFTH CENTURY b.c.

and *lectisternia*. These forms of worship do not, however, seem to have resulted in the naming of days which would be the prerequisite for the inclusion of a day in the *feriale*.[50] I would therefore conclude that, as the style of worship changed over the centuries, fewer and fewer days would acquire names and the *feriale* would cease to grow. It is, however, as far as I can see, impossible to determine which was the last named day to be included before the custom was revived for the Augustalia in 19 b.c.[51] It seems to me quite possible that some of the *feriae* about which we know so little may have been instituted at any time before the date at which *Fasti Ant. Mai.* was drawn.

We might also consider whether any days ever dropped out of the *feriale*. There is no evidence that any did so, and indeed it would be contrary to all we know of Roman religious feeling to cancel *feriae* simply because they were old and neglected by the people. "*Antiquitas proxume accedit ad deos.*" The names of the days would survive if the *feriale* was commonly memorized. It is possible that some of them had associations which preserved them in popular usage. The Volcanalia, for example, was the traditional first day of autumn.[52] Other days not mentioned in our literary sources may have been remembered for similar associations, as Lady Day and

[50] Why did some days acquire names and others not? I suspect there is no logical answer to the question, but that the names came into being from the mysterious process of usage. Why do some people acquire nicknames and others go through life without them? Why in the USA is Independence Day usually referred to as "The Fourth of July," or simply "the Fourth," when our other holidays are given their proper names?

[51] The institution of the Augustalia may have been a piece of conscious archaism calculated to please Augustus, but it departed from some normal calendaric procedures in an interesting way. The date, October 12, is an even number, and comes between two other named days, the Meditrinalia (October 11) and the Fontinalia (October 13). It is the anniversary of the altar of Fortuna Redux, established in honor of Augustus' return to Rome from Syria in 19 b.c., at which the annual sacrifice was performed. The latter fact is a solemn warning against deducing the nature of its rites from the name of a day.

[52] Or at least it was in the time of Ausonius (*Ecl.* 23 [*De Feriis Romanis*] 3). Perhaps this is why the elder Pliny, who worked while others slept, started to do so by lamplight on the Volcanalia (Pliny, *Epp.* 3.5.8). It is reminiscent of the traditional dates on which our grandfathers felt it was proper to begin having fires in bedrooms.

[141]

Michaelmas are best known in Protestant England as the Quarter Days of the business year.

Another factor which would have tended to keep alive the popular knowledge of named days is the peculiarly historical character of the Roman imagination. Whatever the origin of the *feriae* may have been, many of them have been linked with events in Roman legend or history. The outstanding example is the Parilia, which was recognized as a shepherds' festival, but was celebrated, as it still is, as the birthday of Rome. The Regifugium was popularly supposed to celebrate the expulsion of the Tarquins, a sort of Roman Independence Day.[53] The Poplifugia was connected with the sack of Rome by the Gauls, the Consualia with the rape of the Sabine women. The sensational story of Acca Larentia, told to explain the Larentalia, would certainly have caught the popular fancy.

The habit of connecting *feriae* with legendary or historical events, which must have been encouraged by the antiquarians of the republic, probably laid the ground for the last change which came over the calendar as we see it in the *Fasti* of the Julian year. In 45 B.C. the senate honored Julius Caesar by establishing *feriae* on the anniversaries of his victories,[54] which, although they received no names, were marked NP in the *Fasti*. From that time on, the *Fasti* were flooded with *feriae* celebrating events in the lives of the imperial family.[55] It is, I think, this innovation which accounts for the curious fact that none of the *Fasti* inscribed on stone can be dated later than the reign of Tiberius, although some contain a few additional entries made under Claudius.[56] It would seem that to put up *Fasti* in one's house or on a public monument had become a way of demonstrating or evoking loyalty to the regime. A reaction against the anniversary *feriae* began with Caligula, as

[53] This is Ovid's explanation of the day (*Fasti* 2.685-688), and it is given in the *Fasti* of Polemius Silvius, and by Ausonius (*Ecl.* 7.13f.). It seems to be contradicted by Festus in a very fragmentary passage reconstructed on the basis of Paulus' epitome (346f. L.). According to the note in *Fasti Praen.* the same tradition was attached to March 24 whose character was *Q.R.C.F.*
[54] Dio, 43.44.6; Appian, *B.C.* 2.106.
[55] These nameless NP days are discussed in App. 2.
[56] Degrassi, pp. xxiif.

part of his attack on the memory of Augustus: *ac non con-
tentus hac Augusti insectatione Actiacas Siculasque victorias,
ut funestas p. R. et calamitosas, vetuit sollemnibus feriis cele-
brari.* (Suet., *Calig.* 23.1). Claudius in 43 abolished many
feriae, according to Dio (60.17.1) because they were interfering with business. He may also have been tired of the reminders of his predecessors' triumphs. These gestures did not
cure the senate, however, for in 58 it decreed that the days on
which Artaxata had been taken and the victory reported should
become *dies festi.* This flattery of Nero, according to Tacitus,
elicited from a senator an acid comment on the interference of
religion with business (*Ann.* 13.41). Tacitus also reports an
episode which indicates an awareness on the part of the Senate
that a new emperor, unrelated to the Julio-Claudians, might
not appreciate the state of the *Fasti.* At a meeting in 70, before
Vespasian returned to Rome, the senators were preparing for
his advent. Tacitus tells us (*Hist.* 4.40) among other items:
*sorte ducti per quos redderentur bello rapta, quique aera legum
vetustate delapsa noscerent figerentque, et fastos adulatione
temporum foedatos exonerarent modumque publicis impensis
facerent.* This praiseworthy effort to reduce flattery and expense by the same act should have pleased Vespasian, but the
holidays must have continued to increase, for both Nerva (Dio,
68.2.3) and Marcus Aurelius (*Hist. Aug.* 10.10) were forced
in the interests of economy and efficiency to reduce their numbers again. Even so, in the calendars of the late empire[57] the

[57] The *Fasti* of Philocalus, preserved in manuscript, was written in
A.D. 354. See Degrassi, no. 42, and H. Stern, *Le Calendrier de 354. Étude
sur son texte et sur ses illustrations* (Paris 1953). The *Fasti* of Polemius
Silvius (Degrassi, no. 43), also in manuscript, was written in A.D. 448/9.
These *Fasti* vary considerably from those of the early empire in that
they omit some elements, notably the characters of the days, and add
other material, which in the case of Polemius is often Christian. There
are also several *ferialia* of the empire which are designed for special
groups and therefore vary from the *Fasti* (see Degrassi 276-283 for those
found in Italy). The most interesting is the papyrus *Feriale Duranum*,
which was used by the Roman garrison of Dura on the Euphrates in the
early third century A.D. The most recent publication is in *The Excavations
at Dura-Europos. Final Report V, Part 1* (New Haven and London
1959) 191-212. See also A. D. Nock, "The Roman Army and the Roman
Religious Year," *HThR* 45 (1952) 187-252.

[143]

birthdays of emperors, dead and living, are recorded, constant reminders for all men of the ancient and remote power which controlled their lives. They have replaced the character letters of the republican calendar, which reminded a Roman of his rights as a citizen and of his duty to Rome and her gods.

APPENDIX 1

ROMAN INTERCALATION

The ancient sources from which our knowledge of the Roman method of intercalation is derived are diverse in character and date. The primary contemporary evidence for the pre-Julian calendar is contained in *Ant. Mai.*, which gives us, in its thirteenth column, the intercalary month (see Pls. 1, 4, and pp. 25f.). We find more or less detailed accounts of the method in writers of the Empire, Plutarch, Censorinus, Solinus, Ammianus, and Macrobius. The similarity of the wording in the Latin texts suggest that all of them were based to some extent upon a common source, perhaps the lost *De Anno* of Suetonius. The theoretical and often confused accounts given by these authors must be checked for actual practice by evidence of another type, the incidental references in the historians, in Cicero and other writers, and by dated documents preserved in inscriptions. Their probability must also be considered in the light of the astronomical facts. Before discussing the major problems involved, I present for easy consultation the basic evidence from the authors, omitting a few passages which refer only to the Julian calendar. I should, however, make one introductory comment on the nature of the evidence. The descriptions of intercalation given here were written by men in a situation very similar to our own. They were trying to understand from literary evidence a system which had been abandoned generations or centuries before their own days, and to explain how it originated. It is a characteristic of the human mind to try to impose order on disorderly facts, and even to impose order where none existed. Ancient scholars, like their descendants, may well have gone too far in interpreting the facts of the past in the light of the knowledge of their own day, and thus have made what they considered a well-regulated system of intercalation out of what had actually been a rule of thumb, trial and error, method of adjusting the calendar.

In the discussion which follows the texts, evidence will be cited by the numbers under which the texts are here listed.

[145]

1. Cicero, *De Legibus* 2.29:
quod ad tempus, ut sacrificiorum libamenta serventur fetusque pecorum, quae dicta in lege sunt, diligenter habenda ratio intercalandi est, quod institutum perite a Numa posteriorum pontificum neglegentia dissolutum est.

2. Cicero, *Fam.* 7.2.4:
nos hic in multitudine et celebritate iudiciorum et novis legibus ita distinemur ut cotidie vota faciamus ne intercaletur, ut quam primum te videre possimus.

3. Cicero, *Att.* 5.9.2:
hoc tibi ita mando, ut dubitem, an etiam te rogem, ut pugnes, ne intercaletur.

4. Cicero, *Att.* 5.13.3:
quoniam Romae manes, primum illud praefulci atque praemuni, quaeso, ⟨ut⟩ simus annui, ne intercaletur quidem.

5. Cicero, *Att.* 5.21.14:
cum scies, Romae intercalatum sit necne, velim ad me scribas certum, quo die mysteria futura sint.

6. Cicero, *Att.* 6.1.12:
Quinto togam puram Liberalibus cogitabam dare; mandavit enim pater, ea sic observabo, quasi intercalatum non sit.

7. Cicero, *Fam.* 8.6.5 (from Caelius about Curio):
Levissime enim, quia de intercalando non obtinuerat, transfugit ad populum et pro Caesare loqui coepit. . . .

8. Varro, *De Lingua Latina*, 6.13:
Terminalia, quod is dies anni extremus constitutus: duodecimus enim mensis fuit Februarius et cum intercalatur inferiores quinque dies duodecimo demuntur mense.

9. Livy, 1.19.6 (referring to Numa):
atque omnium primum ad cursus lunae in duodecim menses discribit annum; quem quia tricenos dies singulis mensibus luna non explet desuntque ⟨sex⟩ dies solido anno qui solstitiali circumagitur orbe, intercalariis mensibus interponendis ita dispensavit, ut vicesimo anno ad metam eandem solis unde orsi essent, plenis omnium annorum spatiis dies congruerent.
(On this passage see p. 123 n. 13.)

10. Livy, 43.11.13:
hoc anno intercalatum est: tertio die post Terminalia kalendae intercalariae fuere.

11. Livy, 45.44.3:
Intercalatum eo anno; postridie Terminalia *kal.* intercalariae fuerunt.

12. Plutarch, *Numa* 18.1f.:

Ἥψατο δὲ καὶ τῆς περὶ τὸν οὐρανὸν πραγματείας οὔτε ἀκριβῶς οὔτε παντάπασιν ἀθεωρήτως. Ῥωμύλου γὰρ βασιλεύοντος ἀλόγως ἐχρῶντο τοῖς μησὶ καὶ ἀτάκτως, τοὺς μὲν οὐδ' εἴκοσιν ἡμερῶν τοὺς δὲ πέντε καὶ τριάκοντα τοὺς δὲ πλειόνων λογιζόμενοι, τῆς δὲ γινομένης ἀνωμαλίας περὶ τὴν σελήνην καὶ τὸν ἥλιον ἔννοιαν οὐκ ἔχοντες, ἀλλ' ἐν φυλάτ-τοντες μόνον, ὅπως ἑξήκοντα καὶ τριακοσίων ἡμερῶν ὁ ἐνιαυτὸς ἔσται. Νομᾶς δὲ τὸ παράλλαγμα τῆς ἀνωμαλίας ἡμερῶν ἕνδεκα γίνεσθαι λογιζόμενος, ὡς τοῦ μὲν σεληνιακοῦ τριακοσίας πεντήκοντα τέσσαρας ἔχοντος ἡμέρας τοῦ δὲ ἡλιακοῦ τριακοσίας ἑξήκοντα πέντε, τὰς ἕνδεκα ταύτας ἡμέρας διπλασιάζων ἐπήγαγε παρ' ἐνιαυτὸν ἐπὶ τῷ Φεβρουαρίῳ μηνὶ τὸν ἐμβόλιμον, ὑπὸ Ῥωμαίων Μερκηδῖνον καλούμενον, εἴκοσι καὶ δυοῖν ἡμερῶν ὄντα. καὶ τοῦτο μὲν αὐτῷ τὸ ἴαμα τῆς ἀνωμαλίας μει-ζόνων ἔμελλεν ἰαμάτων δεήσεσθαι, μετεκίνησε δὲ καὶ τὴν τάξιν τῶν μηνῶν·

13. Plutarch, *Caesar* 59.1f.:

Ἡ δὲ τοῦ ἡμερολογίου διάθεσις καὶ διόρθωσις τῆς περὶ τὸν χρόνον ἀνωμαλίας φιλοσοφηθεῖσα χαριέντως ὑπ' αὐτοῦ καὶ τέλος λαβοῦσα γλαφυρωτάτην παρέσχε χρείαν. οὐ γὰρ μόνον ἐν τοῖς παλαιοῖς πάνυ χρόνοις τεταραγμέναις ἐχρῶντο Ῥωμαῖοι ταῖς τῶν μηνῶν πρὸς τὸν ἐνιαυτὸν περιόδοις, ὥστε τὰς θυσίας καὶ τὰς ἑορτὰς ὑποφερομένας κατὰ μικρὸν εἰς ἐναντίας ἐκπεπτωκέναι τοῖς χρόνοις ὥρας, ἀλλὰ καὶ περὶ τὴν τότε οὖσαν ἡλιακὴν οἱ μὲν ἄλλοι παντάπασι τούτων ἀσυλλογίστως εἶχον, οἱ δὲ ἱερεῖς μόνοι τὸν καιρὸν εἰδότες ἐξαίφνης καὶ προησθημένου μηδενὸς τὸν ἐμβόλιμον προσέγραφον μῆνα, Μερκηδόνιον ὀνομάζοντες, ὃν Νομᾶς ὁ βασιλεὺς πρῶτος ἐμβαλεῖν λέγεται, μικρὰν καὶ διατείνουσαν οὐ πόρρω βοήθειαν ἐξευρὼν τῆς περὶ τὰς ἀποκαταστάσεις πλημμελείας, ὡς ἐν τοῖς περὶ ἐκείνου γέγραπται.

14. Suetonius, *Jul.* 40:
Conversus hinc ad ordinandum rei publicae statum fastos correxit iam pridem vitio pontificum per intercalandi licentiam adeo turbatos, ut neque messium feriae aestate neque vin-demiarum autumno conpeterent; annumque ad cursum solis

accommodavit, ut trecentorum sexaginta quinque dierum esset et intercalario mense sublato unus dies quarto quoque anno intercalaretur. quo autem magis in posterum ex Kalendis Ianuariis novis temporum ratio congrueret, inter Novembrem ac Decembrem mensem interiecit duos alios; fuitque is annus, quo haec constituebantur, quindecim mensium cum intercalario, qui ex consuetudine in eum annum inciderat.

15. Dio, 40.47.1f.:

Κἀκ τούτου οὔτε τι ἄλλο χρηστὸν συνέβη, καὶ ἡ ἀγορὰ ἡ διὰ τῶν ἐννέα ἀεὶ ἡμερῶν ἀγομένη ἐν αὐτῇ τῇ τοῦ Ἰανουαρίου νουμηνίᾳ ἤχθη. καὶ τοῦτό τε αὐτούς, ὡς οὐκ ἀπὸ ταὐτομάτου συμβὰν ἀλλ' ἐν τέρατος λόγῳ γενόμενον, ἐθορύβει, καὶ ὅτι βύας ἐν τῇ πόλει καὶ ὤφθη καὶ συνελήφθη, ἄγαλμά τέ τι ἐπὶ τρεῖς ἡμέρας ἵδρωσε, καὶ λαμπὰς ἐκ τῶν νοτίων πρὸς ἀνατολὰς διέδραμε, καὶ πολλοὶ μὲν κεραυνοὶ πολλοὶ δὲ καὶ βῶλοι λίθοι τε καὶ ὄστρακα καὶ αἷμα διὰ τοῦ ἀέρος ἠνέχθη.

16. Dio, 40.62.1f.:

συχνὸν οὖν ἐκ τούτου χρόνον ἄλλοτε ἄλλαις σκήψεσιν, ὥστε μηδὲν αὐτῶν τὸ παράπαν κυρωθῆναι, κατατρίψας ἀγανακτεῖν τε προσεποιεῖτο, καὶ ἠξίου μῆνα ἄλλον πρὸς τὰς ὑπ' αὐτῶν δὴ νομοθεσίας ἐπεμβληθῆναι. τοῦτο δὲ ἐγίγνετο μὲν ὁσάκις γε καὶ καθῆκον ἦν, οὐ μέντοι καὶ κατ' ἐκεῖνο συνέβαινεν, ὥσπερ που καὶ αὐτὸς ἅτε ποντίφιξ ὢν ἠπίστατο. ὅμως δ' οὖν δεῖν τε αὐτὸ γενέσθαι ἔλεγε, καὶ τοὺς συνιερέας ὅσον ἀπὸ βοῆς ἐξεβιάζετο· καὶ τέλος μὴ δυνηθεὶς αὐτοὺς πεῖσαι συγκαταθέσθαι οἱ, ὥσπερ οὐδὲ ἐβούλετο, οὐδ' ἄλλο τι διὰ τοῦτο ψηφισθῆναι ἐπέτρεψεν,

17. Dio, 48.33.4:

ἔν τε τῷ πρὸ τούτου ἔτει θηρία τε ἐν τῇ τῶν Ἀπολλωνίων ἱπποδρομίᾳ ἄνδρες ἐς τὴν ἱππάδα τελοῦντες κατέβαλον, καὶ ἡμέρα ἐμβόλιμος παρὰ τὰ καθεστηκότα ἐνεβλήθη, ἵνα μὴ ἡ νουμηνία τοῦ ἐχομένου ἔτους τὴν ἀγορὰν τὴν διὰ τῶν ἐννέα ἡμερῶν ἀγομένην λάβῃ, ὅπερ ἀπὸ τοῦ πάνυ ἀρχαίου σφόδρα ἐφυλάσσετο· καὶ δῆλον ὅτι ἀνθυφῃρέθη αὖθις, ὅπως ὁ χρόνος κατὰ τὰ τῷ Καίσαρι τῷ προτέρῳ δόξαντα συμβῇ.

18. Solinus, 1.34-47:

Tunc ergo primum cursus anni perspecta ratio, quae a rerum origine profunda caligine tegebatur. nam ante Augustum Caesarem incerto modo annum conputabant, qui apud Aegyptios quattuor mensibus terminabatur, apud Arcadas tribus, apud Acarnanas sex, in Italia apud Lavinios tredecim, quorum annus trecentis septuaginta quattuor diebus ferebatur. Romani

initio annum decem mensibus computaverunt a Martio auspi-
cantes, adeo ut eius die prima de aris Vestalibus ignes ac-
cenderent, mutarent veteribus virides laureas, senatus et
populus comitia agerent, matronae servis suis cenas ponerent,
sicuti Saturnalibus domini: illae ut honore promptius obse-
quium provocarent, hi quasi gratiam repensarent perfecti
laboris: maximeque hunc mensem principem testatur fuisse,
quod qui ab hoc quintus erat Quintilis dictus est, deinde
numero decurrente December sollemnem circuitum finiebat
intra diem trecentesimum quartum: tunc enim iste numerus
explebat annum, ita ut sex menses tricenum dierum essent,
quattuor reliqui tricenis et singulis expedirentur. sed quoniam
ratio illa ante Numam a lunae cursu discreparet, lunari com-
putatione annum peraequarunt, quinquaginta et uno die auctis.
ut ergo perficerent duodecim menses, de sex mensibus superi-
oribus detraxerunt dies singulos, eosque quinquaginta istis et
uno diebus adnexuerunt, factique quinquaginta septem divisi
sunt in duos menses, quorum alter viginti novem, alter viginti
octo dies detinebant. sic annus habere quinque atque quinquaginta et trecentos dies coepit.

Postmodum cum perspicerent temere annum clausum intra
dies quos supra diximus, quandoquidem appareret solis
meatum non ante trecentesimum sexagesimum quintum diem,
abundante insuper quadrantis particula, zodiacum conficere
decursum, quadrantem illum et decem dies addiderunt, ut
ad liquidum annus diebus trecentis sexaginta quinque et
quadrante constaret, hortante observatione inparis numeri,
quem Pythagoras monuit praeponi in omnibus oportere. unde
propter dies inpares diis superis et Ianuarius dicatur et
Martius: propter pares Februarius quasi ominosus diis inferis
deputatur. cum itaque haec definitio toto orbe placuisset,
custodiendi quadrantis gratia a diversis gentibus varie intercalabatur, nec umquam tamen ad liquidum fiebat temporum
peraequatio. Graeci ergo singulis annis undecim dies et
quadrantem detrahebant, eosque octies multiplicatos in annum nonum reservabant, ut contractus nonagenarius numerus
in tres menses per tricenos dies scinderetur: qui anno nono
restituti efficiebant dies quadringentos quadraginta quattuor,
quos embolismos vel hyperballontas nominabant. quod cum

initio Romani probassent, contemplatione numeri parilis offensi neglectum brevi perdiderunt, translata in sacerdotes intercalandi potestate: qui plerumque gratificantes rationibus publicanorum pro libidine sua subtrahebant tempora vel augebant. cum haec sic forent constituta modusque intercalandi interdum cumulatior, interdum fieret imminutior, vel omnino dissimulatus praeteriretur, nonnumquam accidebat, ut menses qui fuerant transacti hieme, modo aestivum modo autumnale tempus inciderent.

Itaque C. Caesar universam hanc inconstantiam, incisa temporum turbatione, composuit, et ut statum certum praeteritus acciperet error, dies viginti unum et quadrantem simul intercalavit: quo pacto regradati menses de cetero statuta ordinis sui tempora detinerent. ille ergo annus solus trecentos quadraginta quattuor dies habuit: alii deinceps trecentenos sexagenos quinos et quadrantem. et tunc quoque vitium admissum est per sacerdotes. nam cum praeceptum esset, anno quarto ut intercalarent unum diem, et oporteret confecto quarto anno id observari, antequam quintus auspicaretur, illi incipiente quarto intercalarunt, non desinente. sic per annos sex et triginta cum novem dies tantummodo sufficere debuissent, duodecim sunt intercalati. quod deprehensum Augustus reformavit, iussitque annos duodecim sine intercalatione decurrere, ut tres illi dies, qui ultra novem necessarios temere fuerant intercalati, hoc modo possent repensari. ex qua disciplina omnium postea temporum fundata ratio est.

19. Censorinus, *De Die Natali* 20.1-10:

1 XX. Sed ut hos annos omittam caligine iam profundae vetustatis obductos, in his quoque qui sunt recentioris memoriae et ad cursum lunae vel solis instituti quanta sit varietas, facile est cognoscere, si quis vel in unius Italiae gentibus, ne dicam peregrinis, velit inquirere. Nam ut alium Ferentini alium Lavinii itemque Albani vel Romani habuerunt annum, ita et aliae gentes. Omnibus tamen fuit propositum suos civiles annos varie intercalandis mensibus ad unum illum verum naturalem-
2 que corrigere. de quibus omnibus disserere quoniam longum est, ad Romanorum annum transibimus.

Annum vertentem Romae Licinius quidem Macer et
postea Fenestella statim ab initio duodecim mensum fuisse
scripserunt: sed magis Iunio Gracch*ano* et Fulvio et Varroni et Suetonio aliisque credendum, qui decem mensum
putaverunt fuisse, ut tunc Albanis erat, unde orti Romani.
3 Hi decem menses dies CCCIIII hoc modo habebant: Martius XXXI, Aprilis XXX, Maius XXXI, Iunius XXX,
Quintilis XXXI, Sextilis et September tricenos, October
XXXI, November et December *tricenos*; quorum quat-
4 tuor maiores pleni, ceteri sex cavi vocabantur. Postea
sive a Numa, ut ait Fulvius, sive, ut Iunius, a Tarqui-
nio XII facti sunt menses et dies CCCLV, quamvis luna
XII suis mensibus CCCLIIII dies videbatur explere. sed
ut unus dies abundaret, aut per imprudentiam accidit,
aut, quod magis credo, ea superstitione qua impar nume-
5 rus plenus et magis faustus habebatur. Certe ad annum
priorem unus et quinquaginta dies accesserunt; qui quia
menses duo non explerent, sex illis cavis mensibus dies
sunt singuli detracti et ad eos additi, factique dies L*V*II,
et ex his duo menses, Ianuarius undetriginta dierum, Februarius duodetriginta. atque ita omnes menses pleni et
inpari dierum numero esse coeperunt, excepto Februario,
qui solus cavus et ob hoc ceteris infaustior est habitus.
6 Denique cum intercalarium mensem viginti duum vel viginti trium dierum alternis annis addi placuisset, ut civilis annus ad naturalem exaequaretur, in mense potissi-
mum Februario inter terminalia et regifugium intercalatum est, idque diu factum priusquam sentiretur annos civiles aliquanto naturalibus esse maiores. Quod delictum
ut corrigeretur, pontificibus datum negotium eorumque ar-
7 bitrio intercalandi ratio permissa. Sed horum plerique
ob odium vel gratiam, quo quis magistratu citius abiret
diutius*ve* fungeretur aut publici redemptor ex anni mag-
nitudine in lucro damnove esset, plus minusve ex libidine intercalando rem sibi ad corrigendum mandatam ultro
8 qu*ia* depravarunt, adeo aberratum est ut C. Caesar pontifex maximus suo III et M. Aemilii Lepidi consulatu, quo
retro delictum corrigeret, duos menses intercalarios dierum LX*V*II in mensem Novembrem et Decembrem inter-

poneret, cum iam mense Februario dies tres et viginti in-
tercalasset, faceretque eum annum dierum CCCCXXXXV,
simul providens in futurum ne iterum erraretur: nam intercalario mense sublato annum civilem ad solis cursum
9 formavit. Itaque diebus CCCLV addidit X, quos per
septem menses, qui dies undetricenos habebant, ita distribuit, ut Ianuario et Sextili et Decembri bini accede-
rent, ceteris singuli; eosque dies extremis partibus mensum adposuit, ne scilicet religiones sui cuiusque mensis
10 a loco summoverentur. Quapropter nunc cum in septem
mensibus dies singuli et triceni sint, quattuor tamen illi
ita primitus instituti eo dinoscuntur quod nonas habent
septimanas, ceteri tres omnes*que* reliqui quintanas. Praeterea pro quadrante diei, qui annum verum suppleturus
videbatur, instituit ut peracto quadriennii circuitu dies
unus, ubi mensis quondam solebat, post terminalia intercalaretur, quod nunc bissextum vocatur.

20. Ammianus Marcellinus, 26.1.7-14:

7. Qui cum venisset accitus, inplendique negotii . . . . . .
praesagiis, ut opinari dabatur, vel somniorum adsiduitate,
nec videri die secundo, nec prodire in medium voluit, bissextum vitans Februarii mensis, tunc inluciscens, quod aliquotiens
rei Romanae fuisse norat infaustum. cuius notitiam certam
ple*nius* designabo.

8. Spatium ann*i* vertentis id e*ss*e, periti mundani motus et
siderum definiunt veteres, inter quos Meton et Euctemon
et Hipparchus et Archimedes excellunt, cum sol perenni
rerum sublimium lege, polo percurso signifero, quem
ζῳδιακόν sermo Graecus appellat, trecentis et sexaginta
quinque diebus emensis et noctibus, ad eundem redierit
cardinem, ut (verbo tenus) si a secunda particula elatus
Arietis, ad eam dimensione redierit terminata. 9. sed anni
intervallum verissimum, memoratis diebus et horis sex ad
usque meridiem concluditur plenam, annique sequentis erit
post horam sextam initium, porrectum ad vesperam. tertius
a prima vigilia sumens exordium, ad horam noctis extenditur
sextam. quartus a medio noctis ad usque claram trahitur
lucem. 10. ne igitur haec conputatio variantibus annorum
principiis, ut quodam post horam sextam diei, alio post sex-

tam excurso nocturnam, scientiam omnem squalida diversitate
confundat, et autumnalis mensis inveniatur, quandoque ver-
nalis, placuit senas illas horas quae quadriennio viginti col-
liguntur atque quattuor, in unius diei noctisque adiectae,
transire mensuram. 11. hocque alte considerato, eruditis
concinentibus multis, effectum est, *ut* ad unum distinctumque
exitum, circumversio cursus annui revoluta, nec vaga sit nec
in*certa*, nulloque errore deinceps obumbrata, ratio caelestis
appareat *et* menses tempora retineant praestituta. 12. haec
nondum extentis fusius regnis, diu igno*ra*vere Romani, perque
saecula multa, obscuris difficultatibus inplicati, tunc magis
errorum profunda caligine fluctuabant, cum in sacerdotes
potestatem transtulissent interkalandi, qui licenter gratificantes publicanorum vel litigantium commodis, ad arbitrium
suum subtrahebant tempora vel augebant. 13. hocque ex
coepto emerserunt alia plurima, quae fallebant, quorum
meminisse nunc supervacuum puto. quibus abolitis, Octavi-
anus Augustus Graecos secutus, hanc inconstantiam correcta
turbatione conposuit, spatiis duodecim mensuum et sex
horarum magna deliberatione collectis, per quae duodecim
siderum domicilia, sol discurrens motibus sempiternis, anni
totius intervalla concludit. 14. quam rationem bissexti
probatam, etiam victura cum saeculis Roma, adiumento
numinis divini fundavit. proinde pergamus ad reliqua.

21. Macrobius, *Sat.*1.12.38–14.15:

38 Haec fuit a Romulo annua ordinata dimensio qui,
sicut supra iam diximus, annum decem mensium, dierum vero quattuor et trecentorum habendum esse constituit, mensesque ita disposuit ut quattuor ex his tri-

39 cenos singulos, sex vero tricenos haberent dies. sed cum
is numerus neque solis cursui neque lunae rationibus
conveniret, non numquam usu veniebat ut frigus anni
aestivis mensibus et contra calor hiemalibus proveniret,
quod ubi contigisset, tantum dierum sine ullo mensis no-
mine patiebantur absumi quantum ad id anni tempus ad-
duceret quo caeli habitus instanti mensi aptus inveniretur.

13 Sed secutus Numa, quantum sub caelo rudi et saeculo
adhuc impolito solo ingenio magistro comprehendere

[153]

potuit, vel quia Graecorum observatione forsan instruc-
tus est, quinquaginta dies addidit, ut in trecentos quinquaginta et quattuor dies, quibus duodecim lunae cursus
2 confici credidit, annus extenderetur. atque his quinquaginta diebus a se additis adiecit alios sex retractos illis
sex mensibus qui triginta habebant dies, id est de singulis singulos, factosque quinquaginta et sex dies in
3 duos novos menses pari ratione divisit, ac de duobus
priorem Ianuarium nuncupavit primumque anni esse
voluit, tamquam bicipitis dei mensem, respicientem ac
prospicientem transacti anni finem futurique principia;
secundum dicavit Februo deo, qui lustrationum potens
creditur. lustrari autem eo mense civitatem necesse erat,
4 quo statuit ut iusta dis Manibus solverentur. Numae
ordinationem finitimi mox secuti totidem diebus totidem-
que mensibus ut Pompilio placuit annum suum compu-
tare coeperunt; sed hoc solo discrepabant, quod menses
5 undetricenum tricenumque numero alternaverunt. paulo
post Numa in honorem imparis numeri, secretum hoc et
ante Pythagoram parturiente natura, unum adiecit diem
quem Ianuario dedit, ut tam in anno quam in mensibus
singulis praeter unum Februarium impar numerus ser-
varetur. nam quia duodecim menses, si singuli aut pari
aut impari numero putarentur, consummationem parem
facerent, unus pari numero institutus universam putatio-
6 nem imparem fecit. Ianuarius igitur Aprilis Iunius Sextilis September November December undetricenis cen-
sebantur diebus et quintanas nonas habebant, ac post
idus in omnibus a. d. septimum decimum kalendas compu-
7 tabatur. Martius vero Maius Quintilis et October dies tricenos singulos possidebant. nonae in his septimanae erant
similiterque post idus decem septem dies in singulis
usque ad sequentes kalendas putabantur, sed solus Februarius viginti et octo retinuit dies quasi inferis et deminutio
8 et par numerus conveniret. cum ergo Romani ex hac
distributione Pompilii ad lunae cursum sicut Graeci
annum proprium computarent, necessario et intercala-
9 rem mensem instituerunt more Graecorum. nam et Graeci
cum animadverterent temere se trecentis quinquaginta

quattuor diebus ordinasse annum—quoniam appareret
de solis cursu, qui trecentis sexaginta quinque diebus et
quadrante zodiacum conficit, deesse anno suo undecim
dies et quadrantem—intercalares stata ratione commenti
sunt, ita ut octavo quoque anno nonaginta dies, ex quibus tres menses tricenum dierum composuerunt, inter-
10 calarent. id Graeci fecerunt, quoniam operosum erat
atque difficile omnibus annis undecim dies et quadrantem
intercalare. itaque maluerunt hunc numerum octies multi-
plicare, et nonaginta dies, qui nascuntur si quadrans
cum diebus undecim octies componatur, inserere in tres
menses, ut diximus, distribuendos. hos dies ὑπερβαίνοντας,
11 menses vero ἐμβολίμους appellitabant. hunc ergo ordinem Romanis quoque imitari placuit, sed frustra, quippe
fugit eos diem unum, sicut supra admonuimus, additum
a se ad Graecum numerum in honorem imparis numeri.
ea re per octennium convenire numerus atque ordo non
12 poterat. sed nondum hoc errore comperto per octo annos
nonaginta quasi superfundendos Graecorum exemplo com-
putabant dies, alternisque annis binos et vicenos, alternis
ternos vicenosque intercalantes expensabant intercala-
tionibus quattuor. sed octavo quoque anno intercalares
octo affluebant dies ex singulis quibus vertentis anni numerum apud Romanos super Graecum abundasse iam dixi-
13 mus. hoc quoque errore iam cognito haec species emen-
dationis inducta est. tertio quoque octennio ita inter-
calandos dispensabant dies, ut non nonaginta sed sexaginta sex intercalarent, compensatis viginti et quattuor
diebus pro illis qui per totidem annos supra Graecorum
14 numerum creverant. omni autem intercalationi mensis
Februarius deputatus est quoniam is ultimus anni erat,
quod etiam ipsum de Graecorum imitatione faciebant.
nam et illi ultimo anni sui mensi superfluos interserebant
dies, ut refert Glaucippus qui de sacris Atheniensium scrip-
15 sit. verum una re a Graecis differebant. nam illi confecto
ultimo mense, Romani non confecto Februario sed post
vicesimum et tertium diem eius intercalabant, Termi-
nalibus scilicet iam peractis. deinde reliquos Februarii
mensis dies, qui erant quinque, post intercalationem

[155]

subiungebant, credo vetere religionis suae more, ut Febru-
16 arium omni modo Martius consequeretur. sed cum saepe
eveniret ut nundinae modo in anni principem diem, modo
in nonas caderent—utrumque autem perniciosum rei
publicae putabatur—remedium quo hoc averteretur
excogitatum est, quod aperiemus si prius ostenderimus
cur nundinae vel primis kalendis vel nonis omnibus cave-
17 bantur. nam quotiens incipiente anno dies coepit qui
addictus est nundinis, omnis ille annus infaustis casibus
luctuosus fuit, maximeque Lepidiano tumultu opinio ista
18 firmata est. nonis autem conventus universae multitu-
dinis vitandus existimabatur, quoniam populus Romanus
exactis etiam regibus diem hunc nonarum maxime cele-
brabat quem natalem Servii Tullii existimabat quia, cum
incertum esset quo mense Servius Tullius natus fuisset,
nonis tamen natum esse constaret, omnes nonas celebri
notitia frequentabant: veritos ergo qui diebus praeerant,
nequid nundinis collecta universitas ob desiderium regis
19 novaret, cavisse ut nonae a nundinis segregarentur. unde
dies ille, quo abundare annum diximus, eorum est per-
missus arbitrio qui fastis praeerant, uti, cum vellent,
intercalaretur, dum modo eum in medio Terminaliorum
vel mensis intercalaris ita locarent, ut a suspecto die
celebritatem averteret nundinarum. atque hoc est quod
quidam veterum rettulerunt non solum mensem apud
20 Romanos verum etiam diem intercalarem fuisse. quando
autem primum intercalatum sit varie refertur. et Macer
quidem Licinius eius rei originem Romulo adsignat. Antias libro secundo Numam Pompilium sacrorum causa id
invenisse contendit. Iunius Servium Tullium regem primum intercalasse commemorat, a quo et nundinas insti-
21 tutas Varroni placet. Tuditanus refert libro tertio Magistratuum decem viros, qui decem tabulis duas addiderunt,
de intercalando populum rogasse. Cassius eosdem scribit
auctores. Fulvius autem id egisse M'. Acilium consulem
dicit ab urbe condita anno quingentesimo sexagesimo
secundo, inito mox bello Aetolico. sed hoc arguit Varro
scribendo antiquissimam legem fuisse incisam in columna
aerea a L. Pinario et Furio consulibus, cui mensis inter-

calaris adscribitur. haec de intercalandi principio satis
relata sint.

14 Verum fuit tempus cum propter superstitionem intercalatio omnis omissa est: non numquam vero per gratiam sacerdotum, qui publicanis proferri vel imminui consulto anni dies volebant, modo auctio, modo retractio
dierum proveniebat et sub specie observationis emergebat
2 maior confusionis occasio. sed postea C. Caesar omnem
hanc inconstantiam temporum vagam adhuc et incertam
in ordinem statae definitionis coegit, adnitente sibi M.
Flavio scriba, qui scriptos dies singulos ita ad dictatorem
retulit ut et ordo eorum inveniri facillime posset et in-
3 vento certus status perseveraret. ergo C. Caesar exordium novae ordinationis initurus dies omnes qui adhuc
confusionem poterant facere consumpsit, eaque re factum
est ut annus confusionis ultimus in quadringentos quadraginta tres dies protenderetur. post hoc imitatus Aegyptios, solos divinarum rerum omnium conscios, ad numerum solis, qui diebus trecentis sexaginta quinque et qua-
4 drante cursum conficit, annum dirigere contendit. nam
sicut lunaris annus mensis est, quia luna paulo minus
quam mensem in zodiaci circumitione consumit, ita solis
annus hoc dierum numero colligendus est quem peragit
dum ad id signum se denuo vertit ex quo digressus est,
unde annus vertens vocatur, et habetur magnus, cum
5 lunae annus brevis putetur. horum Vergilius utrumque complexus est:

Interea magnum sol circumvolvitur annum.

hinc et Ateius Capito annum a circuitu temporis putat
dictum, quia veteres an pro circum ponere solebant, ut
Cato in Originibus: *arator an terminum*, id est circum ter-
6 minum, et ambire dicitur pro circumire. Iulius igitur Caesar decem dies observationi veteri super adiecit, ut annum
trecenti sexaginta quinque dies, quibus sol zodiacum
lustrat, efficerent, et ne quadrans deesset, statuit ut quarto quoque anno sacerdotes, qui curabant mensibus ac
diebus, unum intercalarent diem, eo scilicet mense ac loco
quo etiam apud veteres mensis intercalabatur id est ante

quinque ultimos Februarii mensis dies, idque bissextum
7 censuit nominandum. dies autem decem, quos ab eo addi-
tos diximus, hac ordinatione distribuit. in Ianuarium et
Sextilem et Decembrem binos dies inseruit, in Aprilem
autem Iunium Septembrem Novembrem singulos; sed
neque mensi Februario addidit diem, ne deum inferum
religio immutaretur, et Martio Maio Quintili Octobri ser-
vavit pristinum statum, quod satis pleno erant numero, id
8 est dierum singulorum tricenorumque. ideo et septimanas
habent nonas, sicut Numa constituit, quia nihil in his
Iulius mutavit: sed Ianuarius Sextilis December, quibus
Caesar binos dies addidit, licet tricenos singulos habere
post Caesarem coeperint, quintanas tamen habent nonas, et
ab idibus illis sequentes kalendae in undevicesimum rever-
tuntur, quia Caesar quos addidit dies neque ante nonas
neque ante idus inserere voluit, ne nonarum aut iduum
religionem, quae stato erat die, novella comperendina-
9 tione corrumperet. sed nec post idus mox voluit inserere,
ne feriarum quarumque violaretur indictio, sed peractis
cuiusque mensis feriis locum diebus advenis fecit. et
Ianuario quidem dies quos dicimus quartum et tertium
kalendas Februarias dedit, Aprili sextum kalendas Maias,
Iunio tertium kalendas Iulias, Augusto quartum et tertium kalendas Septembres, Septembri tertium kalendas
Octobres, Novembri tertium kalendas Decembres, Decem-
10 bri vero quartum et tertium kalendas Ianuarias. ita
factum est ut, cum omnes hi menses, quibus dies addidit,
ante hanc ordinationem habuissent mensis sequentis kalendas ad septimum decimum revertentes, postea ex
augmento additorum dierum hi qui duos acceperunt
ad nonum decimum, qui vero unum, ad octavum decimum
11 haberent reditum kalendarum. feriarum tamen cuiusque
mensis ordo servatus est. nam sicui fere tertius ab idibus
dies festus aut feriatus fuit et tunc a. d. sextum decimum
dicebatur, etiam post augmentum dierum eadem religio
servata est, ut tertio ab idibus die celebraretur, licet ab
incremento non iam a. d. sextum decimum kalendas sed
a. d. septimum decimum, si unus, aut a. d. octavum
12 decimum, si duo sunt additi, diceretur. nam ideo novos

dies circa finem cuiusque mensis inseruit, ubi finem omnium quae in mense erant repperit feriarum, adiectosque
omnes a se dies fastos notavit, ut maiorem daret actioni-
bus libertatem, et non solum nullum nefastum sed nec
comitialem quemquam de adiectis diebus instituit, ne
13 ambitionem magistratuum augeret adiectio. sic annum
civilem Caesar habitis ad limam dimensionibus constitutum edicto palam posito publicavit; et error huc usque
stare potuisset, ni sacerdotes sibi errorem novum ex
ipsa emendatione fecissent. nam cum oporteret diem qui
ex quadrantibus confit quarto quoque anno confecto
antequam quintus inciperet intercalare, illi quarto non
14 peracto sed incipiente intercalabant. hic error sex et
triginta annis permansit, quibus annis intercalati sunt
dies duodecim cum debuerint intercalari novem. sed hunc
quoque errorem sero deprehensum correxit Augustus,
qui annos duodecim sine intercalari die transigi iussit,
ut illi tres dies qui per annos triginta et sex vitio sacer-
dotalis festinationis excreverant sequentibus annis duode-
15 cim nullo die intercalato devorarentur. post hoc unum
diem secundum ordinationem Caesaris quinto quoque incipiente anno intercalari iussit et omnem hunc ordinem ae-
reae tabulae ad aeternam custodiam incisione mandavit.

22. Servius, *Aen.* 5.49:

NISI FALLOR non quasi nescius dixit, sed propter anni confusionem, quae erat apud maiores. nam ante Caesarem qui
nobis anni rationem composuit, quam hodieque servamus,
intercalabantur decem dies, ut etiam in Verrinis legimus
scilicet lunae non congruente ratione. (Servius or his source
must be thinking of *Verr.* 2.2.129, in which Cicero describes
the Greek method of intercalation. The passage has no bearing on the Roman method. Where Servius got the idea that
the Romans ever intercalated ten days, I cannot discover,
but he may have confused intercalation with the ten days
which Caesar added to the year.)

23. *Dig.* 50.16.98 (Celsus):

Cum bisextum kalendis (kalendas?) est, nihil refert, utrum
priore an posteriore die quis natus sit, et deinceps sextum

[159]

kalendas eius natalis dies est: nam id biduum pro uno die habetur. sed posterior dies intercalatur, non prior: ideo quo anno intercalatum non est sexto kalendas natus, cum bisextum kalendis (kalendas?) est priorem diem natalem habet. Cato putat mensem intercalarem additicium esse: omnesque eius dies pro momento temporis observat extremoque diei mensis Februarii adtribuit Quintus Mucius. Mensis autem intercalaris constat ex diebus viginti octo.

It is clear from the evidence given above that in the pre-Julian calendar the intercalary month was inserted after the Terminalia, *a.d. VII Kal. Mart.* (February 23)[1] and that the Regifugium and Equirria, which in ordinary years were celebrated on *a.d. VI* and *a.d. III Kal. Mart.* (February 24 and 27), were celebrated on *a.d. VI* and *a.d. III Kal. Mart. mense intercalario.*[2] So much is generally agreed,[3] but the length of

[1] See above, in the statement of evidence, items 8, 10, 11, 19 (section 6), 21 (sections 13.14f. and 14.6).

[2] The Regifugium is listed in the intercalary month in *Ant. Mai.* The last days of the month are missing, but, if the Regifugium is given, the Equirria must have been too.

[3] For a slight variation on this pattern, see Mommsen's theory discussed below. A. Magdelain ("Cinq jours épagomènes à Rome?" *REL* 40 [1962] 201-227) has suggested that, until the beginning of the year shifted from March to January (which he assumes happened in 153 B.C.), the Terminalia was the last day of February, and the five days which followed, including the Regifugium and the Equirria, were epagomenal, that is, independent of any month, like the last five days of the Egyptian year which had 12 months of 30 days each. He thinks that in intercalary years 22 or 23 days were inserted between the Terminalia and the epagomenal days. He recognizes that such a scheme would be inconsistent with a true lunar calendar, and assumes that the pre-Julian calendar was preceded by a calendar in which the months were not lunar, but arbitrary divisions of time. Aside from the author's interpretation of texts, which fails to convince me, I find two major weaknesses in his argument. In the first place it leaves no room in the development of the Roman calendar for a true lunar year based on observation, although the ceremonies of the Kalends and the length of the pre-Julian year indicate that they must have grown out of such a year. In the second place, if the epagomenal days were not assimilated into February until after 153 B.C., they would surely have been recorded, or at least mentioned, in the *Fasti* of Fulvius, which was written in the early second century B.C. It would be strange if all knowledge of such an exotic detail had disappeared, especially when the change would have been made during the lifetime of some of the writers who provide us with other data about the calendar. Magdelain bases his argument primarily on Celsus' quotations of Cato and Mucius (see above, item 23), which seem to me

the intercalary month has been the subject of dispute. We are posed with the problem of reconciling the fact that *Ant. Mai.* gives us an intercalary month of 27 days with the statements of Censorinus (item 19, section 6) and Macrobius (item 21, section 13.12) that 22 or 23 days alternately were inserted in February after the Terminalia, and that the last five days of February followed these intercalated days, a process which would produce intercalary months of alternately 27 or 28 days. Before the discovery of *Ant. Mai.*, most scholars accepted the idea that the intercalary month always began on the day after the Terminalia and varied from 27 to 28 days.[4] There is, however, evidence that the month did not always begin on the same day. Livy in one passage (item 11) says that it began *postridie Terminalia*, but in another (item 10) he reports: *tertio die post Terminalia kalendae intercalariae fuere*, that is, the month began on the day after February 24, instead of the day after the 23rd. The simplest interpretation of these assorted bits of evidence is that the intercalary month always had 27 days,[5] but when it was desirable to add 23 days, instead of 22, to the year, February was allowed to continue through the 24th, instead of stopping on the 23rd. In this case, the 24th would have been an ordinary day, and the Regifugium would have been celebrated, as in other intercalary years, on *a.d. VI Kal. Mart. mense intercalario*.[6] This last point is, I think, demonstrated by the fact that Livy (item 10) identifies the intercalary Kalends

---

to deal only with the legal problem of the person who was born on the *bisextum* or in the intercalary month, and to have no wider application. He quotes Varro's statement (see above, item 8) that the Terminalia was the last day of the year, but omits the last clause, which seems to limit the statement to intercalary years. Many of the points made by Magdelain, including his association of the five days with the length of the interregnum, were made by E. T. Merrill, "The Roman Calendar and the Regifugium," *CP* 19 (1924) 20-39.

[4] This interpretation was given by Ideler, in his *Handbuch der mathematischen und technischen Chronologie* (Berlin 1826) 2.56-64, which was for a long time the basic work in its field.

[5] When Celsus (see above, item 23) says it has twenty-eight days, he must be referring to the Julian calendar. Cf. Mommsen (*RC*² 23) who cites the Greek version in which *mensis intercalaris* is translated as February.

[6] Cf. Degrassi, p. 315 and my article "The Intercalary Month in the Pre-Julian Calendar," *Collection Latomus* 58 (1962): *Hommages à Albert Grenier*, 1174-1178.

[161]

of this type as *tertio die post Terminalia*, rather than *postridie Regifugium*, which would have been the natural expression, if the Regifugium had been held on the 24th. Such a conclusion is further supported by the fact that *Ant. Mai.* records the Regifugium in the intercalary month, which would have been misleading if it had not regularly been celebrated then.

If this interpretation is correct we can see why, even though February often lost only four days, Varro (item 8) can say that the last five days were deducted from February, and Macrobius (item 21, section 13.15) says that five days were added to the intercalary month.[7] These statements have been taken as evidence that the length of the intercalary month varied, but since all the days after the Ides of the month were dated *a.d. Kal. Mart.*, it would never have occurred to anyone that its last five might be the lost days of February, if they had not been identified by the celebration of the Regifugium and the Equirria. Since the Regifugium was held on *a.d. VI Kal. Mart.* both in ordinary and in intercalated years, it and the four following days in the intercalary month would naturally appear to be identical with the similarly dated days in February. The true situation would be further obscured by the change which intercalation would produce in the dates of all the days after the Ides of February. Either the 24th or the 23rd would become *pridie Kal. Interk.* and the preceding days would run back to either *a.d. XII* or *XI Kal. Interk.*

It is not surprising that Censorinus and Macrobius should have made a mistake in trying to explain the peculiar features of a calendar with which they had never lived. It is quite probable that they had never even seen the pre-Julian *Fasti*, which must have disappeared very rapidly as soon as they became obsolete. That Varro should have erred in dealing with facts which must have been familiar to him from boyhood seems more peculiar, until we consider the context of his statement that five days are taken from February. He is explaining the name of the Terminalia. Ignoring the day's connection with the god Terminus and the rites connected with terminal stones, he asserts that the Terminalia was established as the last day of

---

[7] Mommsen argued (*RC*[2] 22) that these passages referred only to the years in which 22 days were added.

the year,[8] explaining that February had been the twelfth month and that when intercalation takes place, the last five days are subtracted. It would have been awkward for Varro to add "but of course sometimes February loses only four days and then the Terminalia isn't the last day." It was perhaps the same tenderness for his derivation which led him to omit the Regifugium from the chronological list of *feriae* which he was presenting. His reference to the Equirria, which follows, might be taken by his readers to refer not to the *feriae* of February 27 but to that of March 14. If my argument as to the length of the intercalary month is correct, Varro's insistence on his five days and his derivation of the Terminalia may have been the ultimate cause of the confusion of later writers. I have the impression that one did not lightly question his authority.

The theory as to the method of intercalation which I have presented is based on the scheme given by Mommsen in his *Römische Chronologie*[2] (18-25), with one major difference. He believed that, when the intercalary month began after the 24th of February, the Regifugium was celebrated on its usual day, February 24, not in the intercalary month.[9] The discovery of *Ant. Mai.*, with the Regifugium in the intercalary month, led Mancini, in his publication of *Ant. Mai* in *NS*

[8] Although in literature the god Terminus was associated with periods of time, the ritual of the Terminalia, in so far as we know it, is related only to the cult of the boundary stones (*termini*) (Ovid, *Fasti* 2.639-682; Paulus, 505 L.; Prudentius, *Contra Symm.* 2.1006-1011; Plutarch, *Numa* 16.1, *Q.R.* 15). Anyone who has ever tried to survey boundary lines will understand why this rite should have been carried out at the end of the winter, when the undergrowth is lowest and least likely to obscure markers. If the rite really had had anything to do with the end of the year, it probably would have been moved, in spite of Terminus' notorious stubbornness. Varro is the only writer who states explicitly that the Terminalia was ever the last day of the year. Ovid says only *tu quoque sacrorum, Termine, finis eras* (*Fasti* 2.50). Augustine says that Janus and Terminus are connected with *initia rerum temporalium finesque* (*C.D.* 7.7). Modern scholars who have accepted Varro's statement for other than intercalary years do not seem to realize the calendaric problems which it raises.

[9] This theory was accepted by a few, notably Marquardt (*Römische Staatsverwaltung* [Leipzig 1885] 3.284f.), and is the basis of the discussion of the calendar of 65 B.C. to 45 B.C. in Drumann-Groebe, *Geschichte Roms*[2] (Leipzig 1906) 3.755-827. Even after the discovery of *Ant. Mai.* it was rejected by Wissowa ("Bruchstücke des Römischen Festkalender," *Hermes* 58 [1923] 392) and by Leuze, 132f.

(1921) 122-124, to emend Mommsen's scheme by transferring the Regifugium to this position in all intercalary years. At the same time, however, Mancini made the impossible suggestion that the last days of February became the *first* days of the intercalary month, and that the Regifugium was moved in order to prevent its coinciding with either the last day of February or the intercalary Kalends. He had not observed that there is no way of differentiating one undated day from another except by the events which occur on it. Mancini, in my opinion, was correct in his location of the Regifugium, but for the wrong reason.

Mommsen developed his theory of intercalation in order to explain the two passages in Livy cited above, and to refute the explanation of these which was then popular. Ideler had noted that the intercalary Kalends might fall on the day after February 24th, but interpreted this as an example of an unusual type of intercalation mentioned by Dio and described by Macrobius.[10] The latter states (item 21, section 13.16-19) that the Romans believed that, if the first day of the year coincided with *nundinae*, the whole rest of the year would be marked by misfortune, as was the case in 78 B.C., and that they tried to prevent *nundinae* from coinciding with the Nones, in order to avoid a dangerously large crowd. In order to keep *nundinae* away from the first day of the year, or from any Nones, those who supervised the calendar were allowed to intercalate at their discretion the 355th day of the year (the one day by which the pre-Julian year exceeded the 354-day year of the Greeks), as long as they put it *in medio Terminaliorum vel mensis intercalaris*. This, he adds, is why certain ancient writers report that the Romans had had an intercalary day as well as an intercalary month. Dio, in reporting the events of 52 B.C., comments on the unlucky coincidence of January 1 with the market day (item 15). Later (item 17) he tells us that a day was intercalated in 41 B.C. to prevent, in 40 B.C., the occurrence of the coincidence, which had been carefully avoided since early times. He adds that this day must have been dropped out again, to preserve harmony with the Julian calendar. On the basis of these statements Ideler argued that, in the year in

[10] See reference in n. 4.

which, according to Livy, the intercalary month began after February 24, an extra day had been inserted for the purpose and in the way described by Dio and Macrobius, and that this day would later have been dropped out. It is difficult to see why the Romans should have devised such an extraordinarily inconvenient way of coping with their problem, when they could simply have changed the day of the *nundinae* when necessary. In fact, Dio says (60.24) that the day of the *nundinae* actually was changed in A.D. 44, on account of "certain religious rites," and adds that this happened often. Ideler's theory, however, provided scholars of the nineteenth century with a splendid basis for the ingeniously complicated calculations with which books on the chronology of the Roman republic abound.

The theory that in the pre-Julian calendar a single day could be intercalated assumes that the superstition described by Macrobius and Dio was prevalent in the period of the republic, and that the special form of intercalation to which it gave rise was practiced from an early period. Actually, as Mommsen pointed out, there is no evidence for this assumption except the passage in Livy (item 10), which is not specific, and can be interpreted quite differently. The first date mentioned in connection with the superstition is 78 B.C., the year of the *tumultus Lepidianus* referred to by Macrobius. Since it was the coincidence of January 1 and *nundinae* in that year that confirmed the superstition, it is obvious that no special intercalation was used to avoid it. The same is true of the year 52 B.C., mentioned by Dio.[11] It is not until 41 B.C., after the introduction of the Julian calendar, that we hear of any precautions being taken to avoid the coincidence. It is true that Dio says in his account of 41 B.C. that it had been avoided from of old (ὅπερ ἀπὸ τοῦ πάνυ ἀρχαίου σφόδρα ἐφυλάσσετο), but his own statement in relation to 52 B.C. belies him. Evidence that the Romans of the republic did not intercalate single days, as well as a month, may be found in a passage in Cicero (*Verr.* 2.2.129), in which he explains in great detail the Greek method of adding and then subtracting days in order to adjust

[11] It is perhaps worth noting that 52 B.C. was an intercalary year. See p. 171.

their calendar. If in 70 B.C. the Romans had been used to a similar system, Cicero's careful explanation would have been unnecessary.

There are, moreover, signs of confusion in Macrobius' statement that make one hesitate to accept it at its face value. He identifies the odd day which may be intercalated as the 355th day of the year, without apparently realizing that, according to his own previous calculations, that day was part of the regular pre-Julian year and could not therefore be added to it. The phrase by which he defines the location of the intercalated day, *in medio Terminaliorum vel mensis intercalaris*, inspires the feeling, not unfamiliar to his readers, that he was copying, or miscopying, a source, without any real grasp of what it meant. Inasmuch as the Terminalia was a single day, I do not see how another day could be put in the middle of it. The whole phrase is hard to interpret. If he meant that the day was put between the Terminalia and the intercalary month, he chose a very peculiar way of saying it, and I do not think that the Latin as it stands can be forced into that meaning.[12]

That the Romans of the first century B.C. did entertain superstitious fear of the coincidence of *nundinae* with the

[12] If the text is emended (see Magdelain, *op.cit.* [n. 3] 210, n. 1) to read: *in medio Terminaliorum ⟨et⟩ mensis intercalaris* and *in medio* is translated "between," then *in medio* followed by two nouns in the genitive must be taken as synonymous with *inter* governing two nouns in the accusative. I have not, however, been able to discover in classical Latin an example of *in medio* used for *inter*. If, as originally suggested by Dodwell (cited by Ginzel, 2.245, n. 1) we read *in medio Terminaliorum et Regifugii vel mensis intercalaris*, we have the same problem of Latinity and a further ambiguity. Ginzel seems to interpret this as meaning that the day was placed between the Terminalia and the Regifugium, *or* in the intercalary month, while Magdelain implies that it was put between the *feriae* in ordinary years, or between the Terminalia and the intercalary Kalends. As the text stands, the only possible explanation, as far as I can see, of what the Latin actually says is that Macrobius thought the Terminalia lasted for several days, and that the extra day could be put in the middle of them, or in the intercalary month. Just as the seven days of the Saturnalia had embraced and obscured the *feriae* which followed its original single day, the Terminalia in the fourth century A.D. may have come to be used collectively of the period which also, according to the *Fasti* of Philocalus, contained the Feralia (February 21), the Caristia (February 22), the Regifugium (February 24), in intercalary years the *bisextum*, and Ludi circenses (February 25), and the *natalis divi Constantini* (February 27, replacing the Equirria).

Kalends of January seems clear from the evidence of Dio. I would, however, be inclined to attribute the origin of this superstition not to native belief, but to the influence of astrology and its teaching on the lucky or unlucky character of the days of the planetary week, according to which the character of the first day of the year affected the whole year.[13] The planetary week was known in Rome certainly by the Augustan period.[14] It would not be surprising if the steadily increasing immigration into Rome from the eastern end of the Mediterranean had early in the first century introduced the superstitions connected with the week. In their new environment these would easily be adapted to Roman institutions such as the *nundinae*.

In view, therefore, of the lack of evidence prior to 78 B.C. that the superstition existed in Rome, and since there is a possible explanation for its origin in the first century, I prefer to agree with Mommsen in rejecting the theory that during the republic the Romans ever intercalated single days in order to avoid unlucky coincidences. It is, however, possible that, if the intercalary year began sometimes on the day after the Terminalia and sometimes on the next day, the recurrence of the extra day after the Terminalia might have suggested the existence of an intercalary day alluded to by Macrobius. Writers of the Empire would be all the more prepared to accept this idea, because, in the Julian calendar, the single intercalary day, the *bisextum*, was inserted between the Terminalia and the Regifugium.

For the historian it is perhaps less important to determine the precise length of the intercalary month, or the existence of an intercalary day, then to find out how often intercalation

---

[13] For a detailed account of the relation between New Year's Day, the day of the week, and the consequent character of the year, see Lydus, *De Mensibus* 4.10 (75f. Wuensch). Cf. F. Boll, *Sternglaube und Sterndeutung* (Leipzig 1926) 159, 178f. When this particular relationship was invented by the astrologers is uncertain, but the general principle of chronochrators seems to be late Hellenistic. The idea that the planet of New Year's Day would affect the character of the whole year certainly could have developed quite quickly from the concept of the relation of the planet to the day of the week.

[14] See Degrassi, p. 326 and "Un Nuovo Frammento di Calendario Romano e la Settimana Planetaria di Sette Giorni," *Atti del III Congresso Internazionale di Epigrafia Greca e Latina (1957)* (Roma 1959) 95-104 = *Scritti Vari di Antichità* (Rome 1962), 1.681-691.

took place and whether it followed a regular pattern. Modern scholars have expended enormous efforts on this problem, winding their way through intricate and detailed calculations to establish systems of intercalation.[15] Unfortunately no two of these systems agree, and historians have had to accept one or another as the basis of a chronology. This lack of agreement in a field that has been studied for centuries suggests that the evidence now available is inadequate for a solution. Indeed, since the late nineteenth century no major effort has been made to solve the problem.[16] All I hope to do in this discussion is to point out the reasons why the problem is difficult.

If there is one thing on which the ancient evidence agrees, it is that Roman intercalation was highly irregular until the introduction of the Julian calendar. The ancient authors who try to explain this situation attribute it not so much to the method of intercalation itself as to superstition, or to the negligence of the pontifices and to their deliberate manipulation for ulterior motives (items 1, 13, 14, 18, 19, 20, 21). While I hold no brief for the pontifices, who were surely sometimes influenced by political or financial considerations, I feel that so sweeping an accusation is hardly fair to them. We all have a tendency to suspect dishonesty or self-interest in officials who are probably only ignorant or incompetent. Censorinus and Macrobius tell us that intercalation was supposed to take place in alternate years, and indeed the length of the intercalary period suggests that this was the original intention of those who devised the method.[17] If, however, either my own or the generally accepted interpretation of the republican method of intercalation is correct, it would have been quite impossible for the pontifices to have intercalated regularly every other year without throwing the calendar into far worse confusion than

[15] For a bibliography of work on Roman chronology since A.D. 1540, see Soltau, *RömChron* 13-18. For a discussion of the major theories of the nineteenth century, see Ginzel, 2.218-273 *passim*.

[16] Cf. Drumann-Groebe, *Geschichte Roms*[2], 3.760: "man wird es nicht für Zufall halten dürfen, dass seit dem Jahre 1890 niemand mehr zu der Frage sich geäussert hat. Es scheint, dass wir an dem Punkte angelangt sind, bis zu dem wir mit den heutigen Mitteln kommen können."

[17] For the significance of the number of days intercalated and the errors involved, see Ch. 1, p. 17.

they did. This is because, even if they intercalated only 22 days as a rule, they would still be adding three more days every four years to the calendar year than they should, so that the calendar year would be moving slowly forward in relation to the solar year. The Kalends of January, if it fell on January 1 of our reckoning in one year, would in the next few years fall on January 2, 3, 4, and so on. This gradual shift would not have been obvious at first, I imagine, to people experimenting with a new system, because the slow increment of single days would have been obscured by the fact that in intercalary years the calendar would leap forward in a huge jump and then swing back in the next, ordinary, year. But sooner or later it must have dawned on the pontifices, not to mention all the rest of the Romans, that ceremonies associated with spring were being celebrated in the winter,[18] and that this was the result of over-intercalation. Macrobius tells us (item 21, section 13.13) that in order to counteract this error they devised a cycle of 24 years in the last eight of which they intercalated only 66 days (3 x 22?) instead of 90. No other writer mentions this cycle and I suspect it originated in the mind of some theorist who was trying to explain how the system might have been made to work, and that Macrobius, or his source, assumed that it actually had been used. It seems to me more probable that the pontifices followed the much simpler course of omitting an intercalation or two when they observed that the calendar was inconveniently behind the seasons. This would have kept the calendar in an approximately correct relation to the solar year, and it is clear that, until Caesar spoiled them, the Romans were quite satisfied with an approximate relation.

The pontifices may have been able to keep the calendar in satisfactory order by this empirical method for a long time, but by the beginning of the second century intercalation had obviously been omitted too often. As is pointed out elsewhere

[18] Some of the sources imply that the error grew to the point at which winter months were coming in the summer (item 18), or autumn in the spring (item 20). This seems to me an exaggeration of Suetonius' statement (item 14) that the harvest and vintage *feriae* were not coming in the summer and autumn. I can find no evidence for an error of more than four months, which is bad enough.

(see p. 102), in 190 B.C. the calendar was four months ahead of the year. We do not know whether this resulted from occasional omissions over a long period, or from complete omission over a shorter period, nor do we know why the omission took place. Macrobius, without giving any date, says: *fuit tempus cum propter superstitionem intercalatio omissa est* (item 21, section 14.1). De Sanctis has suggested that the superstition in question might have been related to the hoped-for end of the Second Punic War (cf. Livy, 29.14.1), and that the omission was begun in 203 B.C., to speed the year in which the war would end.[19] He explains the continuation of the omission thereafter simply as the result of inertia. There is another simple reason why intercalation should have been allowed to lapse occasionally. The pontifices apparently did not have to announce whether or not there was to be an intercalary month until the last possible moment (see item 13), presumably the Nones of February. This would be inconvenient enough when Rome's activities were limited to a fairly small area, but when she began to acquire increasing territories, the inconvenience must have increased correspondingly. Generals commanding armies overseas and provincial governors would not hear of the pontifices' decision for weeks or months after the fact. The uncertainties created by this situation are illustrated by some of Cicero's letters from Cilicia (items 3-6). One can imagine the rage of a provincial quaestor who had to correct the dates in all his records for a couple of months when he heard of the intercalation. Caesar's experience with this nuisance in Gaul and elsewhere may have had more to do with his reform of the calendar than did his zeal for scientific accuracy.

These considerations lead me to the unhappy conclusion that, unless a flood of new evidence is forthcoming, it will not be possible to determine, in more than a few cases, which years of the Roman republic were intercalary and which were not. Consequently we cannot as a rule expect to be able to work out a precise equation between dates according to the pre-

[19] See pp. 376-379 of his useful *Appendice Cronologica* in *Storia dei Romani* 4.1 (Turin 1923) 368-406.

Julian calendar and dates in the Julian or Gregorian calendars, unless we have external data such as the solar eclipse of 190 B.C. It may however be worthwhile to list here those years for which there is definite ancient evidence of intercalation:

260 B.C.   *Fasti Triumphales*, Degrassi, *I.I.* 13.1, p. 548
236 B.C.   *Fasti Triumphales, ibid.*, p. 549
189 B.C.   Livy, 37.59.2
177 B.C.   *Fasti Triumphales*, Degrassi, *op.cit.*, p. 555
170 B.C.   Livy, 43.11.13
167 B.C.   Livy, 45.44.3
166 B.C.   *Fasti Triumphales*, Degrassi, *op.cit.*, p. 556
? 164 B.C.   *SIG*[3] 664. The *senatus consultum de Delo* refers to a meeting of the senate called on the intercalary Ides by the praetor Q. Minucius, but the year of his praetorship is not certain. See Broughton, *MRR* 1.440, n. 1.
83 B.C.   Cicero, *pro Quinctio* 79
52 B.C.   Asconius, *In Milonianam* 30, 31.
46 B.C.   Item 14. For the extra intercalation in this *annus confusionis ultimus*, see also items 19 and 21, section 14.3f.

I would suggest that to these there might be added the years in which the *Fasti Triumphales* record triumphs as taking place on the Quirinalia or the Terminalia, instead of dating them in the usual way. These are the only *feriae* used in this way in the *Fasti*, and there must be some reason for the peculiar usage. When Cicero uses the Terminalia as a date in a letter, one may argue that it was because he did not know whether the pontifices had intercalated,[20] but in the case of a record made after the event this explanation will not hold. If, however, the intercalary month could begin after either February 23 or February 24, dating by the *feriae*, which at least always came on the same day after the Ides, would be more precise than dating by the days preceding the intercalary Kalends. For one of these years, 167 B.C., Livy actually dates the triumph on the Quirinalia (45.43.1) and later tells us that the year was

[20] Cf. Degrassi, p. 329.

intercalary (item 11), which, while it is not conclusive, is corroborative evidence. The years in question are 361, 350, 322, 276, 273, 175, and 167 B.C. On the basis of the same reasoning I would also add 94 B.C., on the evidence of the date *a.[d.]* *X Termina[lia]* in an inscription which records a decree of that year (*CIL* 1² 2.682; Degrassi, *ILLRP*, 719).

APPENDIX 2

THE CHARACTERS OF THE DAYS

To those familiar with the *Fasti*, the following discussion may
seem unnecessarily detailed, but I have so often had difficulty in
understanding the reasoning behind readings in the publication
of inscriptions that I felt it would be helpful to be explicit.
For the convenience of the reader, each day is identified by
the modern date, in Arabic numerals. Immediately after this
date I have given the character letter which I believe the day
carried in the republican calendar. This is followed by its
Roman date, including when necessary the equivalent date in
the Julian calendar. Below is given the evidence of the individual *Fasti*, including notations which explain a change in the
character. The *Fasti* are identified by the abbreviations used
by Degrassi in his publication *Inscriptiones Italiae* XIII, 2. For
their full titles and for variant titles used in other publications
see pp. 187-90.

For those not familiar with inscriptions I should explain
that square brackets indicate that the words or letters which
they enclose have been supplied by the editor where parts of
the inscription are missing or illegible. Letters in parentheses
are the completion of words which occur in the inscription in
abbreviations. Common abbreviations which have not been filled
out are:

ex s(*enatus*) c(*onsulto*)   *cos.* = *consul* or *consulibus*
dedic(*ata*) or *dedic*(*atum*)   *pontif*(*ex*) *max*(*imus*)
trib(*unicia*) *potest*(*ate*)   *imp*(*erator*)

GROUP I
(Days changed to NP in the Julian calendar)

January 16 **C**
   (*a.d. XV Kal. Febr.* = *a.d. XVII Kal. Febr. anni Iuliani*)

    NP *Feriae* [*e*]*x s.c. quod eo die aedis* C[*o*]*ncordiae in foro
       dedic. est.* VERUL.
    C   ANT. MAI., MAFF., PRAEN., CAER., OPP.

January 17 **C**

(*a.d. XIV Kal. Febr. = a.d. XVI Kal. Febr. anni Iuliani*)

NP *Feriae ex s.c. quod eo die Augusta nupsit divo Aug[us]t(o).* VERUL.

C ANT. MAI., MAFF., PRAEN., CAER., OPP.

February 5 **N**

(*Non. Febr.*)

NP *Feriae ex s.c. quod eo die imperator Caesar Augustus pontifex maximus trib. potest. XXI cos. XIII a senatu populoque Romano pater patriae appellatus.* PRAEN.

No other *Fasti* preserve a character letter for this day, but it must originally have been N, because Nones are always either F or N, and when in other months they begin, or form part of, a series of N days, they are always N themselves. Since every day in February through the 14th is N, the Nones also must have been N.

February 9 **N**

(*a.d. V Id. Febr.*)

NP VERUL.

N ANT. MAI., MAFF.

Verul. gives no explanation for NP, and the letter may, as the original editors suggest, be a stone cutter's mistake, but such a mistake is unlikely in the middle of a series of N days. Probably it marks an anniversary for which we have as yet no evidence.

March 6 **C**

(*pridie Non. Mart.*)

NP *hoc die Caesar pontif. maxim. fact. est.* MAFF. *Fe[riae ex s.c. quod eo die i]mp. Caesar August. pont. m[ax. factus est Quiri]nio et Valgio cos. II viri ob [eam rem immolant p]opulus coronatus feriatus [agit.]* PRAEN.

In all other months except February and July, in which it is part of an N series, the day before the Nones is C. This was probably the case in March also. If the *comitia sacerdotum* which elected Augustus *pontifex maximus* on this day in 12 B.C. followed the rules for the *comitia tributa* from which it was derived (see p. 37), the evidence of the *Fasti* would not only explain why the day became NP but would support the identification of its character as C.

March 27 **C**

(*a.d. VI Kal. Apr.*)

F *Fer(iae) quod eo die C. Caes. vicit Alexand.* CAER.

NP *hoc die Caesar Alexand. recepit.* MAFF. NP *feriae quod eo die C. [Caesar] Alexandriam recepit.* VERUL.

March 27 shares a peculiarity with August 9 and September 3 and 23. All are *feriae* commemorating events related to the imperial family, but while in the majority of Julian Fasti they are NP, in a few they are F. *Ant. Mai.* preserves only September 3, there marked C. September 23 must have been C in the republican calendar because on that day the *comitia* was held in 167 B.C. (Livy, 43.16.12). If any of these days had been F in the republican calendar they would have been completely inconsistent with its pattern of F days. Nevertheless Mommsen (*CIL* 1². 1, p. 295) and Wissowa (RK² 572, 582, 586), before the discovery of *Ant. Mai.*, classified all four republican days as F, while Leuze (108 n. 2, 115, 116 n. 3), discussing the new evidence of *Ant. Mai.* for September 3, was inclined to think they had all been C. Degrassi in his pre-Julian calendar lists September 3 and 23 as C and March 27 and August 9 as F (344; cf. 331, 345). He explains the F assigned by some *Fasti* to the September days by suggesting that Caesar had given them this character in 45 B.C. (331). This, of course, is possible, but the motive is obscure, and it leaves the abnormality of the other two days even more striking. It seems to me more probable that in the republican calendar all four days had been C, and that the F characters in the Julian Fasti are simply errors. This was the conclusion reached by Leuze who pointed out that in the Julian calendar the nundinal letters for March 27 and September 23 are both F, and might have been repeated by a careless stone cutter.

April 6 N
(*a.d. VIII Id. Apr.*)

NP MAFF. NP *f(eriae) q(uod) e(o) d(ie) C. Caesar C. f. in Africa regem [Iubam devicit]* PRAEN.
N ANT. MAI.

The character N harmonizes with that of the series which begins on the Nones of April.

April 27 C
(*a.d. IV Kal. Mai.*)

Note that this day did not change its date in the Julian calendar, although by our reckoning it is April 28, because Caesar added his extra day, marked F, to April before *a.d. V Kal. Mai.* so that only the previous days were affected. Degrassi gives it as April 28.

NP MAFF. NP *feriae ex s.c. quod eo* [*die signu*]*m et* [*ara*] *Vestae in domu imp. Caesaris Augu*[*sti po*]*ntif. ma*[*x.*] *dedicata est Quirinio et Valgio cos.* PRAEN.

C ESQ. C *fer*(*iae*) *q*(*uod*) *e*(*o*) *d*(*ie*) *sig*(*num*) *Vestae in domo P*(*alatina*) *dedic.* CAER.

C is the character which fits the republican pattern of days. The designer of *Caer.* seems to have forgotten to use the new character letter.

May 12 C
(*a.d. IV Id. Mai.*)

NP *Lud*(*i*) *Mart*(*i*) *in circ*(*o*). MAFF.
C ANT. MAI., VEN., TUSC.

On these games, see Degrassi, pp. 456f.

June 26 C
(*a.d. V Kal. Quinct.* = *a.d. VI Kal. Iul. anni Iuliani*)

NP *Fer*(*iae*) *ex s.* [*c. q*]*uod e*[*o*] *die* [*imp. Caes*(*ar*)] *Augus*[*tus ado*]*p*[*tav*]*it* [*sibi*] *filiu*[*m Ti. Caesarem*] *Aelio* [*et Sentio cos.*]. AMIT.
C VEN., MAFF., ESQ., MAG.

July 4 N
(*a.d. IV Non. Quinct.*)

NP MAFF. NP *Fer*(*iae*) *ex s.c. q*(*uod*) *e*(*o*) *d*(*ie*) *Ara Pacis Aug*(*ustae*) *in camp*(*o*) *Mar*(*tio*) *constituta est Nerone et Varo cos.* AMIT. NP [*Ara P*]*acis August*(*ae*) [*c*]*onstituta.* ANT. MIN.

Since in the republican calendar all other unnamed days between the 1st and 9th of July are N, the 4th probably was too.

July 12 C
(*a.d. IV Id. Quinct.*)

NP MAFF. NP *Fer*(*iae*) *quod* [*e*]*o die C. Caesar est natus.* AMIT. NP *Divi Iul*(*ii*) *natalis.* ANT. MIN.
C ANT. MAI., TUSC., LATER.

According to Dio (47.18.6) Caesar was actually born on July 13, but the celebration was shifted to the 12th because a Sibylline oracle forbade the worship on the 13th of any god but Apollo, of whose games this was the main day.

August 1 F
(*Kal. Sext.*)

NP *Feriae ex s.c. q*(*uod*) *e*(*o*) *d*(*ie*) *imp. Caesar divi f. rem public(am)* *tristissim[o]* *periculo liberat.* AMIT. NP *F(e-riae)* *ex s.c.* *[quod eo die imp. Caesar rem pu]bli(cam)* *tristiss(imo)* *p[e]riculo [libera]vit.* ARV. MAN. POST. NP *Augustus Alexandream recepit. Ti. Clau[di Caesaris Augusti natalis.]* ANT. MIN. NP *Feria[e ex s.c.] q(uod) e(o) d(ie) imp. Cae[sar Aug. rem publicam tristissimo periculo liberavit.]* PRAEN.

F ARV. MAN. PR.

August 2 F
(a.d. IV Non. Sext.)

NP *Feriae quod eo die C. Caes(ar) C. f. in Hispa(nia) citer(iore) et quod in Ponto eod(em) die regem Pharnacem devicit.* AMIT. NP *Divus Iul(ius) Hisp(ania) vic(it).* ANT. MIN. NP (or N. The edge of the fragment crosses the letter.) *Hoc die [Caesar in Hispania] cit(eriore) vicit.* MAFF.

N *Feriae quod hoc die imp. Caesar Hispaniam citeriorem vicit.* VALL.

F ANT. MAI.

Out of the ten months of the republican year for which the character of the day after the Kalends is known (all except August and September) in seven months it is the same as the Kalends, either F (four times) or N (three times). In March, when the Kalends are NP, the day after is F. In June and October the Kalends are N, and the day after is F. Since according to *Arv. Man. Pr* the Kalends of August were F, it is almost certain that the day after was also F.

August 5 F
(Non. Sext.)

NP ANT. MIN.

F MAFF., AMIT.

See discussion of August 6.

August 6 F
(a.d. VIII Id. Sext.)

NP ANT. MIN.

N VIA GRAZ.

F ANT. MAI., MAFF., VALL., AMIT., LATER.

Ant. Min. gives no explanation for assigning NP to these days, and in the case of August 6 the evidence for F is overwhelming. Moreover, in the eight months in which the characters of these days are certain, the Nones and the day following always have the same character, either

F or N. The Nones are never NP. We may then claim that if August 6 was F, so was August 5. What then accounts for the NP in ANT. MIN? Mommsen attributed it to a festival of the empire for which we have no other evidence, and Degrassi accepts this explanation (pp. 353, 359, 368f.). It seems to me more probable that we have here a mistake on the part of the stone cutter of *Ant. Min.*, who was remarkably careless, capable of omitting one whole day (October 13). In the Julian calendar the sequence of character letters for August 7-10 is C C NP NP, and the letters for August 3 and 4 are both C. If the cutter carved all the character letters, working downwards in the column, before he put in the other entries for each day, his eye could easily have slipped from the C C of August 3 and 4 to the C C of the 7th and 8th, and have continued by giving the NP of the 9th and 10th to the 5th and 6th, instead of the correct F. It is not likely that he would have troubled to correct his slip, inasmuch as he was content to leave E for EN on October 14 and December 12. I am therefore inclined to believe that August 5 and 6 were F, not only in the republican calendar, but in the Julian calendar as well.

August 9   **C**
(*a.d. V Id. Sext.*)

NP VALL. NP *Hoc die Caesar Hispali* [sic, for Pharsali] *vic(it)*. MAFF. NP *Fer(iae) q(uod) e(o) d(ie) C. Caes(ar) C. f. Pharsali devicit*. AMIT. NP *Divus Julius Phars(ali) vicit*. ANT. MIN.
F LATER. [*Feriae*] *quod e(o) d(ie) v[icit C. Caesar Pharsali*]. ALLIF.
   See discussion of March 27.

August 10   **C**
(*a.d. IV Id. Sext.*)

NP *Feriae quod eo die arae Cereri matri et Opi Augustae ex voto suscepto constituta[e] sunt Cretico et Long(o) c[os.]*. AMIT. NP *Feriae. Arae Opis et Cereris in vico iugario constitutae sunt*. VALL. NP *Feriae Cereri et Opi Aug*. ANT. MIN.
C MAFF., ALLIF.

August 28   **C**
(*a.d. III Kal. Sept. = a.d. V Kal. Sept. anni Iuliani*)

NP *H(oc) d(ie) ara Victoriae in curia dedic(ata) est*. MAFF.

NP *Fer(iae) ex [s(enatus) c(onsulto)] q[uo]d e(o) [d(ie) ara Victoriae] de[d]icata est.* VAT.

NF PIGH.*

C ALLIF., PINC.

 * PIGH is known only from a manuscript copy of the original inscription, in which NF occurs where NP is the normal reading, and can safely be ignored.

August 29 C
(*pridie Kal. Sept.*)

NF *Nat(alis) Germanic(i).* PIGH.

C MAFF., MAG., VAT., PINC.

 Note that this day is *pridie Kal. Sept.* in both the republican and the Julian calendars, but becomes August 31 in the Julian calendar, because Caesar inserted two F days before it, thus changing the dates of the preceding days, but leaving the last day of the month unchanged. This is true of the last day of each month to which days were added. For NF, see note on August 28.

September 2 F
(*a.d. IV Non. Sept.*)

NP MAFF., VALL., NP *Feriae ex s.c. imp. Caesaris h(onoris) c(ausa) quod eo die vicit Actium.* ARV. MAN. POST. NP *Fer(iae) ex s.c. quod eo die imp. Caes(ar) divi f. Augustus apud Actium vicit se et Titio cos.* AMIT.

N ANT. MIN.

F ARV. MAN. PR. Probably also ANT. MAI. but only the bottom of the vertical stroke remains.

 Since, if the Kalends are F, the second day of a month is also F (see discussion of August 2) and September 1 is F, September 2 must also be F.

September 3 C
(*a.d. III Non. Sept.*)

NP MAFF., ANT. MIN., NP *Feriae* VALL. NP *Fer(iae) et supplicationes aput omnia pulvinaria quod eo die Caes(ar) divi f. vicit in Sicilia Censorino et Calvis(io) cos.* AMIT. NP *Feriae et supplicationes ad omnia pulvinaria.* ARV. MAN. POST.

F ARV. MAN. PR.

C ANT. MAI.

 For the argument in favor of C, given by *Ant. Mai.*, see the discussion of March 27.

September 12 N
(*pridie Id. Sept.*)

NP VALL. ARV.?
N MAFF., AMIT., SAB., V. DEI SERP.
C ANT. MIN.
F TAUR.

Vall. has no note explaining its NP. Either this is an error, or refers to *feriae* otherwise unknown. The latter is improbable, because *Amit.* and *Ant. Min.* are dated later than *Vall.*, but do not recognize the day as NP. If *Vall.* is incorrect this leaves us with a choice between N, C or F. One would expect it to be C, for there is no other example of a single N day for *pridie Id.* in any month or of an F day on this date. On the other hand, *Ant. Min.* is unreliable, while *Maff.* and *Amit.* have very few identifiable errors, and I see no justification for rejecting their evidence. *Taur.* is so brief that its reliability cannot be determined. Mommsen and Degrassi list the day as N, and I have followed their example, noting the departure from the normal pattern.

September 17 **C**
(*a.d. XIV Kal. Oct.* = *a.d. XV Kal. Oct. anni Iuliani*)

NP *Fer(iae) ex s.c. q(uod) e(o) d(ie) divo Augusto honores caelestes a senatu decreti Sex. Appul(eio) Sex. Pomp(eio) cos.* AMIT., V. DEI SERP. NP [*Augusto honores*] *cael(estes) d[ecreti.]* ANT. MIN.
C MAFF., VALL., SAB.

September 23 **C**
(*a.d. VIII Kal. Oct.* = *a.d. IX Kal. Oct. anni Iuliani*)

NP *h(ic) d(ies) Augusti natalis. lud(i) circ(enses)* MAFF.
NP *F(eriae) ex s.c. q(uod) e(o) d(ie) imp. Caesar Augustus pont. ma[x.] natus est.* ARV. MAN. POST.
NP *Nata. . . .* VALL.
NF *Nat. Aug. Epul.* PIGH.
F ARV. MAN. PR., SAB. F *Fer(iae) ex s.c. quod is dies imp. Caesar(is) natalis est.* PINC.

For the argument in favor of C, see the discussion of March 27. Augustus was born in 63 B.C. and there is no way of telling whether the event actually took place on *a.d. IX Kal. Oct.*, the date recorded in the Julian calendars and in other Latin sources (Velleius, 2.65.2; Suet., *Aug.* 5; Gellius, 15.7.3; *CIL* 6.9254; 12.4333) which would in 63 B.C. have been September 22, or on *a.d. VIII Kal. Oct.*, that is September 23, which became *IX Kal. Oct.* in the Julian calendar. *A.d. VIII Kal. Oct.* (Julian)—September 24 by our reckoning—was sometimes included in the birthday celebration, which leads one to suppose (cf. Mommsen, *CIL* 1².1. pp. 329f. and Degrassi, p. 513) that Augustus was actually born on that date of the republican year, but that he celebrated the anniversary on the new date, *IX Kal. Oct.*, and that the following day was included out of respect for the old date. That some confusion on the point existed is indicated by an inscription from Forum Clodi, dated A.D. 18, which, like one from Narbo (*CIL* 12.4333), orders celebrations for both days, but, contradicting the *Fasti*, identifies *a.d. VIII Kal. Oct.* as the birthday (*CIL* 11.3303. Cf. Mommsen *loc.cit.*). Augustus' well known devotion to Apollo may have been the motive for his decision to celebrate on the new date. According to the Julian calendars, September 23 was the dedication day of the temple of Apollo, which was consecrated in 431 B.C. by one C. Julius Mento (Livy, 4.29.7). A comparison of *Ant. Mai.* with the Julian calendars shows that, when the Julian reform changed the numbering of the days *before the Kalends* in the seven months affected, all religious observances continued to fall on the same days *after the Ides*, although they now had new dates. Therefore, if Augustus had continued to celebrate his birthday on *a.d. VIII Kal. Oct.*, it would no longer have coincided with the dedication day of the temple of Apollo which now fell on *a.d. IX Kal. Oct.* In order to preserve the pleasing coincidence he had to accept the new date.

September 24　**C**
　(*a.d. VII Kal. Oct.* = *a.d. VIII Kal. Oct. anni Iuliani*)

　　N　PIGH (for NF?)
　　C　ANT. MAI., MAFF., SAB., PINC., ARV., C *Feria[e]*. . . . VALL.
　　　　See the discussion of September 23.

October 1　**N**
　(*Kal. Oct.*)

　　NP　ARV.
　　N　ANT. MAI., MAFF., PAUL., AMIT.
　　　　The NP of *Arv.* is not explained, and is almost certainly an error. (Cf. Mommsen, *CIL* 1². 1, p. 289 and Degrassi p. 355.) There is no evidence for any republican character other than N, but it should be noted that, like *Kal. Jun.*, this is one of the rare examples of an isolated N day.

October 12　**C**
　(*a.d. IV Id. Oct.*)

AUGUST(ALIA) NP MAFF., ANT. MIN., SAB. AUG(USTALIA) NP *Fer(iae) ex s.c. q(uod) e(o) d(ie) imp. Caes. Aug. ex transmarin(is) provinc(iis) urbem intravit araq(ue) Fort(unae) reduci constit(uta).* AMIT.

C ANT. MAI., PL. M. FANTI., TAUR.

This is the only named day in the *Fasti* which can be shown to have received its name in the Augustan period, and its creation is perhaps the greatest honor ever given Augustus. It is also remarkable because the day has an even number, while all other named days except Regifugium and Equirria (March 14) fall on odd-numbered days.

GROUP 2

(Days whose characters are uncertain)

January 9 AGONIUM **NP**
(*a.d. V Id. Ian.*)

This is the only day in the year for which none of the *Fasti* record a character letter. Since it precedes the Ides, it might well be N (see p. 34), but since May 21 and December 11 are also called Agonia and are NP, it is more probable that January 9 was also NP.

February 21 FERALIA **F** or **FP**
(*a.d. IX. Kal. Mart.*)

F ANT. MAI., MAFF.
FP CAER., VERUL.

This day, together with April 23 and August 19, presents a very knotty problem. Each is marked F by two *Fasti*, and FP by two, or three, others. In *Ant. Mai.* February 21 and April 23 are F, and August 19 is FP, while NP is given to April 23 by *Maff.* and to August 19 by *Vall.* The crux of the problem is that we no more know the meaning of FP than we do that of NP. There is general agreement only that the F stands for *fastus*. The variety of notation in the *Fasti* suggests that the Romans were not sure on this point either. In the most recent comment on FP, Degrassi (pp. 334f.), like Leuze (p. 123), prefers Mommsen's explanation that it stands for *fastus principio* and that these days were *fissi*, like those marked Q.R.C.F., but were *fasti* at the beginning of the day. The weakness of this interpretation is that it suggests by analogy that NP should mean *nefastus principio*, a proposition that for many years no one has been willing to accept. Neither does it explain the diversity of opinion among the *Fasti* as to

[182]

which of the three days was FP. It would perhaps be simplest to accept the evidence of *Ant. Mai.* on the basis of its early date, but that would still leave us with the problem of FP, and of why the two Vinalia should have different characters, when in all other cases of duplicated named days (the two Carmentalia, the three Lemuria, the two Lucaria and the two Consualia) the days have the same character. In the present state of our knowledge the problem seems to me insoluble. Since, however, it is probable that the days were F in some aspect at least, I am inclined to list them in the F category tentatively, and to hope for the discovery of another republican calendar which might give us a clue. The problem of why a named day, other than Kalends or Nones, should be F at all is discussed elsewhere (see pp. 76f.).

March 19 QUINQUATRUS **NP**
(*a.d. XIV Kal. Apr.*)

NP ANT. MAI., CAER., VAT., PRAEN.
N MAFF.
The date after the Ides (see p. 34), combined with the weight of the evidence, makes NP probable.

April 19 CERIALIA **NP**
(*a.d. XII Kal. Mai. = a.d. XIII Kal. Mai. anni Iuliani*)

NP CAER.
N MAFF.
In *Ant. Mai.* and *Esq.* only part of the N is preserved so that one cannot say whether it was N or NP, but the date after the Ides makes NP the more probable.

April 23 VINALIA **F** or **FP**
(*a.d. VIII Kal. Mai. = a.d. IX Kal. Mai. anni Iuliani*)

F ANT. MAI., PRAEN.
FP CAER.
NP MAFF.
For discussion see February 21.

May 7 **F**
(*Non. Mai.*)

N ANT. MAI., MAFF.
F VEN.
Mommsen (*CIL* 1². 1, p. 294) accepted F on the grounds that the majority of Nones are F, and attributed the N of *Maff.* to a confusion with the N of May 9th. After the publication of *Ant. Mai.*, Degrassi rejected F for

[183]

N (p. 350), but, as we have seen in the discussion of August 6, the Nones and the day following normally have the same character, and therefore, since May 8 is certainly F, May 7 should also be F. Moreover, the evidence of *Ant. Mai.* loses some of its force when one looks at Mancini's reconstruction (see Pl. 1). The fragment which Mancini assigned to this position contains only an N preceded by an upright stroke which is probably part of the right leg of the last N of NON. The stroke cannot be part of the right leg of a nundinal letter H because there is no sign between the letters of the vertical guide line incised in the plaster on the right edge of the column of nundinal letters. The N in the fragment must therefore be a character letter following the name of a day. But there is no reason that I can see why the fragment must be given to May 7. It could just as well follow the Nones of February or June. I am therefore inclined to agree with Mommsen's argument and call May 7 an F day.

June 11   MATRALIA **N** or **NP**
(*a.d. III Id. Jun.*)

NP ANT. MAI.
N MAFF., VEN.

The date before the Ides suggests that N may be correct, as does the position within a series of N days which includes a named day, the Vestalia, marked N. One might argue that the copyist of *Ant. Mai.* had made a natural mistake in giving the Matralia the character commonest for named days. One could equally well say that the fact that the Matralia was in a series of N days had led to a mistake in *Maff.* I am, on the whole, inclined to accept N. Degrassi (p. 468) accepts NP.

June 13   **NP**
(*Id. Jun.*)

NP or N ANT. MAI., MAFF.
N VEN.

The evidence is uncertain. This portion of *Maff.* is preserved only in the manuscript copies, of which one gives NP and the others N. In *Ant. Mai.* the right leg of the N comes at the very edge of a fragment so that one cannot tell whether or not it had the loop which would make it NP. *Ven.* never uses NP at all, but applies N indiscriminately to named and unnamed days. Since, however, all other Ides are NP, it is more than probable that June 13 was NP.

June 14 **N**
(*a.d. XVII Kal. Quinct. = a.d. XVIII Kal. Iul. anni Iuliani*)

N ANT. MAI., MAFF., VEN.
F TUSC.
    In the majority of months the day after the Ides is F, but here an N day would be the last in a series of N or NP days, followed by a day of which the first part was N (June 15 Q.S.D.F.). It is probable that *Tusc.* is in error and June 14 was N.

August 19 VINALIA **F** or **FP**
(*a.d. XII Kal. Sept. = a.d. XIV Kal. Sept. anni Iuliani*)

FP ANT. MAI., MAFF., AMIT.
F   ALLIF., ANT. MIN.
NP VALL.
    For discussion see February 21.

September 15 **N**
(*a.d. XVI Kal. Oct. = a.d. XVII Kal. Oct. anni Iuliani*)

N MAFF., SAB., AMIT., V. DEI SERP., TAUR.
C VALL., ANT. MIN.
    This day is in the same situation as September 12, but is even more peculiar. There is no other example in the calendar of an N day later than *XVII Kal.*, unless it precedes a named day. To find one between an F and a C day, on a date which by all the rules should be C, is extraordinary enough to make it very suspect. On the other hand, *Maff.* and *Amit.*, which give N, are generally reliable, and *Ant. Min.* certainly is not, which leaves *Vall.* alone to carry the burden of proof for C. Therefore September 15 was probably N, perhaps because it was the first day of the circus games of the Ludi Romani, although no such restriction on activities is imposed for the corresponding day of the Ludi Plebeii. Cf. Degrassi, p. 510.

October 6 **C**
(*pridie Non. Oct.*)

C ANT. MAI., MAFF., PAUL., AMIT., ARV.
N ANT. MIN.
    Here, as on October 8, *Ant. Min.* provides the only evidence against the normal character for the day, and may be disregarded. Mommsen suggested that the error must have arisen from the fact that this is the date of the defeat of the Romans by the Cimbri in 105 B.C. (*CIL* 1². 1, p. 294), but as there is no other case of a day being marked N because it is the anniversary of a defeat, this is

[185]

not probable. Plutarch (*Luc.* 27.7) specifically says that the Romans called the day μελαίνα, or *dies ater*, which is not the same as *dies nefastus*.

October 16 **F**
(*a.d. XVII Kal. Nov.*)

F MAFF., SAB., AMIT., ANT. MIN., V. DEI SERP.
EN ANT. MAI.
Since the day after the Ides is normally F or, less often, N, the evidence of *Ant. Mai.* may here be questioned. An analogy is found in January 14, but this day, like all the other seven certain EN days, precedes a named day, and October 16 does not. If in the republican calendar October 16 had been EN, the evidence of five *Fasti* suggests that it was changed in the Julian calendar. Degrassi maintains (pp. 334, 355) that this is what happened, and that the change was made by Caesar. This seems to me improbable. Macrobius tells us that Caesar made his new days F so as to provide more time for the courts (1.14.12), but he does not mention an alteration of the character of any old days. If Caesar had altered any, surely he would have chosen C days, not an EN day on which there was a sacrifice, for, as Macrobius points out (1.14.9; 1.15.8), he was careful not to disturb any old religious rites by his innovations. I would therefore judge that the copyist of *Ant. Mai.* made the easy mistake of repeating the notation of the 13th and 14th on the 15th and 16th, and that, as indicated by the five Julian *Fasti*, the day was originally F. Wissowa (*Hermes* 58 [1923] 381f.) rejected EN but Leuze (124f.) accepted it.

December 4 **C**
(*pridie Non. Dec.*)

C AMIT., OPP.
F ANT. MIN.
The day before the Nones is usually C, sometimes N, never F.

December 15 CONSUALIA **NP**
(*a.d. XVI Kal. Ian. = a.d. XVIII Kal. Ian. anni Iuliani*)
NP MAFF., PRAEN., AMIT.
EN ANT. MAI.
For discussion see December 17.

December 17 SATURNALIA **NP**
(*a.d. XIV Kal. Ian. = a.d. XVI Kal. Ian. anni Iuliani*)

[186]

NP AMIT.

EN ANT. MAI.

    The attribution of EN to a named day is unique among all the *Fasti* now known, and seems highly improbable. I am convinced that *Ant. Mai.* is wrong, but I cannot imagine how such an extraordinary error was made. Wissowa (*Hermes* 58 [1923] 381) rejected EN but Leuze (123f.) considered it possible, suggesting that it was changed to NP in the Julian calendar. Degrassi follows Leuze (p. 357).

December 19   OPALIA **NP**

(*a.d. XII Kal. Ian.* = *a.d. XIV Kal. Ian. anni Iuliani*)

NP MAFF., AMIT., OST.

N ANT. MAI.

    The date of a named day after the Ides combines with the weight of evidence to make NP probable. One cannot help feeling that the copyist of *Ant. Mai.* had become very tired.

THE FASTI

The following list of inscriptions containing *Fasti* cites them according to the numbers under which they occur in Degrassi, *Inscriptiones Italiae*, XIII, 2. For each inscription I have given its full title, followed by the abbreviation. Where Degrassi's title differs from former usage, I have given the variant title in parenthesis. For the convenience of those who may not have Degrassi's publication, I have also identified the inscriptions in Mommsen's publication of the *Fasti*, in the second edition of *CIL* 1, or, for those more recently discovered, I have cited the most convenient sources.

1. *Fasti Antiates maiores* (or *Veteres*) = *Ant. Mai.*
   G. Mancini, *NS* (1921) 73ff.; Degrassi, *ILLRP* 9
2. *Fasti fratrum Arvalium* = *Arv.*
   CIL 1².1, III, pp. 214ff.
3. *Fasti Pinciani* = *Pinc.*
   CIL 1².1, V (for VI), p. 219
4. *Fasti Plateae Manfredo Fanti* = *Pl. Fanti*
   CIL 1².1, XIX, 9, p. 252
5. *Fasti Sabini* = *Sab.*
   CIL 1².1, VII, p. 220
6. *Fasti Venusini* = *Ven.*
   CIL 1².1, VIII, pp. 220f.

7. *Fasti Palatii Urbinatis = Pal. Urbin.*
   CIL 1².1, XIX, 11, p. 252
8. *Fasti Caeretani = Caer.*
   CIL 1².1, II, pp. 212f.
9. *Fasti Cuprenses = Cupr.*
   CIL 1².1, XIX, 2, p. 251
10. *Fasti Maffeiani = Maff.*
    CIL 1².1, IX, pp. 222-228
11. *Fasti Esquilini = Esq.*
    CIL 1².1, I, p. 210
12. *Fasti magistrorum vici = Mag.*
    CIL 1².1, XIX, 7, p. 210. For fragments discovered later, see
    G. Mancini, *Bullettino comunale* 58 (1935) 35-79; A.
    Degrassi, *I.I.* 13.1, 20
13. *Fasti Oppiani = Opp.*
    (*Fasti Oppiani minores*)
    CIL VI, 32494
14. *Fasti Lateranenses = Later.*
    Degrassi, *Athenaeum* 25 (1947) 127-139
15. *Fasti Tusculani = Tusc.*
    CIL 1².1, IV, p. 216
16. *Fasti Ostienses = Ost.*
    NS (1921) 251-257
17. *Fasti Praenestini = Praen.*
    CIL 1².1, XI, pp. 230-239. For fragments discovered later
    see Leuze, 98-101
18. *Fasti Vallenses = Vall.*
    CIL 1².1, XII, pp. 240f.
19. *Fasti Paulini = Paul.*
    CIL 1².1, XIII, p. 242
20. *Fasti Viae Ardeatinae = V. Ardeat.*
    CIL 1².1, XIX, 12, p. 252. For fragments discovered later, see
    Degrassi, *Athenaeum* 25 (1947) 132-139, and *I.I.* 13.2, 20,
    pp. 154f.
21. *Fasti Foronovani = Foronov.*
    CIL 1².1, XIX, 10, p. 252
22. *Fasti Verulani = Verul.*
    C. Scaccia Scarafoni, G. Mancini, *NS* (1923) 194-206

23. *Fasti Vaticani = Vat.*
  CIL 1².1, xiv, p. 242
24. *Fasti Allifani = Allif.*
  CIL 1².1, v, p. 217
25. *Fasti Amiternini = Amit.*
  CIL 1².1, xv, pp. 243-245
26. *Fasti Antiates Ministrorum domus Augustae = Ant. min.*
  (*Fasti Antiates*, until the discovery of *Fasti Antiates maiores*)
  CIL 1².1, xvii, pp. 247-249
27. *Fasti Viae dei Serpenti = V. dei Serp.*
  (*Fasti Oppiani maiores*)
  NS (1894) 242-247, *CIL* vi, 32493, xiii
28. *Fasti Viae Graziosa = V. Graz.*
  CIL 1².1, xix, 6
29. *Fasti Pighiani = Pigh.*
  CIL 1².1, xvi, p. 246
30. *Fasti aedis Concordiae = aed. Conc.*
  CIL 1².1, xix, 1, a and b, p. 250
31. *Fasti insulae Tiberinae*
  CIL vi, 32502, xxii
32. *Fasti Viae Principe Amedeo = V. Princ. Am.*
  CIL 1².1, i, p. 210 (with *Fasti Esquilini*)
  CIL vi, 2302, viii
33. *Fasti Farnesiani = Farn.*
  CIL 1².1, xviii, p. 250
34. *Fasti Viae Lanza. = V. Lanza.*
  CIL 1².1, xix, 3, p. 251
35. *Fasti Viae Tiburtinae = V. Tiburt.*
  CIL 1².1, xix, 4, p. 251
36. *Fasti Quirinales = Quir.*
  CIL 1².1, xix, 5, p. 251
37. *Fasti Nolani = Nol.*
  Degrassi, *Atti del terzo Congresso internazionale di epigrafia* (Roma 1957) 95-104 = *Scritti vari di antichità*, 681-691
38. *Fasti Fandozziani = Fandozz.*
  CIL 1².1, xix, 8, p. 252
39. *Fasti Tarentini = Tarent.*
  Published for the first time in *I.I.* 13.2

40. *Fasti Guidizzolenses* = *Guidizz.*
CIL 1².1, xx, p. 253
41. *Fasti Lanuvini* = *Lanuv.*
D. Vaglieri, *NS* 1907, pp. 125f.
42. *Fasti Furii Philocali* = *Fil.*
CIL 1².1, xxi, pp. 254-278
43. *Fasti Polemii Silvii* = *Silv.*
CIL 1².1, xxii, pp. 254-279
60. *Fasti Tauromentani* = *Taur.*

A fragment was discovered in 1962 (at Taormina in Sicily) and inserted in *I.I.* 13.2 as an *Additamentum*, at the last moment before publication, through the courtesy of Dr. G. Manganaro, who has published it and some additional fragments in *Archeologia Classica* 15 (1963) 13ff., and in *Cronache di Archeologia e di Storia dell'Arte* 3 (1964) 38ff. Although *Taur.* contains only a few days, it is of great importance, as it is the only known example of the Roman *Fasti* to have been discovered outside of Italy. Heretofore it has been believed (see Degrassi, p. xxi) that the *Fasti* were not set up in the provinces.

APPENDIX 3

NUNDINAE AND THE *TRINUM NUNDINUM*

The word *nundinae* is the feminine plural of an adjective *nundinus* which is formed from the combination of *novem* and the root **dinom* (day), and describes something which occurs every nine days.[1] The form distinguishes the regularly recurring Ninth Day from other days and periods of time related to the number nine. The *Nonae* of each month is the ninth day before the Ides. A *novemdiale sacrum* is a nine-day period of religious observances, like the modern novena, used under special circumstances.[2] Nine-day periods occur elsewhere in Roman religion. The *Feriae Sementivae*, for example, were celebrated on two days separated by seven days, thus totaling nine.[3] The *dies parentales* ran from the 13th to the 21st of February.[4] The announcement of the Compitalia, and perhaps of other *feriae conceptivae*, was made nine days before the actual celebration (Gellius, 10.24.3). On the ninth day after his birth (*dies lustricus*) a boy was purified and named (Macrobius 1.16.36). In view of this predilection for the nine-day period it is not surprising that at a very early date the Romans should have chosen to use every ninth day for the purpose of a town meeting at which public affairs could be settled, and private business, including a market, could be

---

[1] Walde-Hofmann, *Lateinisches Etymologisches Wörterbuch*[3], vol. 2 (Heidelberg 1954) 188. Cf. Ernout-Meillet, *Dictionnaire étymologique de la langue Latine*,[4] vol. 2 (Paris 1960) 447, s.v. *novem*. For parallels to the Roman nine-day periods see W. H. Roscher, "Die enneadischen und hebdomadischen Fristen und Wochen der ältesten Griechen," *Abhandlungen der K. Sächsischen Gesellschaft der Wissenschaften, Phil. Hist. Klasse*, 21 (1903) No. 4.

[2] That the *novemdiale sacrum* continued through nine days is shown by Livy's account of its origin for the expiation of the prodigy of a rain of stones (1.31.4): *mansit certe sollemne ut quandoque idem prodigium nuntiaretur feriae per novem dies agerentur.*

[3] Lydus, *De Mens.* 3.9 (42 Wuensch).

[4] See Degrassi's commentary on these days, or Warde Fowler, *RF* 306-310.

attended to.[5] They may well have inherited the practice from the Latin peoples from whom they were descended.[6] When the *nundinae*, as we have seen, ceased to be the occasion for *comitia*,[7] and the *legis actiones*, which were restricted to *dies fasti* and *nundinae*, became obsolete, the market survived as the characteristic feature of these days, with the result that, in Latin literature, the commonest meaning for *nundinae* is market, and the words derived from it such as *nundinor* and *nundinatio* are all connected with buying and selling. Eventually all connection with the number nine was forgotten, and in the Empire we find that *nundinae* can be held at any interval.[8]

One factor that must have accelerated the shift in the meaning of the word was the adoption of the seven-day planetary week, which was known in Rome certainly in the Augustan period and perhaps earlier.[9] This week assigned each day its own name, *dies solis, dies lunae*, etc., which made it a very convenient device for reckoning time. Its common use is demonstrated in certain inscriptions in which the *nundinae* of various neighboring towns are dated by the planetary days.[10] It is interesting to note that in these inscriptions eight towns are listed, as though the system of market days had originally been determined by the old count for *nundinae* and then been transferred to the seven-day week. The adoption of the week probably accounts also for three *Fasti*[11] which, in addition to the usual nundinal letters, have an extra column in which the letters A to G, instead of A to H, are repeated, reflecting a period when both systems were in use.

If the *nundinae* were important enough in Roman life to

[5] For the activities on *nundinae* and their early history, see Ch. 5, pp. 84-88 and Ch. 6, pp. 103-106.

[6] Or the practice may have come from the Etruscans. Macrobius in commenting on the Nones, remarks that the Etruscans used to greet their king every ninth day, and discuss their own business: *apud Tuscos Nonae plures habebantur, quod hi nono quoque die regem suum salutabant et de propriis negotiis consulebant* (1.15.13). Macrobius sometimes seems to confuse Nones and *nundinae*.

[7] As the result of *Lex Hortensia* in 287 B.C., see Ch. 6, p. 103.

[8] See *CIL* 8.270 for *nundinae* on *a.d. IV Non.* and *a.d. XII Kal.* each month.

[9] See Ch. 5, p. 89.

[10] Degrassi, nos. 49 and 53; *CIL* 1², p. 218 and 4.8863.

[11] *Fasti Sabini, Foronovani,* and *Nolani*. See Degrassi, p. 326.

warrant the inclusion of the nundinal letters in the calendar, we would expect that there would be in Latin some word, such as the English "week," which would describe the period from one *nundinae* to the next. This would seem to be the obvious meaning of the very rare word *nundinum*. In the literature of the republic it is found, as far as I know, only in fragments of Lucilius and Varro, and, with one exception, only in the phrase *inter nundinum*, which apparently means "within a *nundinum*," or "between *nundinae*." These fragraments are quoted by Nonius (316f. Lindsay) without context, but they seem to reflect a difference between *nundinae* and days *inter nundinum* in respect to people's behavior.[12] The quotation from Lucilius reads: *paucorum atque hoc pacto si nihil gustat inter nundinum*. This suggests that someone was on a restricted diet which could be relaxed on *nundinae*. Varro is quoted as saying in his *Gerontodidascolus*: *quotiens priscus homo ac rusticus Romanus inter nundinum barbam radebat*. The country man apparently shaved only for *nundinae*, as, according to Seneca (*Ep.* 86.12) he took a bath only on *nundinae*. From Varro's *Taphe Menippou* comes a reference to those *qui in urbe inter nundinum calumniarentur*. Mueller, in his edition of Nonius (320), suggests that these men were being contrasted with those *qui pure viverent rure*, which would be consistent with what Varro says about the origin of *nundinae* in *R.R.* 2, *praef.* 1, but is uncertain. In all these fragments there is some question as to whether we should read *inter nundinum* with the noun in the accusative, or a single word *internundinum* used adverbially. Marius Victorinus (25 Keil) seems to support the latter, although in a slightly different form, when he says: *internundinium scribendum, ut interlunium [et trinoctium] ita internundinium, quod novem dies inter se continuos habeat, non quod nono die sit*. But he also seems to be confused between a *nundinum* or nine-day period, and the *internundinum*, which should be the seven days between *nundinae*. The single word is used, but in the ablative, by Macrobius (1.16.35)

---

[12] Lange (*RA* 1³.364, n. 2) states dogmatically that in these passages *nundinum* is the accusative of the masculine *nundinus* (*dies*) which refers to the market day itself. Nonius does say it is masculine, but the sense of the quotations makes it seem impossible that *nundinum* should mean a single day.

quoting or paraphrasing Rutilius Rufus' description of the change which had come over *nundinae*: *sed haec omnia neglegentius haberi coepta et post abolita, postquam internundino etiam ob multitudinem plebis frequentes adesse coeperunt.* Nonius also quotes one fragment of Varro in which the word *nundinum* occurs without *inter* but the readings are so corrupt that it is impossible to determine the meaning. Lindsay reads (317): *cum decemviri fuissent, arbitrari vi nos nundinum divisum habuisse.* Mueller had emended this to read; *cum decemviri fuissent, arbitrati septenis nos diebus nundinum divisum habere*, taking it to be a reference to the seven days which intervened between two *nundinae*. Mommsen (*Staatsr.*[3] 1.38, n. 4) used a reading *arbitrari binos* as evidence that the *decemviri* each had the fasces for half a *nundinum*. Much as I should like to find a connection between the *decemviri* and the *nundinum*, I think it safer here to refrain from conjecture.

Just as *nundinae* lost its original meaning of ninth day, *nundinum* must have lost its specific meaning of the nundinal period. In fact, in the fourth century A.D. we find that it is being used of quite another period of time, the term served by a *consul suffectus* (Lampridius, *Alex. Sev.* 28 and 43; Vopiscus, *Tacit.* 9). But it seems probable that at some very early period *nundinum* would have come to mean a nine-day period reckoned from any day to the ninth following, instead of from one *nundinae* to the next. This is the natural development for any word which refers to a regularly recurring cycle of time, such as a week, a month, or a year. *The* week runs from Sunday to Sunday, but *a* week can run from Wednesday to Wednesday. The rarity with which *nundinum* occurs alone in Latin would, however, suggest that the word belonged to popular speech, such as might be echoed in the *Satires* of Lucilius and Varro, rather than to the language of literature.

Whereas *nundinum* alone is a very rare word, it occurs more often in the expression *trinum nundinum* or its variant form *trinundinum*. The exact meaning of this expression and its grammatical character have been ardently debated in the past, but without sufficient allowance for the historical situation in which it might have originated, and indeed sometimes without consideration of all the evidence. I will first list the

[194]

sixteen passages from inscriptions, authors, and scholia on which our understanding of the *trinum nundinum* is based, and then consider the problems which they present. I have grouped these passages according to the form in which *trinum nundinum* is found in each.

I. TRINUM NUNDINUM

1. *Senatus consultum de Bacchanalibus*, 22f. *CIL* 1².2, 581; Dessau, *ILS* 1.18; *FIRA* no. 30, p. 241.
   Haice utei in conventionid exdeicatis ne minus trinum nundinum.

2. *Lex Latina Tabulae Bantinae*, 31. *CIL* 1².2, 582; *FIRA* no. 6, p. 84.
   . . . inum nondin. . . .

3. *Lex Tarentina*, 23. R. Bartoccini, "Frammento di Legge Romana Rinvenuta a Taranto," *Epigraphica* 9 (1947) 3-32; G. Tibiletti, "Le Leggi *De Iudiciis Repetundarum* fino alla Guerra Sociale," *Athenaeum* 31 (1953) 5-100, esp. 54f.
   . . . l trinum nundinum contenuo palam prodixerit nondinisq(ue) . . . [proscr]ipta propositaque apud forum fuerit.
   In the inscription only the single letter l is preserved before *trinum*. It is interpreted as an abbreviation of *lex*, but editors differ as to the case of *lex*. Bartoccini read [. . h(anc)] l(egem). See below, p. 201.

4. Cicero, *De Dom.* 41.
   si quod in ceteris legibus trinum nundinum esse oportet, id in adoptione satis est trium esse horarum nihil reprehendo: sin eadem observanda sunt, iudicavit senatus M. Drusi legibus, quae contra legem Caeciliam et Didiam latae essent, populum non teneri.

5. *Ibid.* 45.
   quarta sit accusatio trinum nundinum prodicta die, quo die iudicium sit futurum.

6. Cicero, *ad Fam.* 16.12.3.
   ad consulatus petitionem se venturum, neque se iam velle absente se rationem habere suam; se praesentem trinum nundinum petiturum.

7. Cicero, *Phil.* 5.7-8.
Etiam hanc legem populus Romanus accepit? Quid? Promulgata fuit? Quid? Non ante lata quam scripta est? . . . Ubi lex Caecilia et Didia? Ubi promulgatio trinum nundinum?

8. Priscian, 7.3.9 (292 Keil), quoting Cicero:
sic "caelicolum" pro "caelicolarum" et "trinundinum" pro "trinundinarum." Cicero, *pro Cornelio* 1: *ex promulgatione trinundinum dies ad ferendum potestasque venisset.*

II. IN TRINUM NUNDINUM

Livy, 3.35.1.
Comitia decemviris creandis in trinum nundinum indicta sunt.

III. TRINO NUNDINO (TRINUNDINO)

1. Quintilian, 2.4.35.
aut de (iure) ipsius rogationis, quod est varium, sive non trino forte nundino promulgata sive non idoneo die.

2. *Scholia Bobiensia,* 55 (132 Stangl) (on Cicero *pro Sestio* 55).
saepe hanc ostendi promulgatae legis et latae differentiam. Nam trinundino proponebantur ut in notitiam populi pervenirent: quo exacto tempore ferebant iuris validi firmitatem.

3. Macrobius, 3.17.7.
Post Didiam Licinia lex lata est a P. Licinio Crasso Divite, cuius ferundae probandaeque tantum studium ab optimatibus impensum est, ut consulto senatus iuberetur ut ea tantum modo promulgata priusquam trinundino confirmaretur, ita ab omnibus observaretur quasi iam populi sententia comprobata.

IV. TRINUNDINO DIE

1. Macrobius, 1.16.34.
Rutilius scribit Romanos instituisse nundinas ut octo quidem diebus in agris rustici opus facerent, nono autem die intermisso rure ad mercatum legesque accipiendas Romam venirent et ut scita atque consulta frequentiore populo

referrentur, quae trinundino die proposita a singulis atque universis facile noscebantur. unde etiam mos tractus ut leges trinundino die promulgarentur. (On *octo diebus,* see p. 104, n. 38.)

V. TRINUNDINUM TEMPUS

Scholia Bobiensia, 135 (140 Stangl) (on Cicero, *pro Sestio* 135).

Caecilia est autem et Didia quae iubebant in promulgandis legibus trinundinum tempus observari.

VI. IN TRINIS NUNDINIS

Pliny, *N.H.* 18. 15.

L. Minucius Augurinus, qui Spurium Maelium coarguerat, farris pretium in trinis nundinis ad assem redegit.

VII. TRINIS NUNDINIS

Gellius, *N.A.* 20.1.47-49.

Inter eos dies trinis nundinis continuis ad praetorem in comitium producebantur quantaeque pecuniae iudicati essent praedicabatur. Tertiis autem nundinis capite poenas dabant. . . . Et quidem verba ipsa legis dicam, ne existimes invidiam me istam forte formidare: tertiis, inquit, nundinis partis secanto.

It is clear from these passages that *trinum nundinum* is a period of time. The most obvious meaning of the words is "a triple *nundinum.*" But what is that? Some scholars have argued that it means three successive *nundinae* and that the period is therefore 17 days (3 *nundinae* + 2 × 7 intervening days).[13] Others assume that it means three eight-day "weeks,"

---

[13] Ideler, *Handbuch der mathematischen und technischen Chronologie* (Berlin 1826) 2.137; W. Kubitschek, *Grundriss der antiken Zeitrechnung* (Munich 1928) 134. See also Sontheimer, *RE* 16.65 *s.v.* Monat: G. Tibiletti "Le Leggi *de iudiciis repetundarum* fino alla guerra sociale," *Athenaeum* 31 (1953) 54, n. 4 and in *Diz. Epigraf.* 4. Fasc. 23.708, *s.v.* Lex; Broughton, *MRR* 2.4; W. F. McDonald, "Clodius and Lex Aelia Fufia," *JRS* 19 (1929) 176; A. H. J. Greenidge, *The Legal Procedure in Cicero's Time* (Oxford 1901) 346, 357; G. W. Botsford, *RA* 260, n. 1: "The *trinum nundinum* which included three market days could not have contained less than seventeen days or more than twenty four." Lange

each consisting of 7 days + 1 *nundinae*, making a period of 24 days, which was not anchored to *nundinae*, but might begin and end on any day.[14]

The history of the *nundinae* may provide some answers to these problems. As we have seen (pp. 103-6) in the early days of the republic, on *nundinae* the *comitia* met and civil cases were heard in court. Two passages in the evidence given above (VI and VII) are related to this period. In VII Gellius paraphrases and quotes directly a law of the XII Tables about debtors. After they have been brought before the praetor for the first hearing, they are brought before the praetor again *trinis nundinis continuis*, and *tertiis nundinis* they pay the penalty. Here the use of the plural indicates that, as we would

---

(*RA*[3] 1.364f.; 604; 2.470) thought that originally *comitia* were announced for the third *nundinae* following (*in tertias nundinas*), but that after *comitia* were no longer held on *nundinae*, the form *trinum nundinum* came into use, and the *comitia* were held on the first comitial day after the third *nundinae*, so that the period was 17 plus x days. The only serious attempt to reconsider the problem of the *trinum nundinum* in this century is A. W. Lintott's article "Trinundinum" (*CQ* n.s. 15 [1965] 281-285) which reached me only after I had arrived at the conclusion which I present here. He argues that *trinundinum* means "over three market days" but is not any specific number of days, because a promulgator would have to wait for a *dies comitialis* before he could bring his law to the *comitia*. The weak point in Lintott's carefully reasoned argument is, to my mind, that, like Mommsen, he rejects the evidence that in the early period *comitia* could be held on *nundinae*, and allows for no change in the characters of days during the republic. I cannot agree with his final conclusion, but appreciate very much some of the points which he makes in the course of the article.

[14] Mommsen, in *RC*[2] 240 and n. 25, maintained that the *nundinum* was an eight-day week, and that *nundinae* came once a month on *a.d. IX Kal.* Later he decided that the *nundinae* was the first day of each *nundinum*, but he kept to his definition of the *nundinum* as an eight-day week and argued for a 24-day *trinum nundinum* (*Staatsrecht*[3] 3.373 and n. 1, 375-378). For a fuller statement of his theory see below, p. 204. See also Kroll, RE 17.2.1467 s.v. *Nundinae*; L. R. Taylor, *Party Politics in the Age of Caesar* (Sather Classical Lectures 22, Berkeley 1949) 59, 206f.; A. Berger, *Encyclopedic Dictionary of Roman Law* (*Transactions of the American Philosophical Society*, n.s. 43.2, 1953) 657, s.v. *promulgare*. G. Rotondi (*LPPR* 125f.) declines to come to a conclusion because of the paucity of the evidence, but he stresses the important point that, whatever the length of the *trinum nundinum*, it was the minimum period required between *promulgatio* and *rogatio* in order to secure time for consideration. The magistrate could of course set his *comitia* for a day much later if he wanted to.

expect in the fifth century, the hearings were held on *nundinae*, and that *trinae nundinae continuae* would mean "three successive *nundinae*." The only other passage in which we find the plural used (VI) refers to an episode supposed to have taken place in 439 B.C., and again it seems probable that *in trinis nundinis* means "within the period covered by three *nundinae*," or by the third *nundinae* after the one from which the reckoning began. The story is concerned with the price of grain, and this would be determined best on market days.[15]

Rutilius Rufus (IV) says that the custom of promulgating a law a *trinum nundinum* before the *rogatio* originated in the period when the *rogatio* took place on a *nundinae*. One can assume, then, that at that time the *promulgatio* also would take place on a *nundinae*, and that the *rogatio* would follow three *nundinae* later, *tertio nundino*. This practice, however, would perforce have ended in 287 B.C., when Lex Hortensia, by making *nundinae* into *dies fasti*, prevented them from being used for *comitia*. The *rogatio* would now have to take place on a *dies comitialis*, but to maintain tradition it would still follow the *promulgatio* by the same minimum number of days. It seems probable that actually the custom of holding court and *comitia* on days other than *nundinae* had arisen long before 287 B.C., and that therefore in both areas the use of the period equivalent to, but not identical with, that covered by three *nundinae*, had long been common. It is to this time, before 287 B.C., that I would assign the origin to the expression *trinum nundinum* in the singular, used, instead of the old *trinae nundinae*, to designate a period which did not necessarily begin and end on actual *nundinae*. The *trinum nundinum* would have survived into the late republic because of its association with *comitia*, both legislative and judicial, while the use of the word *nundinae* to reckon a period of time would gradually have died out of legal terminology after the praetor's court began to sit on days between *nundinae*. Farmers and business men

---

[15] Pliny is here referring to the story of Minucius, of which there are several different versions (Livy, 4.12.8-16. 4; Dion. Hal., 12.1-4.6). Most of the story is highly improbable, but this particular detail may well be genuine, and preserved in the idiom of an early period, as the price of grain was regularly recorded in the *Annales Maximi* (Cato, quoted by Gellius, 2.28.6).

may have gone on reckoning by *nundinae* for a long time, but Latin literature does not preserve the record of their language. Against this date for the origin of the independent *trinum nundinum* is II, in which Livy is referring to the elections of the decemviri of 450 B.C. According to my hypothesis, in this period one would expect the expression *in tertias nundinas*. It is interesting that Dionysius, writing of the same period, speaks of *comitia* being set for ἡ τρίτη αγορά (7.58.3; 9.41.4; 10.3.5; 10.35.4) which would correctly translate *tertiae nundinae*. Mommsen asserted that Dionysius (and Plutarch *Cor.* 18), like Priscian (I 8), did not know what *nundinum* meant and mistakenly took it to be the same as the familiar *nundinae*.[16] Others use Dionysius' phraseology to prove that *trinum nundinum* meant literally three *nundinae*, on the assumption that Dionysius understood the Latin expression. There is, as far as I can see, no way of proving either argument. It does, however, seem out of keeping with Dionysius' character to suppose that, if he found a technical expression which he did not understand, he would not have consulted someone who could explain it to him. It is also peculiar that if, on Mommsen's assumption, he was too lazy or stupid to find out, he should have mistranslated *trinum nundinum* into the equivalent of the form which did actually occur in the XII Tables. I am inclined to think that he and Livy both found *in tertias nundinas* in their sources and that, while Dionysius translated it literally, Livy modernized his terminology for the benefit of his readers.

The objection which has in the past been made against interpreting *trinum nundinum* as a period independent of *nundinae* has been supported by the statement made by Priscian (I 8) that *trinundinum* is a contracted form of the genitive plural *trinundinarum*. Those who accept this statement maintain either that with the genitive was understood *tempus*, or that the original genitive was, in ignorance, treated as an indeclinable neuter, which later came to be declined.[17] In the passage which Priscian cites from Cicero, it is true, *trinundinum* might

<hr>

[16] *RC*[2] 240 n. 25; *Staatsrecht*[3] 3.375 n. 2.

[17] E.g. L. Lange, "Die Promulgatio trinum nundinum, die Lex Caecilia Didia und nochmals die Lex Pupia," *RhMus* 30 (1875) 362f.; C. John, "Sallustius über Catilinas Candidatur im Jahr 688," *RhMus* 31 (1876) 410; Kroll, *op.cit.* (n. 14) 1471; Lintott, *op.cit.* (n. 13) 281.

be a genitive dependent on *promulgatio*, but this is so in only two other passages in which the expression is used, and in neither is it necessary. In all the passages listed above, it is possible to construe *trinum nundinum* as either accusative or nominative, and in several it *must* be accusative. In I 6 it is clearly an accusative of the duration of time, modifying *petiturum*. In I 5 we have the same construction, modifying *prodicta die*. In I 1 since *haice* must be the object of *exdeicatis*, I think we have another accusative of time in *ne minus trinum nundinum*, which should mean that the proclamation must be made over a period not less than a *trinum nundinum*. Because of the lacunae in the text of I 3, it is hard to say how it should be interpreted. If Piganiol (*CRAI* [1951] 58-68) and Tibiletti[18] are right in reading . . . [*quei diem ex h*(*ac*)] *l*(*ege*) *trinum nundinum contenuo palam prodixerit*, we have an interesting parallel with the expression in I 5: *trinum nundinum prodicta die*. The law would then provide that someone should set a day (for a trial?) a *trinum nundinum* in the future. In this case *trinum nundinum* would again be an accusative of duration of time, while *nundinisq*(*ue*) in the next phrase would refer to actual *nundinae* during the period, on each of which something is to be published in the Forum. The distinction between the period and the individual *nundinae* is interesting and significant.

We can now look at the passages which are taken as support of Priscian's statement. In I 4 it is argued that *trinum nundinum* must be genitive to balance *trium horarum* in the next clause. I see no difficulty, however, in taking it as a predicate noun defining *quod* and therefore in the nominative. Cicero used the genitive with *esse* in the next clause because there is no word for a period of three hours. If he had been talking

---

[18] See references under 1,3. Tibiletti takes *trinum nundinum* to mean three *nundinae* and translates it and *nundinisque* "per tre mercati consecutivi e in ciascuno dei (tre) singoli mercati." He objects to taking *trinum nundinum* as a period of a certain number of days on the grounds that " 'un periodo consecutivo di *tot* giorni' è espressione confusa." But the confusion disappears, I think, if one takes *contenuo* with *palam* as an adverb modifying *prodixerit*, and translates it "immediately," instead of "consecutively," modifying *trinum nundinum*. If the writer of the law had meant what Tibiletti suggests, the natural way to say it would have been the phrase Gellius uses (see VII), *trinis nundinis continuis*.

about three days he could have used *triduum*, and avoided the rather clumsy genitive. In the other two passages (I 7 and 8) it is difficult not to take *trinum nundinum* as dependent on *promulgatio* but we need not assume, as Priscian seems to do, that therefore it must be in the genitive. In early Latin verbal nouns ending in *-io* frequently govern the same case as do the verbs from which they are formed, and take the accusative.[19] I would suggest that *promulgatio trinum nundinum* is a technical legal term which came into being while this use of the accusative was still common,[20] and, like many other legal terms, survived after the construction had become obsolete in nontechnical language. In conclusion it seems to me a more economical interpretation of the evidence to assume that the word *nundinum* was in common use in early Latin and that a *trinum nundinum* was a triple *nundinum*, than to derive it in a roundabout way from a plural genitive which turns into a neuter substantive, simply on the basis of a single statement by Priscian, who was a grammarian, not an expert on legal terminology.

That *trinum nundinum* meant a period of time, not three market days, is further indicated by the two passages from the *Scholia Bobiensia* (III 2 and V) in which it is used with the word *tempus*. That it was dissociated from actual *nundinae* seems to me to be shown not only by the previous argument but also by the wording of *Lex Tarentina* (I 3) in which, although the *trinum nundinum* has already been mentioned, it is necessary to specify that something shall also be done on *nundinae*.

We can now come back to the question of how many days made up a *trinum nundinum*. It is impossible to give an absolute answer because there is no direct evidence. The confident statements made by scholars who write either on Roman history or Roman law are in reality opinions, which are often influenced by the desire to make the *trinum nundinum* fit into

---

[19] Cf. Plautus, *Amph.* 519; *Men.* 1016; *Poen.* 1308; *Stich.* 283; *Truc.* 623. See Leumann-Hofmann-Szantyr, *Lateinische Grammatik* (*Handbuch der Altertumswissenschaft* 2.2.2, Munich 1965) 2.34.

[20] In an early inscription, giving the rules for behavior in a sacred grove, we find the phrase *manum iniect[i]o estod*, where *manum* must be the object of *iniectio* (*CIL* 1².2.401).

a thesis on some more general topic, or ones which have been accepted on faith from someone else. I can do no more than offer my own opinion, based on a study of the calendar itself, and on the hypotheses I have outlined above.

I have argued that the word *nundinum* was used originally to describe the period from one *nundinae* through the next. On the analogy of *biduum, triduum, biennium, triennium*, it would seem to mean a period of nine days. One must however remember that, unlike *biduum* etc., the *nundinum* was a cyclic period, which repeated itself forever, from *nundinae* to *nundinae*. The period between *nundinae* was called *inter nundinum*, the time within the *nundinum*, or seven days. Therefore one *nundinum* was nine days, including the *nundinae* at the beginning and also the one at the end of the period. In the same way, we commonly think of a week as including two occurrences of the same day. If a librarian says on Wednesday "This book is due in a week" he means it is due on the next Wednesday, and the week here includes eight days. Thus one *nundinum* would include nine days, but two would include not 18 but 17, because the middle *nundinae* would be both the last day of the first *nundinum* and the first one of the second. A triple *nundinum* would then be 25 days, that is four *nundinae* plus 3 $\times$ 7 intervening days.[21] I would guess that in the fifth century, when a law was promulgated, the promulgator would say that the law would be presented *trinis nundinis continuis*, and *tertiis nundinis* the *comitia* would vote on it. Later when *comitia* no longer met only on *nundinae*, the formula could be changed, but the period of time would remain the same. The law would now be promulgated for a *trinum nundinum* and could not be voted on before the last day of that period, the 25th day, or according to our way of counting, on the 24th day *after* the announcement.

Previously I mentioned the two numbers of days most commonly assigned to the *trinum nundinum*. Those who hold that it was 17 days argue that it means 3 *nundinae*. Frequently they do not specify whether or not they think that in the late

---

[21] The only person I know of who has performed this calculation is Lintott (*op.cit.* [note 13] 282) who asks with simple common sense "If a week is nine R(oman) days, surely three weeks will be 25 R(oman) days?" By Roman, Lintott means days reckoned inclusively.

Republic the period was still determined by actual *nundinae*. If they do, they must have forgotten that after 287 B.C. *comitia* could not meet on *nundinae*. The chief objection to the 17-day period, in my opinion, is that it requires one to accept the theory that *trinum nundinum* is the genitive of *trinae nundinae*, for if, as I believe, *nundinum* here means the nine-day period, 17 days would best be described as *binum nundinum*.

The major proponent of the 24-day *trinum nundinum* was Mommsen,[22] who argued for it in his *Römische Chronologie*. He maintained that the *nundinum* was an 8-day week, which originally had been a subdivision of the lunar month determined by the phases of the moon, but had then become an independent unit which continued in a cycle through the year. The *trinum nundinum* was then a period of 3 of these 8-day weeks which make up 24 days. Mommsen explained its origin by the theory that the *comitia* which he believed met on March 24 and May 24 would have been announced on the Kalends of each month, and that therefore it would have become customary to use the same period for the announcement of all *comitia*. At this stage in his thinking Mommsen denied that there was any connection between the *nundinum* and the *nundinae*. He believed that the latter was the name given to *a.d. IX Kal.* in each month, which divided the second half of the month as the Nones (*a.d. IX Id.*) did the first half. The references in the classical authors to the *nundinae* as the market held every ninth day he regarded as an incorrect confusion of the *nundinae* with the nameless first day of the *nundinum*. Subsequently he abandoned this identification of the *nundinae*, and defined it as the first day of the 8-day week, the *nundinum*. He now rejected any evidence that *comitia* had ever been held on *nundinae*,[23] although he still believed that *comitia* were held on March 24 and May 24, which he had previously identified as *nundinae*. If he had accepted the ancient evidence that originally *comitia* and *nundinae* coincided, he would logically have had to abandon his definition of the *trinum nundinum* as a 24-day period, because the last day of such a period would not fall on the third *nundinae* after its announcement but on the day before the *nundinae*.

[22] See n. 14 for references.   [23] Cf. Degrassi, p. 325.

It is unfortunate that we have no clear case of the use of *trinum nundinum* which can settle the question of its length. The invalidation of the *Lex Manilia de libertinorum suffragiis* (see p. 46) is sometimes cited as evidence that it was longer than 17 days. The *rogatio* of this law took place on December 29, 67 B.C. and it was invalidated next day, partly on the grounds of *celeritas actionis* (Asconius 65C). It is argued that the tribune Manilius promulgated the law as soon as he entered office on December 10, 67 B.C.,[24] and that more than 17 days had passed on December 29. Unfortunately, the ancient sources do not state when the *promulgatio* took place. For all we know it might have been only 10 days before the *rogatio*.[25] Again, the first law passed by Clodius in 58 B.C. is cited as evidence for the 24-day period.[26] In this case also we do not know when the *promulgatio* took place, although it is probable that Clodius wasted no time. It is often stated that the *rogatio* took place on January 4, the 24th day after December 10 when Clodius entered office, but this is based on the assumption that the day of the *rogatio* was the third day after the Kalends of January. The relevant passage in Cicero says that, when the Compitalia had fallen on the Kalends of January, the new consul Piso permitted the celebration of the *Ludi Compitalicii*, three days after which Clodius by his new laws destroyed the bulwarks of the republic.[27] Therefore the *rogatio* came not three days after the Kalends but three days after the *Ludi*, which almost certainly were not celebrated on the same day as the Compitalia but afterwards.[28] Since January 5 and 6 are *dies*

[24] Mommsen (*Staatsrecht*[3] 3.376, n. 1) says the *promulgatio* took place "nicht vor und wahrscheinlich am 10 December," and then refers to the twenty days which intervened as insufficient.

[25] Cf. Lintott (*op.cit*. [n. 13] 282) who makes the same point.

[26] Mommsen, *loc.cit*. (note 24).

[27] *In Pisonem* 8f.: *Tu, cum in Kalendas Ianuarias compitaliorum dies incidisset, Sex. Cloelium, qui numquam antea praetextatus fuisset, ludos facere et praetextatum volitare passus es . . . . Ergo his fundamentis positis consulatus tui, triduo post, inspectante et tacente te, a fatali portento prodigioque rei publicae lex Aelia et Fufia eversa est, propugnacula murique tranquillitatis atque oti.*

[28] The Compitalia, which was *feriae conceptivae* and the special holiday of slaves and the lower classes, was officially celebrated on one day, at the end of December or the beginning of January, (Festus 304 L.; Gellius 10.24.3; for actual dates see Dio 36.42.2; Cicero, *Att.* 2.2.3 and

fasti the *rogatio* would probably have had to wait for January 7. Thus the *Lex Clodia* cannot be used as proof of a 24-day *trinum nundinum* but neither is it evidence for a 25-day period.

There is one detail in the calendar itself which I think supports my suggestion of a 25-day *trinum nundinum*. In every month except February the period from the Nones to the last day of the month is 25 days. The Nones, the Ides, *a.d. X Kal.* and *pridie Kal.* all carry the same nundinal letter. This may be purely accidental, but it suggests to me a deliberate use of the nundinal period to give an easily remembered pattern to the months (see pp. 88, 120).

2.3.4; *In Pisonem* 8; *Att.* 7.7.3). Cicero refers to it as *compitaliorum dies* or *compitalicius dies*, and we may assume that in the country only the one day was celebrated, because, whereas he refrains from going to the Alban villa that day so as not to be in the way of the household on the holiday, he has no hesitation about going the next day (*Att.* 7.7.3). However, according to Festus (304 L.), although the *sacra* were performed on the one day, the popular celebration spread over three days. This must, I think, refer to festivities in the city, and specifically to the *Ludi Compitales* or *Compitalicii*. These games were conducted by the *magistri* of the *collegia* whose membership was mainly composed of freedmen and slaves. In 64 B.C. the *collegia*, and consequently the games, were abolished by the Senate. If the games had been part of the *sacra* of the Compitalia, which belonged to the state cult, it would, I am sure, have been impossible for the Senate to have done such a thing. I conclude therefore that the games came on the day or days after the official Compitalia. In the *Fasti* of Philocalus (fourth century A.D.), the *Ludi Compitales* are actually given the fixed dates of January 3-5, although this evidence is too late to be of much value. A minor point of grammar may, however, support my conclusion. In the passage in the *In Pisonem* quoted above (n. 27) Cicero says: *Tu cum in Kalendas Ianuarias compitaliorum dies incidisset, Sex. Cloelium . . . ludos facere . . . passus es.* The use of the pluperfect subjunctive *incidisset* suggests to me that the one day of the Compitalia was over when Cloelius gave the games.

APPENDIX 4

THE DATING OF THE CALENDAR

I shall take up here the major theories as to the date of the pre-Julian calendar which have been proposed since 1863, when Mommsen identified it as the "Calendar of Numa." I should first, however, point out a matter of terminology which sometimes injects an element of ambiguity into this subject. The word calendar can be used in a variety of ways. It may refer to what in Latin would be called *annus*, that is the type of year on which the calendar as a whole is based, which may be lunar, solar or lunisolar, with characteristic lengths of months and method of intercalation. It may also refer to the whole calendar, that is the basic year and the contents of the graphic form, the various days with their names, features and characters. In Latin this would be described as *Fasti*. A third use of the word, common among writers on Roman religion is to restrict it to the written form only, and thus to forget about the basic year. This usage is sometimes limited even further by applying the word only to the list of *feriae* (the *feriale*), omitting from consideration the nundinal letters and the characters of the days. I shall try to make clear in which sense the word was used by the authors whose theories I shall discuss, but I must admit that I have sometimes found this difficult to determine.

Another element in the discussion which may confuse readers of today is the use of topographical evidence. The interpretation of the growth of Rome has changed from generation to generation, and what was once considered valid topographical evidence for the dating of the calendar may now seem invalid. Furthermore, some theories about Roman topography upon careful analysis turn out to have been derived from the evidence of the calendar so that the argument has evolved into a vicious circle.

Mommsen's first detailed studies of the calendar written before 1863 were primarily concerned with the year.[1] In 1859

[1] See "Der älteste Römische Kalender," *Zeitschrift für die Altertums-*

he stated (RC^2 30f.) that the pre-Julian year was introduced by the decemviri in 450 B.C., and that a calendar based on it, indicating the *dies fasti*, was included in the XII Tables. That he was at the same time thinking about the calendar as a whole, presumably in connection with his work on the *Fasti*, is indicated in an article on the *Ludi Magni* and *Romani* which also was published in 1859.[2] As evidence for the date when the *Ludi* became annual, he stated here that he would demonstrate elsewhere[3] that in the *Fasti* only the words inscribed in large letters belonged to the oldest *Festkalender* (*feriale*), and that in his opinion this oldest redaction was made in the period of the decemviri. By 1863 when he published the *Fasti* in the first volume of *CIL*, he had changed his mind. He now states (p. 361) that the material in large letters, including the nundinal letters and the names and characters of the days, constitutes the *tabula dierum fastorum nefastorumque* of King Numa, none of which was changed until Caesar's reform.[4] He discusses the *feriale* in detail (pp. 375f.) and draws up what he calls the *laterculus feriarum anni Numani*, consisting of the 45 named days, the Kalends of March (NP) and all the Ides. As evidence for the date of this *laterculus* he states that no religious ceremony or cult known to have been established later than the reign of Numa can be found in the *feriale*. Since the ritual of the *Tigillum Sororium*, established in the reign of Tullus Hostilius, is omitted, the *feriale* must be dated to the reign of the previous king, Numa. Among cults omitted he mentions that of Juppiter Optimus Maximus, attributed to Tarquinius Priscus, and those of Diana and Fors Fortunae, founded by Servius Tullius. He dismisses as late inventions the associations

---

wissenschaft (1846) no. 53, 417-421, and his *Römische Chronologie* (1858, 2nd ed. 1859). In the *Römische Geschichte* (1854-1856), the calendar is barely mentioned in the sections on religion.

[2] *RhMus* 14 (1859) 79-87, reprinted in 1879 in his *Römische Forschungen* 2.42-57.

[3] To prevent confusion on the part of those who read the reprint, I should point out that in it the original words "ich werde anderswo . . . darlegen" have been changed to "ich habe anderswo . . . dargelegt" with a reference to *CIL* 1, p. 361, which had not been published when the article was written.

[4] The NP days which mark anniversaries received their new characters in and after 45 B.C.

made by ancient authors between certain *feriae* and events in later periods. At the end of this section, however, he adds what appears to be a qualification of this absolute date. He says that his *laterculus* is the one attributed to Numa, that is, the one which contains those *feriae* whose origin has been forgotten (*CIL* 1, p. 376 = *CIL* 1².1, p. 299).

In discussing the characters of the days in the calendar of Numa, he asserts that they were never changed during the republic, but that they do not provide a guide to the actual practice of the late republic. As evidence he says that although the *nundinae*, which he identified as *a.d. IX Kal.* in each month, were made *dies fasti* by the *Lex Hortensia*, many of them have other characters. Also the *fasti* do not indicate when *iudicia* could or could not be held.[5]

Mommsen repeated these conclusions in the second edition of *CIL* 1 (1893), making the history of the calendar more explicit. It was devised by Numa, set up in public by Ancus, reproduced by the decemviri in the XII Tables, with them disappeared from public view, but was part of the *Ius Flavianum* and other later commentaries on civil law (*CIL* 1².1, p. 284).

Mommsen's picture of the Calendar of Numa, one and indivisible, provided a new and unique source of evidence for the early period of Rome which has been fully exploited, especially for the study of early Roman religion. At the same time, once it was accepted, it effectively stopped any further study of the history of the calendar in later periods, since it postulated that from Numa to Caesar the calendar was frozen into immobility. For many years, however, it did not achieve the status of a fact on which further interpretations of other evidence could be built. Older books on Roman religion, when they appeared in new editions, were not revised in the light of Mommsen's theory.[6] P. E. Huschke in his interesting, but bewildering, book *Das alte römische Jahr und seine Tage* (1869) disagreed with Mommsen on many points and specifi-

---

[5] *CIL* 1, pp. 366f. In *CIL* 1².1 this material has been shifted to the introduction, p. 283.

[6] E.g., Preller's *Römische Mythologie* (Berlin 1858 and 1865; 3rd ed., ed. H. Jordan, Berlin 1881-1883), and Marquardt's *Römische Staatsverwaltung* (Leipzig 1885).

cally rejected his identification of the material in large letters (141), dates some named days in the republic (256), and argues for a gradual development of the characters of the days (78f.). Huschke preferred to follow O. E. Hartmann, whose posthumous book, *Der römische Kalender* (1882) edited by L. Lange, had been preceded by his *Ordo Judiciorum* (1859). In the earlier book Hartmann was primarily concerned with the law courts, but the whole first section he devoted to a study of the characters of the days and their influence on the times when the courts sat. As far as I know it is the only detailed study of this topic in the modern literature, and is still of great interest. In it Hartmann saw a gradual development of the characters in response to political events during the republic. In his later book he challenged Mommsen, arguing that the large letters in the *Fasti* do not indicate the date of the material which they record but its importance. He maintained that the named days were listed in the *Fasti* because they were *feriae universi populi communes* and *stativae*. They would have been included in the *Fasti* either when they became important or when they became *stativae*, instead of *conceptivae* (132f.), which might have happened at any time during the republic, although many of the *feriae* were certainly of great antiquity. As to the calendar year, Hartmann believed that an original ten-month year was replaced by a twelve-month year in which intercalation took place in an eight-year cycle but with a full lunar month. This was modified by Servius Tullius who introduced the pre-Julian method of intercalation. At this time January became the first month instead of March, but February remained the last month until the decemviri shifted it to second place in order to bring the beginning of the year into relation with the winter solstice.[7] Although this calendar, including the characters of the days, was written out, it remained a secret in the possession of the pontifices, who added or dropped single days in order to avoid the coincidence of *nundinae* with the Kalends of January and the Nones of all months (see App. 1, pp. 164-67). This made it impossible for the public to anticipate *dies fasti* and *nefasti*, until Flavius published the calendar.

[7] This was based on the passage in Ovid, discussed on pp. 128f.

In a paper written in 1891[8] Wissowa berated, in elegant Latin, the scholars who ignored the source of evidence for the study of Roman religion which Mommsen had opened up for them and persisted in using literary sources. He said of the Fasti: *soli eam nobis monstrant religionis Romanae aetatem quae adhuc immunis erat a graecarum fabularum infectione.* But he dated the calendar simply as prior to the republic. In another paper written in the next year[9] he developed his theory that the gods whose cults were recorded in the *tabula feriarum* were to be included among the *di indigetes*, whom he considered the native gods of Rome. This *feriale* he now dated, since it included the Quirinalia, after the inclusion of the Quirinal Hill within the city, but before the reign of Servius Tullius, because it contains no *feriae* for the cult of Diana on the Aventine founded by that king, or for the cult of Juppiter Optimus Maximus founded in 509 B.C. He thus had lowered the date of the *feriale* considerably from that given by Mommsen, ignoring the absence of the *Tigillum Sororium*, which was crucial for Mommsen.

In 1899 Warde Fowler, in his *Roman Festivals of the Period of the Republic*, accepted both Mommsen's attribution of the pre-Julian year to the decemviri (3, note 3) and his theory that no change was made in the *feriae* during the republic (15). He defined the earliest calendar as the material recorded in large letters in the *Fasti*, and assigned it to "the so-called period of Numa, the period of the early monarchy," prior to the Etruscan dynasty (338).

In 1902 Wissowa in his *Religion und Kultus der Römer* (27f.) repeated his argument for the date of the calendar on topographical evidence, but now defined the lower limit for the date by a collective reference to the Tarquins rather than to Servius Tullius.[10]

In 1904 J. Beloch, in a discussion of the chronology of Greek history in the west, maintained that the pre-Julian year

---

[8] "De Feriis anni Romanorum vetustissimi observationes selectae." *Gesammelte Abhandlungen* (Munich 1904) VII, 154-174.

[9] "De dis Romanorum indigetibus et novensidibus disputatio," *Gesammelte Abhandlungen*, VIII, 175-191.

[10] The argument is reproduced in the second edition (1912) 31.

[211]

was introduced by Flavius in 304 B.C.,[11] and that, before this, the Romans had had a lunisolar calendar like the Greeks.[12] He argued that, if they had had a fixed calendar before 304 B.C., the announcements on the Kalends and Nones would not have persisted up to Flavius' day, and that his publication of the *Fasti* would have been unnecessary.

In 1907 De Sanctis in his *Storia dei Romani* (1.265f. = 1.² 259-261) protested against the tendency of the period by asserting that the *feriale* as it occurs in the *Fasti* was the work of the decemviri, partly on the grounds that the distribution of the days with a preponderance of *dies comitiales* presupposes the needs of the republican form of government rather than those of the monarchy. He also attacked the method of dating the *feriale* on negative evidence, that is the absence of certain cults, pointing out that our information about the *feriae* is too fragmentary, and sometimes incorrect, to be reliable. Later in the same book (2.516-523) there is a detailed discussion of the Roman year. De Sanctis dismisses the ten-month year as an absurd legend. According to him the Romans had at first a twelve-month lunar year in which a lunar month was intercalated. The pre-Julian year was introduced as the basis of the first *written* calendar by the decemviri. De Sanctis emphasizes the importance of the fact that this year is completely independent of the moon, which requires that it should be dated later than the regal period. One should note that, in spite of his opposition to Mommsen's theories on other points, he assumes throughout his discussion that the *feriale* and the character letters form an indivisible unit.[13]

In 1911 Warde Fowler in *The Religious Experience of the Roman People* (94f.) picked up Wissowa's topographical argument and assigned the calendar to the period of the fully developed city which included the Quirinal and Capitoline Hills, before the conquest of that city by the Etruscans.

In 1922 Beloch wrote an article on *"Die Sonnenfinsternis des Ennius und der voriulianische Kalender"* (*Hermes* 57 [1922] 119-133), in which he tried to date the eclipse men-

[11] On Flavius and his calendar see above, pp. 108-18.
[12] *Griechische Geschichte* 3.2.208f.
[13] The comments in *Storia dei Romani* 4.2.1 (Turin 1953) 356-358 indicate that De Sanctis never changed his mind about the calendar.

tioned by Ennius (see p. 126) in 288 B.C. For this purpose he used again the theory he had proposed in 1904, that the pre-Julian year had not been introduced until Flavius published the calendar in 304 B.C. To his earlier arguments he added that the Romans could not possibly have adopted a calendar completely unrelated to the moon as early as the period of the decemviri, long before any Greeks had thought of it.[14]

Apparently in response to Beloch's article, M. P. Nilsson in the same year propounded another theory in an article[15] which has had results out of all proportion to the brevity with which it treats a complex subject. After a brief refutation of Beloch's attribution of the pre-Julian year to Flavius, Nilsson admits that there is evidence for what he recalls a reform of the calendar by the decemviri, but insists that a law referring to intercalation presupposes a cyclic calendar and cannot be referred, as Beloch would have it, to the old lunar calendar nor, as Mommsen argued, to the introduction of the pre-Julian year. He then credits Mommsen with having recognized in the large letters of the *Fasti* the old so-called calendar of Numa, which he distinguishes from the pre-Julian calendar. He attributes to Warde Fowler the statement that the *feriale* must be older than the introduction of the Capitoline cult of Jupiter because it contained *no* festivals of Jupiter. He justifies this expulsion of Jupiter from the *feriale* by observing that the *feriae Jovis* (sic) on the Ides "stehen nicht in der gleichen Linie," presumably, although he does not amplify the phrase, comparing them to the other named days, and adds that Juno is almost missing. He goes on to say that Jupiter and Juno are the patrons of the pre-Julian calendar, because they receive sacrifices on the Ides and Kalends, and that therefore the pre-Julian calendar is under the protection of the Capitoline Jupiter and his companion Juno Regina, who do not occur in the oldest *feriale*. From this he concludes that the pre-Julian calendar

[14] This article treats the problem of the eclipse and the calendar in more detail than the first edition (1904) of *Griechische Geschichte*, and its arguments are incorporated in the second edition (1927).

[15] "Zur Frage von dem Alter des vorcäsarischen Kalenders," *Strena Philologica* (Upsala 1922) 131-136, reprinted with an appendix in *Opuscula Selecta* (Lund 1952) 2.979-987. His theory as to the date was not entirely new. On different grounds, it had been proposed by G. F. Unger, *Zeitrechnung der Griechen und Römer* (*Handbuch der klassischen Altertumswissenschaft*, I, sec. F, Nördlingen 1886) 628f.

with the Ides and Kalends was introduced to Rome at the end of the regal period when the Capitoline temple was built, and that its cyclic character was derived from the Greek calendar. There are many fallacies in Nilsson's argument. He has of course based it primarily on Mommsen's theory of the significance of the large letters in the *Fasti*, and then turned his back on that theory by amputating the Kalends and Ides, always in large letters, from the *feriale*. In his next step he has relied on a misinterpretation of Warde Fowler, who did not say that there were no festivals of Jupiter in the *feriale*, but merely that the Capitoline cult of Jupiter did not appear there, which is a very different matter.[16] It is difficult to see how the Ides and Kalends could have originated with the cyclic pre-Julian calendar when their very nature proclaims that they occur in it as vestigial survivals of a lunar calendar. It is perfectly true that Jupiter and Juno presided over the calendar, but not in the cult forms in which they appeared in the Capitolium. The Jupiter of the Ides has no cult title, he is the *pater ipse* of the Romans, attended by the *flamen Dialis*. Juno of the Kalends is Juno Covella, not Regina. The rites on these days are performed not near the Capitolium but on the arx on the opposite peak of the hill, or in the Regia in the Forum. Nilsson's argument leaves the impression that the Romans had not worshipped Jupiter and Juno before the establishment of the Capitoline cult, an impression which I think any student of Roman religion would reject. It is also difficult to see how Nilsson, an expert on time reckoning, could attribute the pre-Julian year to the influence of the Greek calendar after the comments of Beloch and De Sanctis on its very different character. His initial argument that the law *de intercalando* of the decemviri presupposes a calendar with cyclic intercalation fails to convince me. A true lunar calendar, which he assumes preceded the pre-Julian, requires intercalation and I can see no reason why a law providing for the change from *ad hoc* to cyclic intercalation should not be described as *de intercalando*. What else would one call it?

[16] He was well aware that among the named days not only all Ides are *feriae Jovi* but also both Vinalia, the Meditrinalia, the Poplifugia, and the Larentalia.

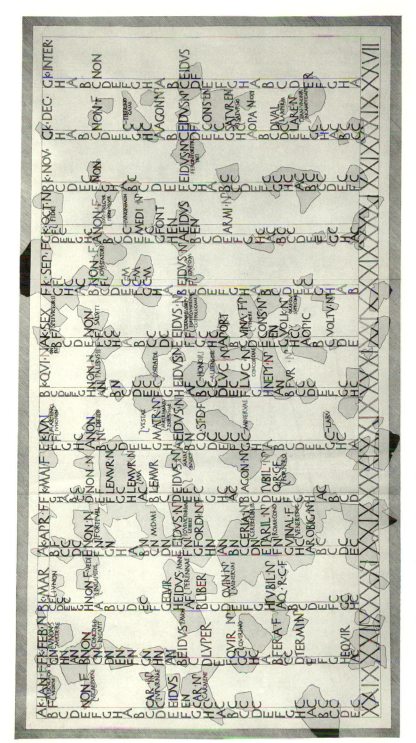

1. *Fasti Antiates Maiores* (after A. Degrassi)

2. *Fasti Amiternini* (after A. Degrassi)

We should note the end result of Nilsson's theory. Instead of using the absence of the Capitoline cult to date the *feriale*, he has used it to date the pre-Julian year at the end of the regal period, leaving the *feriale*, shorn of Kalends and Ides, in a more remote past.

In 1931 F. Altheim, following Wissowa, tried to date the calendar more precisely on topographical evidence.[17] He argued, like Wissowa, that it must have originated after the inclusion of the Quirinal Hill in the city, and that it must be a synthesis of the religious rites of the Septimontium and the Quirinal settlement. From the exclusion of the Capitoline cult he deduced that the calendar must be dated before the Capitoline Hill and the Forum, which it dominates, were part of the city, that is, before the last decades of the sixth century, after the Forum had ceased being used as a necropolis. Furthermore the Capitolium Vetus, the shrine of Jupiter, Juno, and Minerva on the Quirinal, which was older than the great Capitolium, is not mentioned in the calendar. Therefore the calendar must be pushed back to the early sixth century. This argument is weakened by the fact that the rites of the Kalends and Ides were performed on the Capitoline Hill. Just because one cult located on the hill is not mentioned in the calendar, there is no reason to exclude the whole hill. Moreover many of the *feriae* were connected with places in the area of the Forum, and recent excavations have shown that the Forum was inhabited much earlier than has been supposed.

In 1946 K. Hanell published *Das altrömische Eponyme Amt*.[18] The thesis of this book is that the Roman monarchy did not come to an abrupt end with the expulsion of the kings and the institution of two consuls, but that the power of the monarchy gradually diminished during the first half of the fifth century B.C., while from 509 B.C. on an eponymous officer, the

---

[17] *Römische Religionsgeschichte* (Sammlung Göschen 1035, Berlin-Leipzig 1931) 1.26-29. The argument is repeated in later editions, and in his *History of Roman Religion*, trans. H. Mattingly (London 1938). Similar arguments appear in Altheim's *Griechische Götter im alten Rom* (Giessen 1930), but in reverse, as there he uses the calendar as evidence for the topography.

[18] *Skrifter Utgivna av Svenska Institutet i Rom* (Lund 1946) 2. The discussion of the calendar is in ch. 8, 95-117.

praetor maximus, gave his name to the year, as later the two consuls did. In the third century B.C. Roman historians, under the impression that these eponymous officers were consuls, identified the beginning of the list with the founding of the republic and filled in a second name for each year. To support this thesis, it was necessary for Hanell to explain why the eponymous office should have been instituted in 509 B.C. The explanation came readily to hand from Nilsson's association of the pre-Julian year with the Capitoline cult. Hanell argues that the pre-Julian cyclic calendar, modeled on the Greek cyclic calendar, together with the Greek use of eponymous officers for reckoning time, came to Rome with the Capitoline cult, under the influence of Delphi.[19] Hanell has accepted, repeated, and enlarged on Nilsson's theory, without, it would appear, examining it closely.[20] He does not explain, any more than Nilsson did, why the introduction of a new cult of Jupiter should necessitate so drastic an innovation as a new calendar, nor why the influence of Delphi should have inspired a calendar of a type unknown to any Greek in that it broke entirely with the observation of the moon.[21]

In 1949, in an article called "The "Calendar of Numa" and the Pre-Julian Year" (*TAPA* 80 [1949] 320-346), I tried to demonstrate that the festival cycle (*feriale*) in its final form could not have been codified or the *feriae* given their final dates until the introduction of the pre-Julian year in the period of the decemviri. Therefore the festival cycle and the other elements in the calendar represented Rome of the mid-fifth century, not of the sixth century B.C. It will be obvious from what I have said elsewhere in this book that years of further work

[19] This point has not been challenged in most reviews of the book. For exceptions see F. Walbank, *CR* 62 (1948) 83f. and L. R. Taylor, *AJP* 72 (1951) 69-72.

[20] He also cites Nilsson's article to support his idea that before the pre-Julian calendar the Romans had had a year of ten months which had nothing to do with the moon, but Nilsson says (*Opuscula Selecta* 2.985) that the ten-month year would have been lunar, and that two of the natural twelve months were simply unnamed. In his comment below on my article, he states that the Romans must always have had a lunar month (*op.cit.* 986).

[21] For a recent criticism of Hanell's theories about the calendar see E. Meyer, "Zur Frühgeschichte Roms," *MusHelv* 9 (1952) 176-181.

have made me change my mind about many of the ideas presented in the article, although I still believe the pre-Julian year
was introduced by the decemviri. In dealing with the festival
cycle I depended heavily on the theory that the Forum valley
could not have become a center of religious observances until
some considerable time after it had ceased to be a burial ground,
for which I accepted a date about the end of the seventh century
B.C. Recent excavations, however, have shown that the area
was already inhabited before that date, so that my argument
from the topography collapses. My whole thinking about the
calendar at that time was still dominated by Mommsen's concept of its unitary nature. I had not appreciated the implications of Hartmann's suggestion that the large letters in the
Fasti indicated the importance rather than the date of the
material, and I had not realized how much there was to be
learned from the study of the character letters and the nundinal
letters. For a criticism of this article on other scores, see the
appendix to Nilsson's article cited in n. 14.

In 1961, in an article "Notes on the Early Roman Calendar,"[22] E. Gjerstad interpreted the development of the calendar
in terms of his chronology of early Roman history, which
he bases on his archaeological investigations in the Forum
and elsewhere. Much of his interpretation depends on the
conclusions of Nilsson and Hanell, but also departs radically
from them in some particulars. In order to understand it, one
must recall his chronology, which falls into three periods. In
the pre-urban epoch, from the eighth century B.C. to 575 B.C.,
the villages which were established on the Palatine, Esquiline,
Quirinal and Caelian gradually crept down the sides of the hills
and took over much of the Forum valley. In 575 B.C. these
villages were politically united into a single community, an
event which Gjerstad defines as the foundation of the City.
There follow the early and the late regal or archaic periods,

[22] *Acta Archaeologica* 32 (1961) 193-214. The article is briefly re-
sumed in "Legends and Facts of Early Roman History," *Scripta Minora
Regiae Societatis Humaniorum Litterarum Lundensis* 1960-61:2 (Lund
1962) 24-26. I shall touch here only on those parts of Gjerstad's
article which are immediately relevant to the dating of the pre-Julian
calendar. There is a great deal more, for example, a discussion of the
relative dates of the *feriae*, which I cannot go into here.

which terminate in 450 B.C. Since Romulus is only the "fictive eponym" of the city, the early regal period consists of the reigns of Numa, Tullus Hostilius, and Ancus, and the later period covers the reigns of the two Tarquins and Servius Tullius between them. Thus the regal period, instead of beginning with the traditional date for the founding of the city, 754 B.C., begins with Gjerstad's date for the foundation, 575 B.C. and the reigns of the kings are dated correspondingly later than usual, ending with the establishment of the republic in 450 B.C.

According to this system, in the pre-urban epoch the Romans had a lunar year with ten named months and two months which, because they had no *feriae*, were unnamed.[23] Numa introduced a calendar with the same arrangement of months, but standardized the lengths of the months to 29 or 30 days.[24] To this calendar belongs the *feriale*, which contains no rites associated with the Tarquins. The calendar of Numa was under the patronage of Juno Covella and the Jupiter of the Ides, not of the Capitoline Jupiter and Juno, whose cult was introduced, with the *Ludi Romani*, by Tarquinius Priscus in 509 B.C. At the same time Tarquinius introduced the pre-Julian year, which had twelve named months. The cyclic intercalation, however, was devised by Servius Tullius in 472 B.C. and introduced by the *Lex Pinaria* of that year.[25]

[23] He argues that these unnamed months were simply regarded as a second Sextilis and a second September, and that, when the twelve-month year came in, they became September and November, while the old November and December were renamed January and February. This is a most ingenious explanation of the tradition of the ten-month year, but it still does not explain the crucial and perplexing problem of why these two months had no *feriae*, but remained conveniently empty, waiting for the *Ludi Romani* and *Plebeii* to take them over.

[24] There is no evidence, as far as I know, that the Romans used conventionalized lunar months of 29 and 30 days, between the period of their real lunar calendar, and the pre-Julian calendar, although it is possible that, like many other peoples, they did so.

[25] Gjerstad says (209) "Varro's statement that the earliest bill regulating the intercalation was that incised on a bronze column and assigned to 472 B.C. is certainly worthy of serious consideration and there is no reason to doubt its authenticity." But Varro's words, as quoted by Macrobius (1.13.21, for text see pp. 156f.), do not mention regulating intercalation. They simply speak of a law *cui mensis intercalaris adscribitur*. On the other hand, Gjerstad dismisses the evidence for the law

Gjerstad does not say how the pre-Julian year was intercalated before 472 B.C.

This is not the place to discuss Gjerstad's chronology,[26] but we should note what he has done to the date of the calendar. He has accepted Hanell's connection of the pre-Julian calendar with the dedication of the Capitoline temple, but he has slipped the period of the Tarquins forward, so that by dating the calendar to 509 B.C. he puts it at the beginning of the Etruscan dynasty instead of the end. Implicit in his discussion of the divisions of the month is a rejection of Nilsson's assignment of the Ides and Kalends to the pre-Julian year, since he recognizes their position in the lunar calendar. He has added a complication of his own by separating the cyclic intercalation from the first phase of the pre-Julian year, although to most people I think the method of intercalation is the characteristic feature of that year.

In his edition of the *Fasti* (*I.I.* 13.2), published in 1963, Degrassi has discussed briefly a few of the recent attempts to date the calendar (pp. xixf.). He notes the theories of Mommsen and Wissowa, and then comments on those of Nilsson, Hanell and myself. He approves Nilsson's argument, repeated by Hanell, that the *Fasti* must have existed before the decemviri because otherwise the decemviri could not have initiated a law about intercalation, but goes on to say that the original *Fasti* must have been added to and changed before they were finally published in the XII Tables. He accepts as a general principle Mommsen's identification of the earliest *Fasti* as the material in large letters, but suggests that during the republic some changes may have been made in the characters of the days when *feriae* were changed from *conceptivae* to *stativae* (p. xxiv). Although he does not say so in so many words, it would seem that Degrassi has moved away from the unitary concept of the *Fasti*, towards one which would allow the possibility of

---

of the decemviri, which is specifically described as *de intercalando* (Macrobius *loc.cit.*), saying that we do not know "the contents or the purport of the bill."

[26] For a full discussion of Gjerstad's recent work on Rome see A. Momigliano, "An Interim Report on the Origins of Rome," *JRS* 53 (1963) 95-121.

change and development. It is amusing to note that thus, just a century after Mommsen propounded his theory of the date and nature of the Calendar of Numa, the way has opened for a renewal of the type of speculation about the history of the calendar which prevailed before Mommsen's theory dominated the field.

THE ROMAN CALENDAR

RECONSTRUCTED

INDEX

Acca Larentia, 81, 142
M'. Acilius, see *Lex Acilia*
aediles, 80
agere cum populo, see *ius cum populo agendi*
Agonalia, 73
Agonium, 134, 139, 182
alphabet, 113
ancilia, 64n12, 134
Angerona, 81
Anna Perenna, 79
anniversaries, 25, 27, 32, 142, 173-82
Apollo, games, 176; temple, 181
Argei, 134
arx, 20f, 100, 214
astrology, 167
Augustalia, 32, 141, 182
Augustus, birthday, 22, 180f; as *pontifex maximus*, 174. See also Augustalia
M. Aurelius, 143
auspices, 4, 36ff, 95

birthdays, Agrippina, 67n21; Antony, 63n9; Augustus, 22, 180f; Caesar, 176; Constantine, 166n 12; Rome, 79
bisextum, 166n12, 167

Caelian Hill, 217
calendar, Athenian, 15, 121n8; Egyptian, 15, 121n8; Greek, 111 n55, 120, 121n8, 214; lunar, 11-13; solar, 15
  Roman: civil, 3, 5, 16n19n21; literary evidence, 5ff, 121ff; internal evidence, 119f; decemviral, 109-12, 126-30, 208f, 212f, 216f; Flavian, 108-18, 211, 213; Julian, 3, 6, 14, 22, 89, 142ff, 161n5, 165, 167, 173-81 *passim*; lunar, 21, 119, 123, 125f, 130f
  pre-Julian: character, 16-22; introduction, 21n34, 93, 119-30, 207-20; reconstruction, 31-35, 173-81; theories as to date: Altheim, 215; Beloch, 121n8, 211ff;

Degrassi, 219f; Fowler, 211f; Gjerstad, 217ff; Hanell, 215f; Hartmann, 210; Huschke, 209f; Michels, 126n22, 216f; Mommsen, 93f, 207ff; Nilsson, 213ff; De Sanctis, 121n8, 212; Unger, 213n15; Wissowa, 211
  See also calendars, *Fasti*, intercalation, months, year, years
calendars, nature, 3f; bases, 9ff; construction, 11-15; civil, 3, 10, 14, 16n21. See also year, years, months
Caligula, 142f
Capitoline cult, 208, 211, 213-16, 218, 219
Capitoline Hill, 20f, 100, 212, 215
Capitolium, 80, 133, 214f, 219; *Vetus*, 215
Caristia, 166n12
Carmentalia, 73, 134, 183
Castor and Pollux, 80
centumviri, 51
Ceres, 80
Cerialia, 135n45, 183
character letters, vii, 24, 28ff, 173-81, 208, 217
chronocrators, 167n13
chronology, Roman, vii, 165, 168, 170f, 217f
Claudius, emperor, 143
———— Appius Caecus, 108, 118
Clodius, P. Pulcher, 60n56, 94, 205. See also *Lex Clodia*
comitia, 29, 36ff, 67; dates, 42, 45, 58f; on *dies fasti*, 94f, 97; on *nundinae*, 84, 104ff, 198f; and *Ludi*, 41, 83n62; on March and May 24, 204;
  prohibited by: *dies fasti*, 49; *dies nefasti*, 29, 62, 66, 68; *feriae conceptivae*, 39f; *feriae imperativae*, 40, 45; *feriae Latinae*, 45; *nundinae*, 40, 84, 104ff; *supplicationes*, 40, 45f. See also *dies comitiales*
———— *calata*, 38, 47
———— *centuriata*, 36f, 39n7

The Roman Calendar Reconstructed